PRAISE FOR
WINNING GLOBAL MARKETS

"We noticed that the world economy is more and more unscattered by Globalization, which is not flat essentially. This is just what has been put forward by the Kotler brothers and we are very lucky and thankful to have their brilliant insights of 600 world cities generating a high percentage of the world's wealth. It provides Chinese enterprises a new and creative way to audit and make their international marketing strategies."

—**Zhang Ruimin**
CEO, Haier Group, Qingdao, China, the largest
home appliance maker in the world

"An important contribution for policy makers and corporations as the world reorients itself towards a new pattern of geographical concentration in economic activity."

—**Nirmalya Kumar**
Member, Group Executive Council, Tata Sons;
Professor of Marketing at London Business School

"Our company is a global company. Our future is tied to the great urban market centers all over the world. Our problem is how to change the national culture of our company to a truly global culture. The Kotler brothers point the way in their important new book."

—**Adi Godrej**
Chairman, Godrej Group

"Research in economic sciences is preoccupied with business firms and nations. The Kotler book explains why the focus should move to cities. This is further supported by the emerging logic of service as efficient value-in-use through resource integration and co-creation. Cities are the most concentrated and complex networks of service systems created by Man, integrating contributions from businesses, governments and the commons. Business school research and education should take a leading role in this development."

—**Evert Gummesson**
Emeritus Professor of Service Management and Marketing,
Stockholm Business School (SBS), University of Stockholm, Sweden

"A blueprint for any city or municipal leader to generate economic growth with the right combination of tools in their toolbox."

—**Nancy Berry**
Mayor of College Station, Texas;
Home of Texas A&M University

"Philip and Milton Kotler are on a crusade to tackle marketing challenges, and they hold sole authority on it. Investing in growing nations can be challenging, and if you like to expand your influence, *Winning Global Markets* is a step in the right direction."

—**A.J.M. Muzammil**
Mayor of Colombo, Sri Lanka

"A fascinating perspective on why companies must organize their business around global cities instead of organizing around countries and regions. Each chapter generated a new 'a ha' moment for me and made me think differently."

—**Dr. Jagdish N. Sheth**
Charles H. Kellstadt Professor of Marketing,
Goizueta Business School, Emory University

"With a refreshing data-based, analytical perspectives, the Kotlers show how a global firm should appraise what cities to gain a presence, a critical decision in the ever changing world scene."

—**David Aaker**
Vice-Chairman of Prophet;
Author of *Aaker on Branding*

"AVIC International Holdings is expanding our commercial businesses globally. Many cities in Africa, U.S., Latin America, and elsewhere are coming to us with investment opportunities. The Kotler brothers' new book, *Winning Global Markets*, gives us the first systematic method for selecting the best new city markets to enter for our real estate, hotels, airports, department stores and other enterprises."

—**Wu Guang Quan**
CEO, AVIC International Holdings, Beijing, China

"This brilliant book of the Kotler brothers provides Chinese cities with a new perspective to merge into the global innovation of industries, and more important, inspires Wuhan city to become an international city."

—**Mayor Tang Lianzhi**
Wuhan city, the commercial center of central China,
with 10 million city population

"This is an essential book to read for any C-level executives of multi-national corporations wanting to grow and expand in the first third of the twenty-first century. The Kotlers correctly point to the ever more urban global economy and the rapid growth of cities in developing countries as two key trends global CEOs must adapt to in order to lead and thrive in this new century."

—David Houle
Futurist;
Author of *Entering the Shift Age*

"The Kotlers have provided a wonderful guide for both major cities (who will be the largest consumers of products and services) and major organizations (who will be the largest providers of products and services) in tomorrow's changing world."

—Marshall Goldsmith
New York Times best-selling author of *MOJO* and
What Got You Here Won't Get You There

"The increasingly volatile global macro-economic factors and the rapidly changing demographics and environmental aspects constantly challenge businesses, countries, and cities to review and refocus growth strategies and optimize resources. As corporate and city leaders and managers seek winning solutions in the face of such dynamic demands, they will be forced to venture into unfamiliar territory and take less trodden paths as never before. This book provides many facts, insights and thought provoking ideas that will test and transform conventional thinking and lead to the development and implementation of innovative solutions for the challenges that lie ahead. I believe this book will be a much sought-after handbook for company strategists and city marketers as they guide their entities to greater prosperity."

—Amal Cabraal
Former Chairman/CEO, Unilever Sri Lanka;
Director, John Keells Holdings;
Hatton National Bank;
Ceylon Beverage Holdings;
Lion Brewery Ceylon

"Cities are the window into developing economies and the best door to take for entering these burgeoning markets. Philip and Milton Kotler give marketers and strategists a clear look through this window along with compelling advice on how to choose where and how to capitalize on the opportunities in cities."

—George Day
Professor, Wharton School, University of Pennsylvania;
Author of *Strategy from Outside In:*
Profiting from Customer Value

"Global companies must decide carefully in which global cities to plant their resources and future. This book does an excellent job helping companies understand and evaluate different global cities and where they should be."

—**Harsh Mariwala**
Chairman, Marico Ltd., India

"Having managed different business growth strategies in China for twenty years, I know how crucial it is to understand the economics of cities. Companies must carefully choose the urban regions in which to plant their resources, marketing focus, and future. Yet understanding how your choice of cities drives growth is a topic that business schools have not yet grasped. This book does an excellent job helping companies understand and evaluate different global cities and where they should be."

—**SY Lau**
Senior Executive Vice President of Tencent Holding
Company, Shenzhen, China

"I am impressed with the fact that 600 city regions contribute 67 percent of global GDP. Every major global company must plant its roots in these cities."

—**Dr. Chen Bin**
CEO, Continental Hope Group, Chengdu, China

"*Winning Global Markets* is extremely relevant and timely as the majority of the world's population now lives in urban areas. Big cities shape the way we live and connect, and this book shows how marketers can take an active part in this transformation. This is particularly significant for Japan, where consumer behavior is defined by a highly urbanized population in some of the world's largest cities. By describing the role of big cities, Philip and Milton Kotler help us identify synergies between the public and private sectors, to invest in the future and create long-term value for business and society at the same time."

—*Kozo Takaoka*
President and CEO, Nestle, Japan

"This book is a must-read for entrepreneurs and mayors. The Kotler brothers helped us a lot on our aviation park; I believe their new book will bring great value to the market."

—**Jin Qian Sheng**
Director, China (Yanliang) Aviation Industry Base

Winning
Global Markets

Winning Global Markets

How Businesses Invest and Prosper in the World's High-Growth Cities

PHILIP AND MILTON

KOTLER

WILEY

ISBN: 978-1-118-89381-4 (cloth)
ISBN: 978-1-118-89379-1 (ebk)
ISBN: 978-1-118-89383-8 (ebk)

Printed in the United States of America

10 9 8 7 6 5 4 3 2 1

Milton Kotler:
I dedicate my contribution to this book to all of my colleagues at Kotler Management, with offices in Beijing, Shenzhen, Shanghai and Wuhan. Without their devotion to the mission of our company to enhance the marketing skill of Chinese companies and local government authorities, neither our company nor this book would be possible.

Philip Kotler:
I dedicate this book to my nine grandchildren, who will live and thrive in the new world economy of multinationals and megacities: Jordan, Jamie, Ellie, Abby, Olivia, Sam, Shaina, Sapphire, and Dante.

CONTENTS

PREFACE

This is a book that centers on cities and companies. Cities need to grow and prosper. Companies also need to grow and prosper. It turns out that the fortunes of the two entities—cities and companies—are intimately interconnected.

How? A city needs to develop not only an attractive social life but also a strong economic life and future. Much has been written about the social life of cities, but much less has been written about their economic life. A city's economic life depends on its ability to attract and nurture small businesses, medium-size businesses, and large domestic corporations and multinational companies (MNCs). This book focuses on the attraction of MNCs. These businesses carry out research, investment, production, distribution, and sales that drive the city's economy. Cities have gross domestic products (GDPs), just as nations do. We can measure how much GDP a particular city generates. The GDP provides a picture of jobs and household, business, per capita, and median income—all good measures of a city's "economic" condition.

We can also talk about the rate of growth of a city's GDP. If GDP growth is strong, the city is generating new jobs and its citizens prosper. If GDP growth is low, zero, or even negative, the city is barely surviving. Many top cities are falling behind or even failing—such as Detroit and Flint in Michigan; Cleveland, Dayton, and Youngstown in Ohio; and Stockton and Riverside in California—because they stopped being attractive to business. This is a concern to the city's businesspeople, to its jobholders and job seekers, to its politicians, and to its citizens.

Companies are making decisions all the time on where to invest, where to produce their goods and services, and where to sell them. Companies that are growing have to find new locations and choose them carefully. Companies also must periodically reassess the locations of their current economic activities because locations change in their desirability. Many domestic-based companies are facing new competitors who come in with lower prices, better quality, or both, all because of the opening of trade around the world and the facilitation of trade made possible by advances in technology. Domestic companies can't stand still. They have to defend themselves, and they have to move to new, promising locations where opportunities are growing.

Many companies have moved their manufacturing from developed countries to developing countries in their search for lower costs. In doing this, these companies had to evaluate which cities and locations are the best. If French car manufacturer Peugeot wants to expand in the Asian market, where should it establish its new management and production branches? It already has a joint production venture with Dongfeng, based in Wuhan. Should it strengthen its production presence in East China's top cities, such as Shanghai, Hangzhou, or Guangzhou? Peugeot assembles in Bangkok, but should it produce there, as it does in Indonesia?

The economic standing of different cities and metropolitan areas is of primary concern to business leaders and managers, who have to know how much product they can sell locally and trade outwardly, how much they should invest, and where they should invest for the growth of their enterprise. Economic standing is also of primary concern to politicians, who need business growth to generate city revenue to pay the bills they incur and to provide jobs for their citizens.

Successful business owners and managers have to know all dimensions of a city's life: the land and housing costs, the city's amenities and features, the direction in which the city is going in the next 10 or 20 years. Companies need to know who, what, when, where, why, and how buyers purchase goods and services. They have to know the laws and the ease of establishing businesses and trading and exporting goods.

The politicians in a city have to understand what different companies require from a city to operate successfully. Not every company has an interest in a particular city. Every city has to determine its main attractions and which industries, as well as which companies in those industries, can find the city's resources and ambitions a good fit. Politicians need the skills to attract the right businesses to their city and thus generate enough prosperity to pay the city's bills, create jobs for its citizens, and get themselves reelected or reappointed.

Citizens generally know little about the economy of their city. They are concerned with jobs, family, friends, neighbors, and personal pleasures. Scholars and thought leaders have neglected the study of the economy of cities because they thought the key to economic development lay in the policies of nations, not those of cities.

In the last three decades, matters have changed. National governments have pursued a regime of global free trade. Capital investment, consumption, and trade have crossed national borders. Companies in the developed world have moved from thinking exclusively about domestic production and consumption to shifting their manufacturing to the East. This has allowed them to reduce their costs and to fine-tune their marketing and financial strategies so that they engineer high demand for their brands throughout the world and thus achieve maximum market share and profits.

Meanwhile, the developing world has continued to learn how to make money by making things. Developing countries have been learning how to market their goods and services. There has been a great increase in the number of MNCs coming out of the developing world, and arising MNCs from the East are posing strong competitive threats to the long-dominant MNCs of the West.

Rural people have continued to migrate in growing numbers from farms into large cities. Great industrial cities, such as São Paulo and

Jakarta, have grown in the developing world, becoming megacities. Large cities of up to 5 million people and megacities of more than 10 million people have begun to dominate the GDP of nations. In the developing world, massive industrial production has filled old and new cities with rural populations. Developing countries have absorbed investment for infrastructure, manufacturing, natural resources, and trade. They have rapidly urbanized their populations as a vast labor force and developed an indigenous middle class for consumption and a wealthy upper class for investment.

At the same time, great commercial centers in the developed world—such as New York, London, Paris, Stuttgart, Milan, and Tokyo—have sustained their wealth by attracting domestic and global talent and investment for a new mix of industries and creative media.

The massive change of urban market scale has induced the merger of domestic companies to consolidate into massive MNCs, which have come to dominate national GDPs and the gross world product (GWP). By 2010, 8,000 companies around the world generated 90 percent of the GWP. Six hundred cities yielded 50 percent of the GWP. Of these, only 100 cities yielded 38 percent of the GWP. Trend projections only advance this concentration at both ends of the exchange between companies and cities.

From an economic point of view, we are living in a world of MNCs and global cities. Companies and cities have overwhelmed the economic force of nations. Companies and cities constitute the platform of investment decisions by business leaders and marketers and are the major concern of political leaders, who must position their cities in this trend.

Small businesses play an important role in job creation and economic growth but a smaller role in generating economic value. They play an important role in the political and social life of a country but a smaller role in its economic life. Most successful small businesses are absorbed by MNCs.

What happened to the economic development role of the nation-state? Developed nations spent their energy advancing the level of public welfare with deficit spending. They pursued political programs and trade integration and engaged in regional wars. They promoted a marketing and financial system to drive consumption. As sovereign powers, they spent more time planning their relations abroad than they did at home. They let both the real economy and their cities take care of themselves.

The legacy of the West's great wealth and power masked the tectonic shifts in the global economy toward the East until the financial crisis of 2008. That crisis knocked the socks off of the overleveraged developed world and slowed the growth rate of the developing world. Central governments and their central banks provided meager economic stimulus, some by courting self-destructive austerity programs, but they primarily used their energy to save their top banks with cheap money in the hope of restoring a flow of credit for economic stimulus. This did not occur.

While nations were saving their banks, their cities were on their own to repair their economies with expensive bond money, and large companies were on their own to reap the profit of cheap money. Global cities competed with one another to attract MNC investment. Companies used their cash for investment to grow their brands in the developing world, which, unlike the West, was far from saturating its demand.

So we come to the setting for this book. The destiny of the economic world today is in the hands of the interplay between global MNCs and global cities. Our purpose is to assist business leaders to pick the right places for investments in the best global-growth cities and to assist marketing managers to intensify their marketing campaigns to reap the harvest of these investments. Our corollary purpose is to help the political and civic leaders of global cities to attract global MNCs that are choosing among many competing cities. We give some attention to the role that national governments can play to facilitate the economic growth of their top city regions by attracting suitable MNC investment.

Chapter 1 illuminates the economic power of global cities. Chapter 2 examines what cities are doing to maximize their market power. Chapter 3 reveals the immense economic power of MNCs. Chapter 4 investigates how MNCs select new cities for market expansion. Chapter 5 discusses what cities can do to win the competition for MNC investment. Chapter 6 considers how national governments can assist their top cities to grow economically. Chapter 7 examines the social and moral responsibilities of MNCs and cities in the brutal game of economic competition. Finally, Chapter 8 assists marketing managers to strategically and tactically optimize value for their companies in a world of global city markets.

We present a lot of data and case examples to put flesh on the bones of a proposition that the future of marketing depends on how effectively business marketers use the resources of their large companies to win share and profits in the ever-narrowing sphere of concentrated urban global markets. We also explain how city marketers can use the strengths of their cities in the competition to successfully attract global MNC investment for employment, higher income, public revenue, and civil prosperity.

There is nothing permanent in the landscape of an economy. Change occurs all the time. But we can say with confidence that for the next two decades, the global market economy will rest on the interplay of MNCs and large city regions.

ACKNOWLEDGMENTS

Philip Kotler

As an economist trained at the University of Chicago and the Massachusetts Institute of Technology, I focus my attention on how local, national, and international economies interact and operate, paying particular attention to how midsize and large multinational organizations locate their activities and entities—factories, distribution centers, retail outlets, and financial and marketing operations. Among the management thinkers who most influenced my thinking about the activities of multinationals are Peter Drucker, Michael Porter, Gary Hamel, Jim Collins, and Vijay Govindarajan.

For many years I have also been researching how *cities* choose which industries and companies to attract. I formed a research project with professors Irving Rein and Donald Haider of Northwestern University to study this question. We published our findings in 1993 in *Marketing Places: Attracting Investment, Industry, and Tourism to Cities, States, and Nations.* Our book describes the theory and techniques of how cities position, differentiate, and market themselves to an array of interest groups, including companies, employees, citizens, and government organizations. Later we invited different co-authors to join us in researching and publishing how foreign cities operate abroad. I want to acknowledge the distinct contributions of Christer Asplund (Europe, 1999), Michael Hamlin (Asia, 2001), and David Gertner (Latin America, 2006).

As Asia's role grew more prominent in the global picture, I began to focus more attention on developments in Asian cities and regions. I carried out research with Hermawan Kartajaya from Indonesia and Hooi Den Hua and Sandra Liu from Singapore, and we published *Repositioning Asia: From Bubble to Sustainable Economy* (2000) and *Think ASEAN* (2007).

I want to acknowledge Simon Anholt's contribution in starting the journal *Place Branding*, which publishes empirical studies of how cities around the world plan their company attraction and retention campaigns. I want to acknowledge Rainisto Seppo from Finland for his excellent book *Place Marketing and Branding: Success Factors and Best Practices* (2009). I also benefited from discussions with other experts in place marketing, such as Magdalena Florek (Poland), Nina Marianne Iversen (Norway), Joao Freire (Portugal), and Guiseppe Marzano (U.S.).

I am grateful for the ideas and help of the Wiley staff and Richard Narramore, Tiffany Colon, and Susan Cerra of Wiley.

Finally, I want to recognize my wife, Nancy, as my constant inspiration and companion in my work and life.

Milton Kotler

As a marketing strategist who has lived and worked in China for 15 years, I owe my knowledge of Chinese and Asian companies and city economies to my company colleagues, business and local government associates, and well-informed friends throughout China and the West.

Because my company serves Chinese company and local government clients, I have a unique perspective on the country's urban growth, outward investment, and global business perspective. Cao Hu, President, Kotler Marketing China, takes first place in advising me on this book. I thank him for his brilliance in thought and management, and his kindness, patience, and loyalty.

This book also rests on the research assistance and insights of Esther Wang, Au Tong, Yao Mumin, Sam Wang, and Colin Qiaoi of our urban development team. I also learned a great deal from a valued advisor, Qin Yang Wen, of Co-Stone Capital.

My perspectives in this book have been guided by many Chinese CEOs: Zhang Rumin, Haier; Wu Guang Quan, AVIC International Holdings; and Dr. Chen Bin, Continental Hope. They have informed my understanding of the growth of Chinese multinational companies.

I have learned much from the mayors and other local and provincial officials of Zhengzhou, Dalian, Wuhan, Tianjin, and other great cities of China with whom I have worked. They have given me a profound understanding of the urbanization policy and urban and industrial development practices of China.

Many American and European friends and associates have also helped my understanding of the role of cities and multinational companies in the expansion of the global economy. Philip Kotler, my dear brother and marketing mentor, has been the finest co-author with whom to work. Vidur Saghal has been a constant advisor on the cities and companies of India. Hermann Simons has been helpful for Europe. I owe special thanks to my U.S. urban development colleagues: Jeff Lee, an American land designer; architects Ed Feiner and Steve Manlove of Perkins+Will; U.S. developers Alex Green of JStreet Companies in Washington and Stephen Gutman of the Corcoran Group in New York City; and finally, real estate attorney Robert Diamond of Reed Smith, LLC.

I would like to thank the McKinsey Global Institute for tracking the trends of globalization, urbanization, and the changing landscape of multinational business, and for making this rich research material publicly available.

No book of mine can be successfully executed without discussions with my beautiful and brilliant wife, Greta Kotler, a global business manager in her own career.

1 The Economic Power of Global Cities

Companies—midsize and large multinational companies (MNCs) —need to figure out where to sell their goods and services. In their home market, they must decide geographically where to plant their headquarters, regional offices, production, distribution, and sales management. Companies have to choose the right cities, because city advantage is more decisive for business success than national advantage.

As companies move abroad, they decide which nation or nations to produce and sell in and choose specific locations where they intend to carry out their administration, production, distribution, and sales work. If a company chooses to sell in China, where does it locate its headquarters for China? Will it be Beijing, Shanghai, Hong Kong, or any of a dozen other cities? And in each Chinese city where it plans to operate, the company needs to develop specific presences and locations. Choosing a pattern of locations around the world is a gigantic task that can make a major difference in the company's success.

Every nation contains a set of cities that differ in their importance and national and global reach. Some of the world's cities are bigger

1

than many nations. The 2007 Greater Tokyo metropolitan region of $13,500 \, km^2$ had 35 million residents. It was roughly equal to the population of Canada and larger than that of Malaysia, the Netherlands, and Saudi Arabia.[1] Other megacity regions include Shanghai, Beijing, Mumbai, Delhi, New York City, Los Angeles, London, Mexico City, São Paulo, Buenos Aires, Rio de Janeiro, Dhaka, Lagos, Moscow, Cairo, and Istanbul, and they are likewise bigger than many country populations. These cities generate a huge level of gross national income for the nation. Each has extensive economic, political, and social relations with other cities and nations.

We assert that the growth of nations is intimately tied to the growth of their major cities. Top cities have grown faster in gross domestic product (GDP) than the rate of their country's GDP growth. Major cities are the source of a nation's wealth, not the other way around. In the markets of a nation's major cities, investment, trade, and consumption take place.

Yet development economists have spent the last nearly 70 years focusing on nation building and national economic growth, not city growth. Following World War II, the United Nations, World Bank, and International Monetary Fund, as well as the hegemonic powers of the United States and the Soviet Union, pursued policies of building national economies as the route to economic development and growth. Nation building deals with central government policy and structure, military modernization, social planning, large-scale infrastructure, global and bilateral trade agreements, global financial integration, and agricultural support.

When central planners in the Soviet Union, China, India, and other nations propounded central policy and held a tight rein on local initiative, many of their cities declined in economic growth, environmental quality, and social stability. The Soviet Union sank because its cities sank. The same warning could be applied to the United States. The federal government has paid little attention to the economic growth of key American cities. They let the cities economically decay in the face of suburban sprawl, financial liabilities, social engineering, and outmigration of businesses and talent to other parts of the country and offshore. Cities were seen as a place to improve the lot of the poor, not places to launch economic growth. To a lesser extent this was true of Europe, as well.

The net result has been the rise of financially draining central government bureaucracies, sluggish economic growth, political polarization, major corruption, and persistent social upheaval. National resources are politically spread across the regions of a country, with little ability to concentrate resources in top market cities for accelerated growth and greater contribution to national revenue. This attenuation of resources to politically favored regions of the country is one of the economic perils of both democracy and autocracy.

The United States and India are good examples of this. U.S. grants-in-aid programs to states and cities spread federal resources across the nation's cities according to "fairness" criteria that bear no relation to the productive potential of recipient cities. It is too little for too many and never enough for what can spur economic growth. The National Congress Party of India has departed from an earlier policy of targeted infrastructure investment designed to stimulate economic investment to embrace a policy of guaranteed income and discounted grain to the countryside (at 10 percent of the market price). The result is a reduction from 9.3 percent GDP growth (2010–2011) to 5 percent GDP growth (2012–2013).[2] Because central governments are generally not able to invest resources in key growth cities, local city governments and city regions have been forced to step up to the plate and initiate investment promotion programs.

A good example is the work that Mayor Michael R. Bloomberg undertook to improve the economic prosperity of New York City. Later we describe the many initiatives he undertook to strengthen New York City's role in the global economy. After his 11 years as mayor of the city, he created a high-powered consulting group to use his vast fortune to help reshape cities around the world. He views large cities as laboratories for large-scale experiments in economic development, public health and education, and environmental sustainability.[3]

This idea of stressing the key importance of major cities in the growth of a nation's GDP is also on U.S. President Barack Obama's mind. On December 13, 2013, Obama met with more than a dozen new mayors and mayors-elect and told them that the "nation's cities are central to the economic progress of the United States" and that he wanted "to work with mayors to provide an environment that makes them [the cities] key job creation hubs."[4]

There are strong reasons why global companies must focus investment on growing cities in the developing world. Major cities in the United States and Europe are declining in population, and their consumption, trade, and investment are weakening. They cannot be relied on by Western MNCs to provide sufficient markets for business growth and adequate return to shareholders. The fastest-growing cities are in developing countries, especially in Asia and Latin America, which are having rapid growth of their middle and affluent classes. This is where money can be made, and both developed- and developing-country MNCs and large domestic businesses are exploiting these opportunities. Western MNCs must move more aggressively before they are outpaced by new developing-country MNCs.[5]

We repeat: Midsize and large cities in developing countries generally have a growth rate exceeding that of their host countries.[6] The sum total of a nation's top cities comprises the greatest part of its GDP. In developed countries, cities provide as much as 80 percent of the national GDP. In the United States, cities contribute 79 percent of the national GDP. In developing countries, the range is 40 to 60 percent. Chinese cities contribute 60 percent of the national GDP and 85 percent of China's GDP growth rate. Thirty-five Chinese cities alone contributed just under 50 percent of China's GDP in 2013.[7]

Although many developing nations were in turmoil during the last decades of the twentieth century that precluded investment, they have since stabilized and attracted investment. The road to economic growth is still rocky in the Middle East and in parts of Latin America and Asia, but the major city regions of China, India, Brazil, South Africa, Chile, Colombia, Indonesia, South Korea, Mexico, Singapore, Vietnam, and elsewhere are open for business.

The premise of Western nation building has been that economic development springs from democratic institutions. Although democratic nations such as South Korea, Taiwan, India, Brazil, and Mexico are doing well, autocratic nations such as China, Singapore, Saudi Arabia, and the United Arab Emirates are doing just as well without democratic political institutions. Even Russia, a dubious democracy, is rising from her ashes.

If economic prosperity does not necessarily come from democratic institutions, where does it come from? Beneath the shell of nation building, developing economies have thrived through the rapid growth of cities and their dynamic interplay of rapid urbanization, industrialization, trade, consumption, and education. Cities have grown through external and internal investment, transplanted global industries, indigenous industries, innovative implementation of central government investment and enterprise policies, improved operations and marketing skills, and indigenous entrepreneurial talent and spirit.

National institutions occasionally play a facilitating role in attracting external investment, trade, and consumption, but more often they play an inhibitive role. The leadership and enterprises of the megacities and large cities in the developing world are the engines of local economic growth, which produces added revenue for central governments. The nation does not produce wealth; at best, it facilitates urban growth. Cities grow the wealth of nations. Nations are the beneficiaries of city economies, not the progenitors.

According to 2011 McKinsey Global Institute data, the top 600 cities in the world included 20 percent of the world's population and generated US$34 trillion, or roughly half of the gross world product (GWP). By 2025, the top 600 cities are expected to double their GDP to US$65 trillion and contribute 67 percent to the GWP.[8]

The GDP purchasing power parity (PPP) of developing cities is racing toward the purchasing power of the West. The standard of living today in Shenzhen, China, is equivalent to that in Chicago and has more middle-class households.[9] Living in Shanghai and Beijing is more expensive than living in New York City. From 2007 to 2010, the GDP of large Chinese cities rose from 20 percent to 37 percent of the GDP of large U.S. cities.[10]

By 2025, the distribution of developed- and developing-country GWP contributions will likely be inverted. By 2025, it is estimated by the Paris School of Economics that China will be second to the United States in nominal GDP, with a GDP that is two-thirds the GDP of the European Union (EU) and half that of the United States.[11] The Chinese economy of 2010 was equal to the U.S. economy of 2000. Also by 2025, India is expected to be the sixth-largest economy, equal in GDP to France.[12] The epicenter of global economy is turning from the cities of developed countries to the cities of developing countries.

How can this be? Why is the economic development of Asia and other developing areas eclipsing Western economic dominance? The West expected continuing political and economic domination after the Cold War with the Soviet Union ended, not that economic giants in the developing world would challenge American preeminence.

The answer is simple. Since the rise of nation states in the nineteenth century, comparative politics and economics have been based on national data. Nations were compared by absolute nominal GDP, not GDP PPP or rate of GDP growth. The same still holds for comparative GDP data. Nominal GDP is calculated in U.S. dollars, not in PPP—namely, what it comparatively costs people to live in different countries at the same lifestyle. Nominal GDP in the developed world is a historic legacy. The growth rate of GDP PPP is a contemporary dynamo.

Country data does not reflect differences in city GDP within the country or city contribution to country GDP. For example, in 2011, the top 15 cities in India contributed 56 percent of India's GDP yet only held 7.5 percent of its population.[13] In other words, national GDP data lag behind in-country city data. Cities are growing faster than their countries. Cities are more attractive markets than their countries as a whole. Cities are the economic powerhouses of countries.

PricewaterhouseCoopers[14] estimates that Brazil's annual growth rate in the period 2010–2025 will be less than 3 percent, while the estimate for São Paulo in the same period is an annual growth rate of 4.3 percent, and in Rio de Janeiro the estimated annual growth is 4.2 percent. India's estimated annual country growth rate is 5 percent, while Mumbai and New Delhi are estimated to grow at 6.3 and 6.4 percent, respectively. In the case of China, which is estimated to grow at a 5.5 percent annual rate over this period, its top city growth rate in Shanghai, Beijing, and Guangzhou is expected to exceed this by as much as 10 percent. In 2012, Tianjin's GDP grew at 16.4 percent, while China's GDP grew at 10 percent. In the United States, the 2011 growth rate for San Jose, California, over the previous year was 7.7 percent; Houston grew 3.8 percent; and Midland, Texas, had a 9.5 percent increase in GDP.[15] These well exceed the 2011 U.S. GDP growth rate of 1.7 percent. Which figures should businesses turn to for investment in market expansion—national data or city data?

Economic growth springs not from nation building but from national policies that invite global private investment in industries, trade, and consumption to top-growing cities in both the developed world and the developing world. This investment catalyzes industrialization and commercial development in invested cities. It adds value to urbanization by inviting new skills, improving education, improving infrastructure and technology capacity, advancing household income growth and middle-class expansion, stimulating small-business supplier enterprises, and increasing capital formation, trade, investment, and consumption.

City building, not nation building, has been the key to the rise of emerging markets. The megacities and large cities of the world have an 80 percent higher per capita GDP than that of their host economies.[16] By 2025, only 12 of the top 25 cities with an annual average household income above $20,000 in PPP are expected to be in developed regions, namely, Tokyo, New York, London, Paris, Rhein-Ruhr, Osaka, Los Angeles, Seoul, Chicago, Milan, the Randstad, and Madrid.[17] The other 13 are expected to be in developing regions, namely, Shanghai, Beijing, Moscow, Mexico City, São Paulo, Mumbai, Cairo, Hong Kong, Taipei, Shenzhen, Istanbul, Delhi, and Buenos Aires.

Let's illustrate the power of cities by the example of China. In 1980, Deng Xiaoping, Communist Party leader of China, instituted special economic zones (SEZs) in five Chinese east coast cities to test market economics after decades of state planning. The experimental cities included Shenzhen, Zhuhai, and Shantou in Guangdong Province; Xiamen in Fujian Province; and the entire province of Hainan. These cities became free trade zones, export processing zones, industrial parks, free ports, free economic zones, and urban enterprise zones.

China's first foreign capital inflows to these city zones came not from Western countries but from private offshore Chinese capital in Hong Kong, Singapore, and other overseas Chinese investors. Western corporate and financial investment capital followed. However, not all of these Chinese investors were in capitalist countries. Some were in countries that were Socialist at the time, such as Indonesia.

When the Shenzhen SEZ was organized, the zone consisted of a small fishing town and a trading town of 30,000 people, settled on no more than 3 square kilometers of dilapidated buildings and lacking even a traffic light. A new urban landscape of economic development was to be built on this barren settlement. Shenzhen was the most special of the four SEZs, with the greatest freedom to explore economic policy innovations. By 1982, additional portions of the Shenzhen municipality were added to the SEZ, bringing its population up to 351,871.[18]

By 2000, only eight years after its SEZ designation, Shenzhen reached a population of 7,008,428. By 2010, its population had soared 47.8 percent to 10,357,938,[19] and most of the Shenzhen municipality was subsumed in the SEZ. Its GDP reached US$3,581 per capita by 2012, with a PPP of $23,897.[20] At a 10 percent annual growth rate, Shenzhen's PPP is nearly equal to the 2010 per capita GDP of $29,535 of Chicago. It has already exceeded Cleveland's per capita GDP and at the time of this writing was expected to soon match Philadelphia's per capita GDP.

In short order, the experimental SEZs spread to all cities in China, and great industrial and commercial cities proliferated in Beijing, Shanghai, Chongqing, Chengdu, Tianjin, Wuhan, Xi'an, Guangzhou, and other city regions. Western companies entered these cities' markets independently or as joint ventures in selected industries with state-owned companies, which provided market entry in exchange for investment, technology transfer, and management skills. External investment, along with new internal private and public capital formation, also fueled private and state-owned sector growth. There was vast public and private investment in infrastructure, and within three decades, Chinese cities grew to become some of the largest global economic urban centers and made China the world's second largest economy.

By 2010, China's private sector had generated 65 percent of its GDP and held 40 percent of its capital. The Communist Party built a prosperous market economy with Chinese characteristics. Similar patterns of Western and internal investment followed in other countries to turn the developing cities of Jakarta, Bangkok, Kuala Lumpur, Dubai, Mexico City, São Paulo, and Mumbai into great global cities.

China is now following the pattern of Western investment into China by investing in African cities. Chinese investment in Africa exceeds the investment of the World Bank on that continent. China has developed and used its own capital resources for foreign investments and acquisitions of industrial, property, and commercial companies; technology; and logistical assets in Africa, as well as in other developing regions and developed countries. China pursues direct foreign investment and can financially leverage its capital for foreign investment.

Urbanization

The key to the shift of national wealth from developed to developing countries lies in the rapid urbanization of vast populations of low-wage workers into large cities, which creates compelling production cost advantages to global companies and investors, as well as access to new huge markets. With advances in education and technology, this shift has progressed to value-added supply chains and brands for export and new middle-class domestic consumption.

Jane Jacobs[21] and other urban analysts have pointed out the wealth-creating effect of cities. Although early writers such as Jacobs focused on the urbanization of developed countries, there is today a far larger scale of wealth creation in cities in the developing world. According to McKinsey, "China's economic transformation resulting from urbanization is happening at 100 times the scale of the first country in the world to urbanize—the United Kingdom—and at 10 times the speed."[22] The question that every American has to ponder is whether the United States, with a population of 315 million in 2013,[23] can effectively compete with a 2010 urban developing world of 2.6 billion people.[24]

For the first time in human history, we live in an urban world. More than 50 percent of the world's population lives in cities and generate 80 percent of the GWP. As of 2007, 380 cities of McKinsey's index of

600 top global cities, accounted for 50 percent of the GWP. By 2025, the 600 largest cities are expected to generate 60 percent of the GWP.[25] The 2025 players will change. In the developing world, 136 new cities (100 cities in China alone) will likely enter the 600 city index. One out of every three developed cities in the 2007 index will likely drop from the list. The key element of new wealth creation will derive from consumption, which is expected to rise from 485 million households with an average per capita income $20,000 in 2007 to 735 million households with an average per capita income of $32,000 in 2025.[26]

The Economy of Cities

Cities are intensively productive environments for infrastructure and commercial investment, industrialization, employment, higher-wage migration from rural areas, logistics and trade, educational advancement, property development, consumer marketing and distribution, cultural attraction, and capital formation. Cities and city clusters provide the supply chains for both manufacturing and services industries.

The upside of large cities and megacities is their opportunity for industrial, technology, and commercial investment. They are great company markets for household consumption income and personal career advancement through education and enterprise. They also have downsides of environmental degradation and pressure on natural resources. Large cities pose great challenges of political and administrative management and social harmony.

The consumption taking place in cities is divided among the poor, the low-income consumers, the middle class, and the wealthy upper class, as well as all of their subdivisions. In the emerging 440 developing-market cities, households above $20,000 PPP are expected to rise from 35 percent of households in 2010 to 55 percent of households in 2025. Developing cities will also have a large high-income and wealth class, defined as household income in excess of $70,000 at per annum PPP. This number of high-income households is expected to triple in the developing world's top cities from 20 million in 2010 to 60 million in 2025, representing 60 percent of global growth in urban high-income households and exceeding the number of wealthy households of the developed cities. China alone will likely account for 19 percent of new high-income developing-city households.[27]

Of the 26 anticipated large cities in 2025, with a population of 5 million to 10 million and with a median household income of more than $20,000 (middle-income and high-income classes), 11 cities will likely be in the developing world—Brazil, Russia, India, and China (BRIC countries) and others—whereas the remaining 15 cities will likely be in the developed world.[28] Only 3 of the top 26 large cities are anticipated to be in the United States—New York, Los Angeles, and Chicago. If we turn to the 23 anticipated megacities with a population of more than 10 million and the highest number of middle-income households, McKinsey estimates that only 7 will be in the West—New York and Los Angeles in the United States; London, Paris, and Rhein-Ruhr in Europe; and Tokyo and Osaka in Japan. The remaining 16 megacities will likely be in developing regions—Shanghai, Beijing, and Chongqing in China; Mumbai, Delhi, and Kolkata in India; and Mexico City, São Paulo, Buenos Aires, and Rio de Janeiro in Latin America, plus Karachi, Dhaka, Manila, Moscow, Cairo, and Istanbul. The epicenter of the marketing of all business-to-business (B2B) and business-to-consumer (B2C) companies will likely have shifted from developed to developing regions.[29]

Variances in factors other than income alone, like the age of the population, the number and size of households, and the population's education level, will distinguish the problems and opportunities of doing business in these top cities and the broader McKinsey index of the top 600 cities. Multinational and indigenous companies will need to adjust their strategies and operations to different cityscape profiles.

Business Strategy in City Economies

In her 1984 book *Cities and the Wealth of Nations,* Jacobs brilliantly dismantled national theories of wealth creation by demonstrating in realistic terms that cities and their regions are the true generators of national wealth.[30] She argued that cities grow through different stages: (1) markets for imports, (2) import replacement (jobs), (3) industrial and commercial transplants, (4) technology, and (5) capital formation and investment. She demonstrated how great Western city regions joined with other importing and exporting city regions within a nation to create the wealth of nations. The city region is the core of the national economy. As core cities flourish in import replacement, they begin to export their surplus production and innovations to nearby core cities and then to foreign countries. Imports are continually converted into replacements and exports, and the wealth of city regions grows. When the central city declines in energy and inventiveness, the city region degrades.

Jacobs wrote an earlier book in 1961, *The Death and Life of Great American Cities,* in which she traces the competitive race between cities and city regions within the United States and the various reasons some cities won and others lost.[31] Every city competes for markets, jobs, transplants, technology, and capital. Cities may be permanent, but there is no permanence to their wealth and economic power.

Jacobs witnessed the rise of Tokyo and other major Japanese cities and the rising wealth of Japan. But she did not live to see the economic rise of megacities and large cities in China, India, and the other regions of Asia; São Paulo, Rio de Janeiro, and Mexico City in Latin America; Istanbul and Dubai in the Middle East; or Lagos in Africa. Nor did she live to see the declining economic growth of Tokyo and other major Japanese cities during decades of stagnation in the 1990s and forward or the collapse of Detroit and the economic decline of many prominent American and European cities. But Jacobs has been right all along. The changing economic fortunes of city regions rest on the shifting sands of domestic and global markets, jobs, transplants, technology, and capital.

By the time of Jacobs's 1961 book, the Soviet Union had not collapsed. The new world order of free trade, financial integration, and new global financial instruments were not yet in place. There was no World Trade Organization to facilitate the transformation of protectionist trade to more open trade. China had just begun its rapid market growth in the heart of Communist China. Socialist India had not yet begun market reforms. Multinational corporations had not yet become the global behemoths that they are today. By the time Jacobs died in 2006, the outline of the new world had already appeared. Our book is a tribute to her pioneering work on the wealth of cities and how business and political, social, and personal life must adjust to this new urban world.

Let us look at how Jacobs's five stages shape today's and tomorrow's global economy.

Markets

We have already documented the new landscape of city markets (defining a city as a metropolitan region, just as Jacobs called it a city region). In 2008, there were 80 million middle-class and wealthy-class households in the developing cities of the world's top 600 cities and 172 million such households in the developed world.[32]

Regarding the fastest rate of city GDP growth in 2025, China alone is expected to have 15 of the top 25 greatest city GDP growth rates in the world. Only one U.S. city, Los Angeles, will probably rank in the top 25 GDP growth rates. In terms of the number of households above $20,000 GDP PPP per annum, only New York, Los Angeles, and Chicago in the United States will likely rank in the top 25 cities, matched by Shanghai, Beijing, and Shenzhen in China. More broadly, 12 of the top 25 cities with a household income above $20,000 GDP PPP per annum will likely be in the developing world.[33]

The profile of markets as a factor of wealth has changed from developed to developing countries. This means that the epicenter of consumption is shifting because of a combination of city GDP growth, population size, household number and size, and per capita income.

The key to the growing market consumption of top developing cities is the global reach of multinational corporations in manufacturing, brand power, and retail chains. This is enhanced by the rise of indigenous companies and their production power, styling, advertising, and distribution though their retail chains and malls.

Western multinational B2C and B2B companies initially exported their goods and services to developing cities. In short order, these MNC imports were copied and sold by developing-country companies to businesses and consumers at a lower price. To meet this market threat and to meet export competition, MNCs transplanted their production to host developing cities to protect their brands for host-country markets and to take advantage of low-cost labor that they could export to their home countries and other markets.

MNCs tried to trump indigenous import replacement with patent and copyright protection. This has historically been a hopeless task. Nonetheless, MNC brands took root in host economies, and Western industrial and commercial investments added economic power to developing cities while imperiling the manufacturing economy of their home countries.

Indigenous companies in developing cities not only substituted imports and grew their own brands and position in the marketplace but also began to invest in research and development (R&D) and innovation. By 2011, China became the second-largest export country, after the EU and ahead of the United States.[34] In 2012, Chinese telecommunications giant Huawei invested 13.7 percent of its annual revenue in R&D.[35] By 2013, China had shifted its export profile to value-added products and was competing successfully with MNC products in its domestic markets.

Jobs

There are more jobs in the top developing cities than in the top developed cities. You can fit the 2025 projected population of the five top per capita income developed cities in the world (Oslo, Doha, Bergen, Trondheim, and San Jose) into one job district of Shanghai.[36] Most top-performing per capita cities have small populations and job markets but are rich in natural, human, and financial resources.

Where did these abundant jobs of developing cities come from? Shenzhen grew from a population of 30,000 inhabitants in 1980 to more than 10 million in 2010. Tianjin grew from 7.7 million in 1980 to 11 million in 2012. Mumbai's metropolitan area grew from 8.2 million in 1981 to 13 million in 2012. São Paulo's metropolitan area population grew from 8.5 million in 1980 to 13 million in 2012.[37]

In general, 70 percent of the total population is a working-age cohort. Of this group, 50 percent represent an aging population. Taking the Organisation for Economic Co-operation and Development (OECD) definition of a working-age population as a range from age 15 to age 64, the top-performing GDP cities in the developing world, with their large populations, have high employment growth.[38]

The developing world added 886 million nonfarm jobs from 1980 to 2010, or an increase of 61 percent, versus 164 million new nonfarm jobs in the developed world, or an increase of 9 percent.[39] Annual employment growth in top developing cities is running at a 1 to 2 percent increase annually. By contrast, the top developed cities recorded 2012 unemployment in the following order: Paris at 11.4 percent, Los Angeles at 9.7 percent, London at 9.6 percent, Chicago at 9.5 percent, and New York at 7.7 percent. Since 1980, 50 U.S. metropolitan areas have had a net decline of employment ranging from −1 to −4.9 percent. Although net unemployment over a 30-year period of boom and bust is far less severe than the post–financial crisis job decline, it is evident that recoveries and new booms cannot offset long-term decline. The long-term decline is far worse in Europe.

The job growth rate of top developing cities comes principally from countryside migration to cities for higher wages. The principal factor of city job growth is urbanization. China and India have a long way to go until they meet the 80 percent urbanization level of the developed world.[40]

An additional factor of city job growth is the workforce penetration of the population. Workforce penetration is a ratio of current employment to working-age cohort. Latin America has reached an 80 percent level of workforce penetration.[41] Its stronger rate of GDP growth compared with the United States partly results from higher workforce participation to working-age population. Brazil also has a higher ratio than the United States. U.S. labor force participation has declined from its height of 67 percent in 2000 to 63.2 percent in 2013 and is projected to decline to 60 percent by 2040.[42] Many unemployed working-age Americans have stopped looking for work. One reason is declining economic growth, but another is the vast expansion of jobless benefits over the past two decades. The situation in high-welfare countries of Europe is even worse. In 2012, Italy and Spain had workforce penetration of only 44 percent to their working-age cohorts. France had 51 percent workforce penetration.[43]

Transplants

A large portion of urban population and employment growth in developing-country cities derives from indigenous public and private infrastructure and industrial and services investment. But a major source of this growth since 1980 has been the transplantation of manufacturing from developed city regions to developing city regions.

Many factors, including low wages, improved education and skills training, infrastructure, logistics, local supply, large metropolitan consumer markets, favorable bilateral and global trade policy, and investment incentives of host countries, have joined forces to move the industrial core of the developed world to the developing world.

The epicenter of middle-class consumption and per capita wealth is moving in concert with this industrial and commercial investment shift.

Developing cities are marketing their investment advantage in concert with central and local government policy and monetary, fiscal, and trade support. They compete among one another for foreign direct investment (FDI). Cities primarily market transplants, not central governments. Trade delegations led by mayors from every large city in China send marketing delegations to U.S. cities and European cities to present their investment opportunities. These delegations go to cities in the United States, like San Francisco, Dallas, Atlanta, Chicago, and New York, not to the federal government in Washington, DC.

Investment for industrial transplants and branches is a city-to-city exchange, not a country-to-country exchange. American presidents may trumpet investment and trade accomplishments. But these deals are made on from global city to global city. Country presidents bring delegations of city mayors and business leaders to global cities for business attraction to their own cities.

We can expect a continued hollowing out of manufacturing in the developed world and its passage to developing cities for decades to come.[44] This trend is reflected in the earlier stated reference to comparative city GDP growth in the developed and developing worlds. Higher absolute GDP and per capita income in the West are legacy attributes that will likely wane in coming decades.

Whereas U.S. cities once developed indigenous industries for import replacement from cities of Europe, today the cities of developing regions are attracting transplants and developing indigenous manufacturing for import replacement from the West. The vast scale and rapid pace of this replacement account for the fast growth of developing cities and their consuming classes.

The only hope of economic growth for low-population developed cities is innovation for export. However, this too is expected to be continuously replaced by importing cities of the developing world. China aims to reduce its technology imports from 50 percent to 30 percent by 2020. While China's share of global R&D rose to 12 percent in 2011, U.S. share is global R&D declined from 36 percent to 34 percent.[45] Innovation and productivity are keys to the future balance of economic power between cities of the developed and those of the developing world.

By 2013, major developing countries and their indigenous private and state-owned MNCs and large businesses were financially able to support indigenous innovation. For the Chinese GDP, 60 percent comes from the private sector in China, and 40 percent of China's wealth is in private hands.[46] China's private sector is growing at a faster rate than state-owned companies, and Chinese wealth, public and private, is investing and acquiring businesses in developed cities of Europe, Japan, and the United States for advanced technology, market access, and brand power.

Enterprise transplants are beginning to move in an opposing direction. Huawei is the second-largest telecommunications equipment company in the world. It is privately held and has facilities and operations throughout the world—in Europe, Latin America, South and Southeast Asia, Africa, the Middle East, and even the United States, where its activity is largely blocked by the federal government. Lenovo is the biggest PC maker in the world, and it is publicly listed in Hong Kong. China has vast private, as well as public capital for the global expansion of its city businesses. Chinese enterprises have made many company acquisitions in both Europe and the United States. In the first nine months of 2013, Chinese firms spent a record $12.2 billion on 55 greenfield projects and acquisitions in the United States, well on the way to a new record of Chinese FDI in the United States.[47]

Developing cities have been exporting more goods to developed cities than they have been importing. As a result, there has been a major growth of foreign currency reserves in China and elsewhere in the developing world for global business investment and expansion, which adds to the wealth of the developing cities and nations. The economic hope of developed regions to offset the loss of transplanted industries and jobs is innovative technologies. This brings us to the next element of city economic growth: technology.

Technology

China and many other developing countries require joint venture structures for foreign investment in selected industrial sectors. This is partly for the purpose of adding capital assets and revenue to state-owned companies but also for indigenous partners to learn the technology of high-value production and copy this knowledge for their own branded products and components. Indigenous joint venture partners are also learning how to efficiently manage large-scale business operations and management processes.

MNCs accept this condition of joint venture and technology transfer for the short-term benefit of market access and sales revenue to meet their corporate bottom line. MNCs are constant victims of intellectual property theft, whether by joint partners or third parties. For all of the comment and complaint on this issue, and all of the legal expenses of MNCs to secure intellectual property, little can be done. First, there is nothing new about this; it is the ancient process of import replacement. Furthermore, in a world of Internet information, corporate espionage is not only pecuniary but also malicious fun. Cyber security is a horserace between inventors and pirates, and pirates are often the winners.

Copying is the core of city economic growth. All cities grow by import replacements, which is a fancy phrase for *copying*. No legal system or procedure can stop the heart of city economies from copying and growing. They must reproduce what they import to grow their economies and then export at a low price what they previously imported.

Many Indian companies have copied the art of software from the West, and now Infosys is a world leader in software. Haier has copied General Electric (GE), Electrolux, and Bosh appliances and is now the largest white goods appliance maker in the world.[48] Galanz copied American microwave ovens and by 2007 became the largest microwave oven producer in the world.[49] Not only do developing city regions replace imports for their home market and for export, they also end up producing and even designing the original branded imports they replaced. Western consumer MNCs have become largely marketing organizations, outsourcing design as well as production. Branded retail chains in the West import replacement goods directly as private-label brands.

As Chinese companies absorb more Western technology in their manufacturing base, they also invest in new technologies. From 2009 to 2013, ZTE, formerly Zhongxing Telecommunication Equipment, a Chinese telecommunications equipment and smartphone maker, spent 10 percent of its sales revenue on R&D, far higher than American companies generally.[50] Apple spends only 3 percent of sales on R&D. In addition, the Chinese government invests heavily in R&D. Under the twelfth five-year plan, which runs until 2015, China will likely increase public R&D expenditure to 2.2 percent, and then it will likely increase it to 2.5 percent by 2020. This would put it on par with developed countries. The OECD average in 2011 was 2.3 percent. Increased funding for science in China is planned to reach $36 billion by 2012, up more than 12 percent year on year from 2011. Of this, about 14 percent is being allocated to basic research.

China now leads the world in solar and wind power. It is ahead of the United States in electric car manufacturing and sales. China's overseas direct investment (ODI) is purchasing European machinery manufacturing and technology at a speedy rate. China's Sany acquired

Putzmeister in Germany and is now on par with U.S. and Japanese cement mixers for construction. If there's a race to lead the Internet of things (IoT), China aims to set the pace. Beijing has focused on developing technology by which devices can communicate via infrared sensor, radio-frequency identification, and other machine-to-machine technology. The Chinese Ministry of Information and Technology estimates China's IoT market will hit $80.3 billion by 2015 and then double to $166 billion by 2020. China is also leading in light-emitting diodes and mobile payment technology, as well as advancing to leadership in semiconductor technology, optoelectronics, and grapheme technology. According to the Battelle Institute, the largest manager of scientific laboratories in the U.S., "The growth of China's R&D will far outpace those of the U.S., which has resumed modest growth that is expected to be relatively stable through 2020. . . . At the current rates of growth and investment, China's total funding of R&D is expected to surpass that of the U.S. by about 2020."[51]

What all this means is that Chinese cities like Shenzhen, home to ZTE and Huawei; India cities like Bangalore, home to Infosys; and Mumbai, home to Reliance, are catching up to Western cities in technology and talent, as well as investment, trade, and consumption.

Capital

New York, London, Paris, Frankfurt, Tokyo, and Singapore are still the major global financial centers of capital, but Hong Kong (legally part of China), Shanghai, Beijing, Mumbai, Delhi, São Paulo, and Dubai are not far behind.

The essential matter is that more global investment capital is flowing to the 480 developing cities of the McKinsey 600 index than to its 120 developed cities.[52] Just as the West places its manufacturing offshore, it is placing its investment capital offshore. Western MNCs are keeping billons in profit offshore to invest in developing city regions, instead of bringing these earnings back to their home countries for taxation and limited domestic investment opportunity.

The sovereign wealth funds of developing countries are growing at a faster rate than are surpluses in developed countries, which are largely deficit countries with enormous national and local bond liabilities. The future solvency of the peripheral EU is still open to question, as is the EU currency zone. There is no end to U.S. sovereign debt, which is supported by the U.S. dollar being the preeminent global reserve currency, still settling 80 percent of global trade transactions.

The Chinese renminbi (RMB) is making rapid progress in international trade settlement. The Wall Street Journal Market Watch reported that, according to figures from the Society for Worldwide Interbank Financial Telecommunication, the Chinese yuan surpassed the euro in October 2013 to become the world's second-most-used currency in international trade and finance.[53] Deutsche Bank predicted that yuan trade settlement would increase by 50 percent in 2014.[54]

Within a decade, the Chinese RMB will likely become fully convertible and shake up the financial resources of the developed world. China's trade settlement with Europe is likely to surpass the Asia trade settlement by the end of 2014.[55] Russia and Brazil are settling some of their China trades in RMB, and further bilateral swap agreements with other countries are on their way. These swaps, like the recent Australian dollar–to–China RMB swap, bypass the dollar and reduce the cost of trade. When China's policy makers are ready for the big step of convertibility is anyone's guess, but convertibility is coming.

The most interesting element of capital flows is China's Overseas Direct Investment (ODI). Chinese ODI grew from $3 billion in 2004 to a current level of $87.8 billion in 2012.[56] China is becoming an important investment competitor to the West.

U.S. direct investment abroad exceeded domestic investment in the United States in 1990 and did so by a wider margin than in

1985—$184 billion versus $152 billion. By 2011, the U.S. Direct Investment Position Abroad on a Historical-Cost Basis reached $273 billion and was distributed in the following proportions: 55.6 percent went to Europe, 13 percent went to Canada, 17 percent went to Asia, 13 percent went to Latin America, and 8 percent went to Africa and the Middle East. In summary, 30.8 percent, or $84 billion, went to developing city regions.[57]

As reported by the U.S. Bureau of Labor Statistics, in 2013, U.S. domestic investment during the decade of 1992 to 2002 grew 6.2 percent annually. During the following decade of 2002 to 2012, investment precipitously declined to 0.6 percent annually. Outward decade projection of 4.7 percent annual growth from 2012 to 2022 is hypothetical. The real fact is the actual decline, not the speculative increase.[58]

What this means is that the United States has substantially decreased its capital investment in its city industries and is, in effect, financing industries in developing cities to beat the economic growth of its own cities. Furthermore, investment into rich, developed countries fell by 9.5 percent in the first half of 2012, compared with the same period in 2011.[59] The United States has also given up on European growth.

The top cities of developing countries now receive more than half of global FDI inflows.[60] In the first half of 2012, however, China surpassed the United States and became the world's largest recipient of FDI. This category refers to international investment in which the investor obtains a lasting interest in an enterprise in another country. Most concretely, it may take the form of buying or constructing a factory in a foreign country or adding improvements to such a facility in the form of property, plants, or equipment.[61] In short, global capital is making its bet on the economic growth of developing city regions, rather than that of developed city regions.

Business Strategies for Developing-City Markets

McKinsey reported that in 2012, "Only 19 percent of surveyed business executives were reporting that their company's senior executives were making business location decisions at the city, rather than the country level and that they expect that share to remain constant over the next five years."[62] Furthermore, 36 percent make strategic business expansion decisions based on regional investment and leave the task of allocating investment to cities to working groups. Astonishingly, 61 percent of senior executives don't plan at the city level "because they are perceived as an irrelevant unit of strategic planning."[63] Among senior executives, 52 percent don't use city information in their daily work. If these senior executives are looking for customers, they are overlooking the most salient fact of where customers are. They are not in global countries and global regions but in the cities and city regions of countries.

When MNCs seek locations for improved market access and local talent, only 30 percent report that these decisions are made at a city level.[64] Professionals live in cities, not just in countries. Country-level statistics of professional and management talent, not to mention local market size, cannot identify Silicon Valley, Bangalore, Shenzhen, Tianjin, Wuhan, Jakarta, or Chennai. Maybe old habits can identify Minneapolis, Chicago, Manchester, Munich, Frankfurt, Lyon, or Stockholm, but none of these cities were among the top 23 city regions of high- middle-income households of 2007, and none were anticipated to be in this group in 2025.[65]

Corporate Culture

Senior executives of Western MNCs have been in management positions for decades. It is tough to unlearn a mind-set of 30 to 40 years, especially when that mindset has long been successful. Most U.S. consumer and services MNCs still do much of their business in the United States, but this picture is changing quickly. As of 2011, Walmart still did 76 percent of its business in the United States. Nike does 50 percent of its business in North America. Marriott is still American enough to do 84 percent of its business in the United States, and McKesson, the largest U.S. drug distributor, does 91 percent of its business in the United States.[66]

Still, there is slippage. McDonald's earns 66 percent of its revenue overseas. Apple receives 65 percent of its sales revenue from overseas sales. Even Amazon is seeing 45 percent of its sales overseas. Turning to the industrial sector, we see Intel with 88 percent of its revenue overseas, Dow Chemical at 67 percent overseas, IBM at 67 percent overseas, GE at 54 percent overseas, and Ford at 51 percent overseas.[67]

If we take 50 percent overseas sales as the tipping point for a truly global U.S. MNC, it is likely that we will see most U.S. Fortune 500 and Fortune 1,000 companies selling more than 50 percent abroad by the end of the decade. With the exceptions of Intel, Ford, and IBM selling a small share of foreign sales directly to central and state governments, most of these sales are to municipalities and companies. These procuring companies and consumers are in cities. The largest city destinations of U.S. foreign sales are Western developed countries in Europe, Japan, Korea, and Australia. Although we do not have the figures on the percentage of sales to developing cities, it is a fair bet, with European and Japanese economic stagnation and rapid developing-city growth, that a majority percentage of U.S. multinational foreign sales will shift from developed cities to developing cities before 2025.

It is the strategic challenge of every company to figure out the location change of sales revenue and rates of this shift. Companies have enough research capability to see the city path of their business shift over the coming decade if they accept the premise of city market economies. They need competitive intelligence to see where their

Western MNC competitors are going, when, and how. They have to track the rise and competitive strategies of new emerging-market MNCs and the global city spaces in which they plan to operate.

They have to change the culture of their headquarters and stakeholders to understand two basic changes. First, don't put too many resources in developed city markets. They are declining in consumer and business growth, whereas developing-city markets are growing. Second, forget global regions and countries and focus management talent on city markets, both in the developing and in the developed regions. Western failure to accomplish this business cultural shift will only advance the rise of new MNCs in developing cities and eventually their encroachment in developed cities.

Segmentation

City markets in developing countries are growing at different rates in population, household number and size, household and per capita income, educational level and talent, age distribution, and the mix of supply resources to meet demand. Developing cities with increasing households need residential and commercial property and all the fittings for middle-class living. Cities with high fertility rates need baby products. Those with a rising aging population need advanced health care.

Every midsize and large MNC has to map its product line to the demographics of developing-country city regions. Large companies have to be good geographers and know the top city regions in developing countries that represent the best opportunities for their product line.

Developing cities with high savings cultures are reluctant to spend. Those with spending cultures are ready to buy. Cities with many institutions of higher education and research have a large stock of talent for R&D and innovation. Newer developing cities that have not yet replaced their imports have fewer indigenous competitors than older cities. Cities with agile entrepreneurial political leadership are more inviting to Western MNC entry and growth than bureaucratic cities, which are protectionist toward their own indigenous companies. Some cities have highly suitable and outward looking partners for joint venture and strategic alliances; others are too restrictive, distrustful, and reluctant to deal with Western partners. Every company needs to segment its opportunities and formulate its criteria for ranking the attractiveness of cities.

Targeting

The McKinsey 600 cities index, with its 430 developing cities, is too vast a landscape for strategic investment. Which cities should your business invest in and according to what criteria? What time order and investment scale do you set for your company among these opportunity developing cities?

Below the city level, what demographic segments should you target? Every MNC has diversified product lines for different income, age, gender, education, occupation, and lifestyle group. Which brands are most salient to the changing demographic groups in these fast-growing developing city regions? Which products will have the greatest appeal and least competitive pressures in these growing cities? Which products in your portfolio fit the local culture, and how effectively can these products be localized for maximum consumer appeal? How do you deploy your product line of price points, design, and features for distribution to households and personal shoppers in these different cities?

What mix of distribution channels do you devise? Chinese cities have the highest number of Internet users and fast-growing e-commerce sales. India's cities have a slower rate of e-commerce growth. The United Arab Emirates cities are high wealth centers for luxury goods and travel. They want elegant retail channels. African emerging cities need more standard household goods and services and favor big-box chains. Top Chinese cities have millions of luxury and middle-class consumers, as well as many more in countryside towns and rural districts. The channels have to be highly diversified.

How do you advertise in developing cities with different cultures? Cultural variation and taste differ enormously among cities, even in the same country. The people of the Middle East are highly sensitive and alien to Western outlook. How does a Western product achieve credibility in the massive city region of Cairo?

Sales programs also have to be different. Developing-city consumers are used to bargaining. Everyday low prices do not work in a marketplace of haggling. That did not work for JCPenney when it tried unsuccessfully to abandon its heritage of frequent sales promotions to emphasize celebrity branding, higher prices, and no sales promotions.

How do you price for profit in vast developing cities that have a heritage of flexible pricing and fragmented distribution? What systems do you need to control price flexibility in the distribution chain, as well as the supply chain? The distribution pie has many more slices.

If we have to move from a global regional and country company organization, how do we organize for city regions? If the wealth of companies comes from developing-country city regions, companies have to have senior executives at the city region level. They cannot succeed with tactical work groups. The most promising approach is to target the fastest-growing city region clusters and seat senior management at the city region cluster level.

We are facing a new generation of marketing, different from the past and with an uncertain future. What we do know for certain, as borne out in the data, is that global city regions in the developing world will likely dominate market economies and be a fundamental source of company growth and prosperity. Developed city regions will still play a large role because of their high per capita GDP and their still great store of capital and intellectual and management assets. The new global organization of business will have to meld these diverging worlds. This book addresses these issues in detail and with strategic insight.

Conclusions

Here are some points to remember from this chapter:

- City metropolitan regions are the real generators of national wealth, not the nation.

- Multinational corporations (MNCs) are the major investors in city region growth.

- Urbanization in the developing world is growing rapidly and changing the global business landscape.

- City regions in the developing world are growing faster in GDP, population, and middle-class consumption than are cities in developed countries.

- Developing countries are generating their own MNCs to compete domestically and globally with Western MNCs.

- Western MNCs have to recognize the growing competitive technology of developing countries and their high-talent cities.

- Western MNC culture and leadership has to reflect the increasing percentage of revenues from the developing world.

- MNCs have to target top-growth city metro regions for investment in order to create revenue growth.

- Businesses have to reconfigure their administration, production, and marketing on the basis of the power of city markets, not national markets.

Questions for Discussion

1. Which city metropolitan regions are offering you the most promise for future revenue and growth? In which regions should you make plans for further expansion?

2. Which city metropolitan regions are declining? Where should you consider reducing your investment?

3. Which of your competitors are likely to present the strongest competition in the future? Why?

2 How City Metropolitan Regions Compete in the Global Economy

Although many cities are looking for more growth, their chances of successfully attracting multinational companies (MNCs) depend on their individual extrinsic and intrinsic characteristics. We have identified 11 characteristics that make a difference: the city's or metropolitan region's scale, the nature of its demographics, its logistics, its potential for awarding incentives, and whether it has industrial clusters, good supply chains, a favorable central government policy, social stability, political and civic leadership, institutional strength, and commercial strength. Cities that are blessed with many of these characteristics do better than cities that lack them. Here, we examine and illustrate each characteristic in turn.

Scale

Larger cities, cities with scale and infrastructure and talent resources, are better able to compete for MNCs and large companies than smaller communities. It is unlikely that a small town could offer the size of opportunity that a large business might need. We see most major urban centers in the world extending their market scale and capacities through metropolitan organization and through city region infrastructure agreements to create superior demand and supply conditions for prospective enterprises to perform and prosper.

According to the pioneering work of Bruce Katz and the Brookings Institution's Metropolitan Policy Program,[1] Denver is an outstanding example of transformation. A troubled city in the 1960s and 1970s, Denver moved through careful steps over three decades to become the 21st largest metropolitan district in the United States and 18th in gross metropolitan product (GMP) in 2012.[2]

During the 1960s and 1970s, the flight of white citizens from the city created a ring of prosperous communities and jurisdictions surrounding Denver's declining economy and large minority population. The city sought to annex surrounding unincorporated areas to enlarge its school district and retain a diverse population but to no avail. In 1974, the Poundstone Amendment to the Colorado constitution precluded any jurisdiction from annexing unincorporated areas in surrounding areas unless it was supported by a majority vote of the proposed annexee county. That ended Denver's ability to grow its municipal way out of its economic and social problems.

Denver leadership was forced to find another method of growth. In 1987, the Denver Metro Chamber of Commerce created a new vehicle for economic growth called the Greater Denver Corporation, which was later renamed the Metro Denver Economic Development Corporation. Its purpose was threefold: (1) to create an international airport, (2) to put Denver on the global map as an economic location for jobs, and (3) to develop an economic development program for the metropolitan region.

Because Denver could not annex, it had to make jurisdictional deals. Mayor Federico Pena and Denver business leaders went to the grass roots of adjoining Adams County. They worked out a cooperative plan of shared costs and benefits for Denver and Adams County to build an international airport. Denver agreed to foot the bill for the airport infrastructure if Adams County ceded a portion of its land to Denver for the airport construction. A majority vote by Denver and Adams County voters passed in 1988. Denver gained control of a piece of land in Adams County, and the county gained the commercial advantage of proximity to the airport. These successful metropolitan developments led to a next step of city region growth.

All municipalities and counties in the region realized that a great city had to feature an exciting cultural district. Denver had a zoo, art museum, botanical garden, nature museum, performing arts center, and other cultural and scientific institutions, which it could barely support. The value of these institutions for the attraction of business and talent to the region were evident enough to government and business leaders and voters throughout the region to create a new metropolitan scientific and culture tax district. An ongoing levy of 0.10 percent was set in 1988 to create a $40 million fund to support cultural and scientific institutions in the region.[3] Today, the Denver Zoo is the fourth-most-visited zoo in the United States, and the Museum of Nature and Science has the highest number of paid membership of all museums in America. The Denver Performing Arts Complex is the second-largest performing arts center in the country. In 1989, the district agreed to another ongoing 0.10 percent sales tax levy to finance the construction of a baseball stadium in downtown Denver. The levy was discontinued in 1991 upon the final defeasance of all of its outstanding debt.

Metropolitan consolidation in Denver had one last step to take. In 2004, the mayors, business leaders, and voters of the region approved a sales tax increase to build a metropolitan rapid transit system that would tie the people of the metropolitan region together. The community planned to raise and spend $7.8 billion by 2013. This amount was raised, but additional funds will be needed to compete the rapid transit project.

Today, Denver is a dynamic hub for aviation, aerospace, bioscience, broadcasting and telecommunications, renewable energy, financial services, health care, and information technology. With a population of 2.5 million, it is the twenty-first-largest metropolitan statistical area (MSA) in the United States. Denver ranks fifth in the United States for foreign direct investment (FDI) and, according to Brookings 2011 ranking of economic performance, is ranked 102 among metropolitan regions worldwide. Its median household income ranks eleventh in the United States, exceeding the standard metropolitan areas (SMAs) of Chicago, New York City, Seattle, Philadelphia, Austin, Dallas, and Los Angeles—not bad for a city seen as a loser in the 1960s and 1970s. According to *Forbes,* Denver is the fifth best metropolitan region in the United States for businesses and careers and the seventh-most-wired city in America. The largest employers in Denver include Lockheed Martin, Health One, Frontier Airlines, CenturyLink, Kaiser Permanente, Wells Fargo Bank, Centura Health, DirecTV, and Comcast.[4]

What is most interesting about the progress of Denver is that the city region took a cooperative and collaborative approach to metropolitan regionalization. It was preempted by the Poundstone Amendment from pursuing the aggressive nineteenth- and twentieth-century annexations carried out politically by New York City, Chicago, Philadelphia, Pittsburgh, Boston, and many other major U.S. cities. These cities crushed the independent economies and initiatives of annexed towns and cities and diverted their energy to the central city.[5] In contrast, Denver has flourished by collaborating with its surrounding municipalities and counties to create a region of mutual benefit.

No great city of the world is a single municipal entity. Like Denver, all great cities are city regions, coordinated by metropolitan government organization. Greater Tokyo is the world's most populous metropolitan area, with upward of 35 million people and 13,500 square kilometers (5,200 square miles) of landmass.[6] Metropolitan Tokyo's population is governed and administered in 23 special wards, which are individual cities with local governments. The metropolitan government also administers 39 municipalities in the western part of the metropolitan prefecture and the two outlying island chains. Greater Tokyo is the world's largest urban agglomeration economy, with an annual GDP of US$1.9 trillion,[7] ahead of New York City's metropolitan annual GDP of $1.2 trillion, as of 2012.[8] The city hosts the headquarters of 51 of the Fortune Global 500 companies, the highest number of any city.[9]

The 12 million population of Mumbai, India, and its 4,355 square kilometers (1,681.5 square miles) of land are governed by the Mumbai Metropolitan Region Development Authority, which consists of seven municipal corporations and 15 smaller municipal councils.[10] In Brazil, São Paulo's metropolitan region of 20 million people inhabiting 8,000 square kilometers (roughly 3,089 square miles) is governed by a regional authority comprising 39 municipalities, including the municipality of São Paulo.[11]

Returning to the case of Denver, we see the scale challenge of the 12-county Denver-Aurora Metropolitan Statistical Area against competitive foreign city regions in attracting large company investment for markets, production, wages, and other company benefits. How does Denver's SMA, with about one-tenth the landmass (401.2 square kilometers, or 154.9 square miles) and less than one-quarter of the population of Mumbai, compete with large cities of the world in attracting large company investment?

The most difficult problem that the leaders, planners, and promoters of investment in American and European cities face in attracting

MNC investment is the vast and daunting difference in market scale with metropolitan city regions of the developing world. From a scale perspective, American cities are more inclined to compete for business investment against other American cities of a roughly similar scale range than to compete against the midsize and large city regions of the developing world.

The consequence of this scale disparity in the West is evident. Top U.S. cities get larger as they suck business investment from smaller American cities. The East becomes effulgent with new cities, while the West becomes a wasteland of old cities. We deal later with corrective solutions for this matter.

Demographics

Each metropolitan area has a distinctive combination of demographics, the key ones being population, income, age, education, occupation, ethnicity, and language. Companies in different industries require unique demographic conditions to function effectively. Consider the following:

- Metropolitan regions with a large number of high-income households attract high-end retailers.

- Metropolitan regions with large aging populations and sufficient payment systems are attractive to health care providers.

- Metropolitan regions that have integrated their universities and research institutes into a strong pool of scientific and technical facilities and talent have the best chance of attracting companies with strong investment in research and development.

Sometimes an area decides that its current industries are slowing and that it needs to develop one or more new industries. One of the current attractive industries to develop is information and communications technology (ICT). New York City, notwithstanding its leadership in finance, media, and fashion, is the top city in the United States for high-tech jobs.[12] It is even seeking to expand its high-tech advantage. One of its major decisions was to build a climate that would attract companies in its ICT sector. One step New York City recently took was to form a science and technology collaboration with Cornell University and the Israel Institute of Technology. The educational institutions are planning a $2 billion Cornell University campus and office complex to be located on Roosevelt Island in New York City.[13]

This collaboration will enable New York City to stay ahead of 22 world cities that are trying to catch up and even beat it in ICT dominance, the top 6 of which—Stockholm, London, Singapore, Seoul, Paris, and Tokyo—are fairly close. Further down the chain of the world's top ICT-savvy cities are Los Angeles, Sydney, Beijing, Shanghai, Moscow, São Paulo, Istanbul, Mexico City, Delhi, Cairo, Buenos Aires, Mumbai, Johannesburg, Jakarta, Manila, Dhaka, Lagos, and Karachi. Former Mayor Michael R. Bloomberg and other New York City leaders saw the technology collaboration on Roosevelt Island not simply as an original initiative but as a necessary step in maintaining the city's leadership and keeping ahead of global competition.

Logistics

Cities are busy forming metropolitan authorities to advance their logistic capacity. Many companies need highly interconnected urban centers for conducting efficient production and trade operations. Cities needs convenient rail, road, telecommunications, marine port, and airport facilities to advance a diversity of industries, including manufacturing exports, ICT, tourism, machinery supply chain imports, food processing, and automobile assembly.

After a century of disputes over road, rail, and port connections between New York and New Jersey, both states formed a port district authority in 1921. This interstate compact, called the Port Authority of

New York and New Jersey (PANYNJ), along with the involvement of many counties and municipalities, oversees much of the regional transport infrastructure, including bridges, tunnels, rail, buses, airports, and seaports. The authority manages the bridges that connect New York City to New Jersey, including the Holland Tunnel, Lincoln Tunnel, and George Washington Bridge. It operates the Port Newark–Elizabeth Marine Terminal, which is the largest port on the Eastern Seaboard and the third-largest port in the United States.[14] PANYNJ also manages the LaGuardia, John F. Kennedy, and Newark Liberty international airports. This masterpiece of metropolitan cooperation has played an inestimable role in the economic strength of the New York City region.

Many jurisdictions within and between states plan major logistic centers and throughways. For example, Los Angeles and Las Vegas are working with their respective state and local governments to build a high-speed rail link. These cities want to reap greater mutual benefits in their gaming, information, hospitality, and meeting industries. This rail link would build a new global corridor of service industries.

Logistic developments also have a profound impact on U.S. ports. By the end of 2014, the Panama Canal is scheduled to have completed its greatest expansion, more than doubling its capacity and allowing it to handle the world's most massive ships. Panama City is responsible for the creation of approximately 55 percent of the country's GDP of US$35 billion,[15] with a growth rate higher than the country growth rate of 10.7 percent in 2012. According to the *Wall Street Journal*, "The economy of Panama is slated to continue thriving in 2013 after posting double-digit growth for two straight years as a boom in construction and transportation tied to the expansion of the Panama Canal continues to drive economic growth."[16]

U.S. ports are scrambling to keep up with the expansion of the Panama Canal. State governments and their port authorities all along the Gulf of Mexico and East Coast are seeking to spend billions of dollars building bigger ports in a rush to accommodate the larger ships that will start traveling through the canal. It is a high-stakes investment, and in a sense, they're all competing with one another. The ports that become the first go-to destinations for larger vessels will have a huge competitive advantage over their peers.[17]

On the other side of the world, port development is stirring contention in the relationships among countries. Gwadar Port in Pakistan is a major financial and construction investment by China to gain access to the Indian Ocean. Gwadar is a free-trade port in southern Pakistan. It is vital for oil shipment, because it accommodates about one-third of the world's traded oil. It is a transit route for oil from the Persian Gulf to China. China and Pakistan reached agreement in 2013 to connect Gwadar Port by rail to China.[18] This agreement has caused consternation in India and concern in the United States because of the potential use of the port as a Chinese naval base. China already operates the Gwadar port. The Gwadar Port is very important to the Pakistan economy and will increase its 2012 population of 85,000 to be far larger as Chinese investment increases in the city.[19] Gwadar is of vital importance to Pakistan's ability to attract investment in logistics development.

Incentives

Cities and metropolitan regions compete for the attention of businesses by offering companies a pallet of incentives. These incentives include industrial revenue bonds, tax increment financing for infrastructure, industrial enterprise direct or subsidized loans, site advantages, tax incentives, public utility rate breaks (water, electricity, etc.), and city projects and infrastructure improvements.

Metropolitan areas also offer training for new employees through their network of educational institutions. They plan new districts designed for work, living, and play that attract young professionals. They provide a range of social services that help to integrate a foreign workforce into the host community.

Las Vegas provides many incentive programs to attract new businesses for local economic development and expand the operations of domiciled businesses. The Quick Start Program offers up to $50,000 toward renovating existing structures to conform to current building and fire codes. Another program called the Visual Improvement Program gives rebates to businesses that improve the appearance of their establishments. The Fast Track Program enables city staff to work with owners for fast titles, permits, and licenses. The Las Vegas Redevelopment Agency offers financial assistance for high-rise residential, retail, hotel, and mixed-use projects. The Retail Downtown Las Vegas Program helps developers and brokers to find suitable tenants.[20]

On the other side of the United States, Arlington, Virginia, is across the Potomac River from Washington, DC, and has been successful in attracting businesses and associations that want to be located in the greater Washington area. It secured Boeing's regional headquarters and the relocation from Washington, DC, of the Corporate Executive Board, as well as Netherlands-based Kusters Engineering, the Bureau of National Affairs, the National Association for College Admission Counseling, the National Association of Broadcasters, the National Crime Prevention Association, the Center for Naval Analyses, the Defense Advanced Research Projects Agency, and many other businesses, government agencies, and associations. Washington, DC, is having a tough time keeping its agencies, businesses, and associations in its district.

Every city competes for companies with incentive packages and other business-friendly programs. According to *Forbes*, the top five cities for business in 2013 were Salt Lake City (home to Adobe Systems, Twitter, and eBay) and Provo, Utah; Raleigh, North Carolina; and San Antonio and Austin, Texas.[21]

Cities in other countries refuse to be left out. Toronto's Imagination, Manufacturing, Innovation, Technology program offered a basket of incentives to Coca-Cola that secured Coca-Cola's decision to lease

100,000 square feet of real estate and facilitated the move of the company's Canadian headquarters to Toronto's downtown core.[22]

Singapore also offers a broad menu of incentives to attract businesses. The city-state has been successful in many business sectors, but its attraction of financial institutions is outstanding. According to a 2013 U.K. survey of 300 bankers, 3 out of 10 bankers (27 percent) chose Singapore as their preferred place of work, compared to 22 percent who chose London. Another 20 percent chose Hong Kong, whereas 19 percent preferred New York City. Dubai came in at 13 percent. Such numbers may not be a shock to Wall Street, but they confound many American people and politicians who think U.S. financial services are paramount.[23]

Industry Clusters

Metropolitan areas need to think deeply about which industries they want to attract. It is not enough to attempt to draw in a new foreign car manufacturer. Such a manufacturer may resist considering a metropolitan area unless a cluster of other suppliers, distributors, and financiers also operate in that area. We call this an *industrial cluster*. Professor Michael Porter, in his book *Competitive Advantage*, presents many thoughts on the critical importance of industrial clusters.[24]

Businesses are attracted to industrial cluster environments that nourish their growth through business alliances and knowledge exchange with major companies in their industry. They also benefit from nearby suppliers, as well as collaborations with local universities and their scientific and technological talent, incubators, and educated student output. Businesses value the presence of private equity and other financial investment agents that focus on specific sectors for new venture investment and commercial financing.

Suzhou Industrial Park in Suzhou, China, is an excellent example of the attractive force of industry clusters. Its biotechnology (biotech) zone

has attracted many major global pharmaceutical and biotech companies. It has additional industry zones in ICT, new materials, chemicals,
media, and machinery. In the United States, the Boston metropolitan
region, anchored in Harvard University and the Massachusetts Institute of Technology (MIT), has created the famous Route 128 corridor
of companies in the ICT and health care informatics industries to rival
California's Silicon Valley.

Perhaps the most prominent industrial cluster in the United States
is in Houston, Texas. The energy sector drives the business activity
of Houston. Oil and gas companies are clustered south of the central
business district and in the Woodlands, a master-planned community
27 miles north of downtown. The energy sector accounts for 3.4 percent
of the city's employment, more than five times the national average of
0.6 percent.[25] Refineries and distribution centers cluster near the port,
whereas energy companies and other major employers tend to establish
a presence either downtown or in a submarket like Woodlands.

"Houston is clearly a growth leader," Walter Page, the director of
office research at Property and Portfolio Research in Boston, told the
New York Times. "It was the first major economy in the U.S. to reg-
ister more jobs than it lost in the recession. Employment here is up
3.7 percent since August 2008, when it peaked before declining during
the recession. That compares with New York's gain of just 0.7 percent
from its peak in April 2008 before declining," Mr. Page said.[26]

Supply Chains

Every product and service has an extensive supply chain for production,
sales, and after-sale service and maintenance. These chains are unique
to each industry and to each company within an industry. The supply
chain of production and sales is a cost and quality concern to companies. The after-sale supply chain is a customer satisfaction and loyalty
concern to companies and produces additional revenue.

Supply chains for production are complex, involving many independent businesses that supply parts, components, and systems for the assembly of final branded products that go to market. The classic American automotive production supply chain was Detroit. All three of the top U.S. carmakers were located in the Detroit city region, along with many major parts and component suppliers. The entry of foreign auto production into the southern region of the United States, with its nonunion labor market and lower cost structure, challenged Detroit's auto hegemony. American consumers took to Japanese and European cars with gusto for their high quality and lower price relative to models by the American makers. The unionized supply chain became a competitive disadvantage, because foreign makers brought suppliers to southern production venues in Kentucky, Tennessee, and Alabama.

Even before the financial collapse of 2008 that bankrupted General Motors (GM), American carmakers mitigated union costs and opened some factories in Texas, Kentucky, and business-friendly Indiana. GM and Ford Motor intensified their international expansion to counter declining market share in the United States. GM is flourishing in China with its state-owned partner SAIC Motor. In 2013, GM sold more cars and trucks in China than it did in the United States, and a foreign market outpaced the automaker's domestic sales for the first time in its 102-year history.[27] GM is now doing quite well; the big loser is Detroit.

Supply chains for sales are also complex, involving many independent intermediaries to promote, distribute, sell, and trade products to customers. American sales of foreign-made imports of American apparel brands go through a chain of production and distribution that may begin with textile fabrication in Bangladesh, design in Hong Kong, and cutting and assembly in China; then moves to importers to the U.S. market; and from there spreads to warehouses, wholesalers, distributors, and finally to retailers. Companies of the magnitude of Walmart ship directly from foreign production centers to their own import logistic terminals, on to their own distribution centers in the

United States, and then on to their stores. By owning its distribution and sales chain, Walmart gains great cost savings that enable it to sell to U.S. consumers at the lowest price.

There is also an after-sale supply chain that requires many independent businesses to maintain, repair, and service the purchased brand product. This is of vital importance to high levels of customer satisfaction and brand retention. The linkage of all supply segments is called the *value chain,* and it is paramount to brand companies with respect to quality, innovation, cost, and customer satisfaction.

A city region has to provide competitive supply chain advantages to any company it endeavors to attract to its region. Cities are consolidating regional organizations to amalgamate suppliers into supply chains relevant to the core industries they are trying to build. The 10 largest distribution hubs in the United States are Memphis, Chicago, Houston, Los Angeles, New Orleans, the PANYNJ, Philadelphia, Mobile, Charleston, and Savannah.[28] The distribution hubs play an increasing role in the assembly of final products to retailers, including repackaging, labeling, shipping, and information control.

One major difficulty that cities have in expanding their supply chain capacity is that each city region has a legacy business complex, which may or may not be suitable to new core industries and companies. For example, New York City has to handle the supply chains of three major industries—apparel and fashion, finance, and media. As explained earlier, New York is also leading in technology industry jobs. This poses a difficulty in collective agreement within the city region on the allocation of supply chain resources. As certain core industries decline in a city, there is great pressure to revive them with more dedicated supply chain resources. The tendency of legacy suppliers is to politically support the core legacy industry rather than to make way for suppliers of new core industries.

The legacy auto suppliers of Michigan and northern Ohio are trying to adapt to new generations of auto production, but in this case they are also trying to innovate new uses for their technology. There are fledgling information technology and media start-ups in Detroit, but is uncertain whether Detroit will or can find a new core industry to sustain the large city as auto production is reduced.

The greatest weakness in metropolitan economic development planning and business attraction is the lack of planning knowledge about the supply chain requirements of companies that the metropolitan area is trying to attract. Some metropolitan planning agencies are augmenting their staff with manufacturing and marketing specialists to better organize suitable supply chains for business attraction.

City regions in developing countries have a particular advantage in organizing supply chain clusters, because they are not burdened with legacy industries and legacy suppliers. China has a policy and network of special economic zones (SEZs) that deliberately congregate domestic and foreign supply chains to support global and domestic MNCs and large companies. The Shenzhen SEZ has a network of suppliers for its core ICT industry. Telecommunications giants Huawei and ZTE, formerly Zhongxing Telecommunication Equipment, have grown to global MNC status because the planning authorities of the Shenzhen SEZ solicited the right small or midsize enterprises (SMEs) to supply their industry. Likewise, the strength of the German auto industry rests upon thousands of specialty SMEs that supply parts, components, and systems to the top German auto brands. These SMEs account for 50 percent of the German GDP and 70 percent of Germany's workforce.[29]

The challenges of any global metropolitan region are to understand the quality and cost of its supply chain advantage and then to decide which industries and companies are best served by this advantage.

Central Government Policy

Central government policies and practices play important roles in global business attraction. No matter how attractive a country's cities may be in market size, household income, and available talent, monetary volatility is a major deterrent to investment. Because global companies use local currencies for their business transactions, rapid depreciation of currency value raises import costs for parts and components for assembled products. For example, the fast decline of the Indian rupee in 2013 made it difficult for both foreign and domestic durable goods manufacturers operating in New Delhi, Chennai, Kolkata, and Mumbai, which depend on imported components for the final products they send to market.

The trade policy of a country can impose virtual or real quotas on the volume of import sales. China limits the amount of foreign car imports with a 25 percent tax. Despite this high tax on foreign luxury cars in Beijing, Shanghai, Shenzhen, and other wealthy Chinese cities, foreign luxury carmakers cannot keep up with market demand.[30] These restrictions in foreign trade are also common in India, Indonesia, and many other fast-growing economies.

Regulations are another impediment that city regions face in attracting global companies and supporting indigenous business growth. India in particular is notorious for its cumbersome bureaucracy and costly manufacturing and commercial regulations.

U.S. restrictions on the export of advanced technologies impede the growth of city regions such as Seattle, San Francisco, Silicon Valley, Austin, Raleigh-Durham, Los Angeles, and Washington, DC, which are home to many high-tech companies. For example, officials of Morristown and the Newark–Union MSA in New Jersey, home of Honeywell and other advance technology companies, regularly lobby the U.S. Committee on Foreign Investment to approve American technology sales to China. Mayors and business leaders in Los Angeles are continuously pressing China to reduce its media import restrictions to allow more Hollywood movies into China.

London has relaxed its financial regulatory environment to sustain its preeminence as a global financial center and has attracted many

European, Asian, and U.S. banks and financial service companies. London is vying with Shanghai, Hong Kong, and Singapore to become a major center for trade settlement in the Chinese yuan currency.

Fiscal policy can be a major deterrent to foreign business attraction. The United States has one of the highest corporate income tax rates in the world. This inhibits many foreign companies from producing goods in the United States. Even U.S. companies do not repatriate their foreign profits for investment in American city regions because of the high tax rates. Many countries with low corporate taxes, such as Ireland and Eastern Europe, are more attractive to American manufacturers and software companies than their home country for investment.

One of the stickiest issues of Chinese FDI into the United States is the U.S. protocol for foreign investment. The Committee on Foreign Investment in the United States (CFIUS) has blocked various American cities' efforts to attract Chinese companies, such as the China National Offshore Oil Cooperation (CNOOC), Huawei, Sany, and ZTE, from investing in their markets. Many Chinese companies have a well-founded fear of industrial investment in the United States. The United States is politically hostile to Chinese investment that impinges on a broad definition of national security, particularly in energy, aeronautics, and telecommunications industries. The result of this restrictive regime is that Chinese companies instead spread their wings to cities of Asia, Africa, Latin America, and Europe, and U.S. cities lose this investment opportunity.

Social Stability

Companies need a stable social environment to maintain steady and consistently growing operations. The disorder, violence, and instability of great urban centers such as Cairo, Alexandria, Damascus, Istanbul, Ankara, Athens, and Dhaka have created great difficulty in attracting internal and external investment. In addition, these and other politically volatile city regions cannot withstand the outflow of capital and industries seeking safer havens for investment and company growth.

Before the Rana Plaza building collapsed in Dhaka, Bangladesh, which had a death toll of more than 100 people, American consumer apparel companies, like Walmart, Levi Strauss & Co., and Sears, were reconsidering their production in Dhaka factories that have multiple tenants, most of whom are domestic and not scrupulous about worker safety. The impact of the Rana disaster is impelling the American brands to occupy their own factories so they can control the working environment and safety.

This is a hard trend for domestic apparel makers to follow because of the high cost of limited land and manufacturing capacity. Some U.S. companies want to get away from the dangerous work environment of Dhaka. The Walt Disney Co. announced that it would no longer license production in Bangladesh. Other companies such as Target and Nike have reduced their production in Bangladesh. The Bangladesh Garment Manufacturers and Exporters Association has reported substantial loss to its $20-billion-a-year apparel industry, and the government is strengthening its regulatory control of buildings to safeguard its garment industry, which represents 80 percent of Bangladesh exports.

Cambodia also sees an opening. "With the recent incidents, it's possible that external pressure will be so high that they'll have to shift," Ken Loo, secretary-general of Cambodia's Garment Manufacturers Association, told the *Wall Street Journal*.[31]

Political and Civic Leadership

Investors and businesses are attracted to city regions that have proactive political and civic leaders who welcome and support new business and investment. For example, Rudolph Giuliani turned a decaying and crime-ridden New York City into a world-class city that has attracted domestic and foreign investment at a scale to put the city among the top 10 global cities.[32]

Mayor Richard J. Daley was the mayor of Chicago for 21 years and chairman of the Cook County Democratic Central Committee. During his years in office, he promoted business investment in Chicago and turned a faltering city that had lost major industries into a thriving commercial city with diversified small manufacturing.[33] In 2001, his son and then Mayor Richard M. Daley brought Boeing's corporate headquarters to Chicago from Seattle.[34]

According to a 2013 Thumbtack survey of more than 8,000 small businesses, among the most business-friendly cities in the United States in which to start a new business or expand an existing business, Austin is in first place because of networking, low taxes, and a community culture that embraces new ideas. Virginia Beach is next because it is only half an hour from the world's largest naval station in Norfolk. Virginia Beach's status as a vacation town also enhances its attraction for hospitality. Houston is third, not only because of Texas's light hand in overseeing local regulations and licensing requirements, but also because it abounds with affordable business space. Houston is the fourth-largest city in the United States, but its real estate cost does not reflect its prosperity. It is a low-cost but prominent city for businesses. New York City would cost twice as much.

Colorado Springs is next with its culture of individualism. It has business-friendly regulations and a highly skilled workforce with graduates from important universities in the area. San Antonio is next because of its talent pool of skilled software engineers, who work for 60 percent of the pay of their peers in San Jose, California, but enjoy a less expensive standard of living. You can get a mansion in San Antonio for the cost of an apartment in Silicon Valley.

Nashville follows because its living costs and its taxes are low. It is a great music center and attracts entrepreneurs to invest in its entertainment venues. The Dallas–Fort Worth–Arlington metroplex of 6.7 million people follows on the list because of its low taxes, a business-friendly government, and a high economic growth rate. Raleigh–Durham–Chapel Hill finishes out the top eight because of the talent it draws from Duke University and the University of North Carolina, as well as the talent and business advantage of The Research Triangle and its 7,000 acres of high-tech research and development centers.[35]

Except for Colorado Springs, all of the other top business-friendly cities named in this survey are in the South. Within the United States, there is a tug-of-war between the old cities of New England, the Central States, and the Midwest for attracting new business and expanding current businesses and the far more business-friendly and less-unionized cities of the South and Southwest. Fundamentally, the country has a legacy North and a new-industry South. This poses a great challenge to northern political and civic leaders to keep what they have, let alone gain anything new. Additionally, Unions and civil bureaucracy are more implanted in the North than in the South. There is nothing in sight to change this trend.

We would be remiss to omit the deleterious effect of corruption on the business attractiveness of cities. The political systems in some cities, such as those in Miami and Chicago, are notoriously corrupt. Several past Illinois governors and numerous legislators have been in jail. This is probably the key issue on which Chicago's future turns. Across the world, countries such as Russia are so notorious for corruption that many global companies refuse to make investments there. Numerous MNCs avoid Russia's major industrial and market centers, including Moscow, St. Petersburg, Nizhny Novgorod, Yekaterinburg, and Novosibirsk.

Institutional Strength

Global business needs talented individuals, and these individuals' families need a lifestyle of comfort, good education, wellness, and continuing intellectual and creative exchange. The successful cities and towns along Massachusetts Route 128 thrive with burgeoning new technologies in health care and CIT. Harvard and MIT produce the scientific and technical advancement for these and other industries. Local governments in Massachusetts have created the best public school system in the country to attract talent to the Boston high-tech metropolitan region. Its cultural institutions are also of the highest order.

The vast and prosperous Zhongguancun Science Park in Beijing is rooted in three great universities, Tsinghua, Beida, and Renmin, as well as numerous government scientific and technology institutes. Hundreds of domestic and global high-tech companies have invested heavily in the park and are using its homegrown talent to produce new products and services for domestic and global markets.

Northwestern Polytechnical University and Xi'an Aeronautical University underpin the vitality of the Xi'an metropolitan region as one of China's leading aviation industry centers. Likewise, the Indian Institutes of Technology in engineering and management are located in 16 urban centers, including Chennai, Mumbai, and Delhi. They generate high-level talent for India's major industrial companies, as well as foreign businesses in those cities.

Talented people need a rich cultural life for their inquisitive minds and sensitive tastes. The Lincoln Center in New York revived decaying venues for the performing arts and created a landmark cultural facility for the educated and culturally enlightened audience and philanthropic community of New York City. It is the site of the Juilliard School, which attracts performing arts students from all over the world. Juilliard is constructing a music conservatory in Tianjin, China. The new financial district of Tianjin emulates the cultural richness of Manhattan and wants world-class Western musical training for its educated and culturally keen class. As of 2011, there were 30 million piano students and 10 million violin students in China.[36]

Commercial Strength

Retailers and property developers look for great commercial centers within which to establish a strong presence and build landmark commercial properties. Chicago revived its decaying commerce in the 1980s through the redevelopment of Michigan Avenue as a mecca for American Midwest shoppers. The redevelopment of decaying South Beach turned Miami Beach into a global tourism destination. The revitalization of the Bund in Shanghai has drawn luxury retailers to build signature stores in the waterfront area and make Shanghai the fashion center of China.

Many city metropolitan areas are planning for economic development and competing for businesses and investors to join their hub. The number of choice locations is more ample than the capital resources for investment. Businesses and investors have to make careful location selections to optimize their business growth and return on investment.

Conclusions

Urban centers that seek growth need to review their strengths and weaknesses. They must be realistic about which industries and companies they should seek to attract. An urban center needs a great amount of money to try to attract a new industry, let alone a major company in that industry. That urban center needs to review its standing on 10 factors: scale, demographics, logistics, incentives budget, industrial clusters, supply chain capabilities, central government policies, social stability, political and civic leadership, institutional strength, and commercial strength.

Questions for Discussion

1. Consider your metropolitan area. Name an industry or company that your metropolitan area might find it rewarding to attract.

2. Rate your metropolitan area on each of the 10 factors described in this chapter. Use a rating from 1 to 5, with 5 being best.

3. What are your metropolitan area's major weaknesses in the 10 factors, and what can be done about this?

4. After considering your ratings, would you recommend that your metropolitan area spend money to attract the industry or company you named earlier?

5. Should you consider going after a different industry or company, given your metropolitan area's strengths and weaknesses on the 10 factors?

3 The Real Generators of Wealth

Global Multinational Company Investment

We have made the case that in many nations, an inversion is taking place between the role of the nation and the role of its cities. Most economic thinking in the past has focused on how to build a nation's strength, with the nation's cities reduced to an afterthought. The normal hierarchy is the nation first, then the states or provinces, and finally the cities. This hierarchy made sense when the nation had great economic power and wealth and could dispense it to the states and cities. Today, this makes less sense, given that national treasuries are running dry and cities can no longer depend on the largess of the nation for infrastructure development, loan guarantee programs to local companies, employment and training assistance, and other types of support for companies to grow city economies.

Cities are turning increasingly to large multinational companies (MNCs) to make direct investments in their local economy by locating company headquarters (HQs), regional business centers, business division HQs, research and development (R&D) centers, and production and distribution facilities in their city regions, as well as by participating in public-private partnerships (P3s) for new physical and information infrastructure. Cities are reaching out to the private sector, principally to American and foreign MNCs, for local economic growth.

Let's look at the issue of infrastructure and its impact on local economies. There is a long history of publicly funded infrastructure development in the United States. The Dwight D. Eisenhower National System of Interstate and Defense Highways, federally authorized in 1956, is a national network of freeways that, as of 2010,[1] has a total length of 47,182 miles (75,932 kilometers), making it the world's second-longest freeway system after China's.[2] As of 2010, about one-quarter of all vehicle miles driven in the United States use the interstate system.[3] The original cost authorization of the federal highway system in 1956 was $26 billion ($225 billion in 2014 dollars).[4] This system has contributed vastly to the economic growth of thousands of cities along its routes.

Certain national governments still make large direct investments in highways, ports, dams, electric power, airports, and other vital infrastructure projects, which have an important economic impact on surrounding city regions. The Three Gorges Dam in China cost the China Development Bank US$148 billion by 2008 in construction, relocation, and financing costs.[5] By historic comparison, the Hoover Dam cost the U.S. government $50 million in 1931 dollars, the equivalent of $960 million in 2008 U.S. dollars.[6]

However, within the past two decades, infrastructure projects in both developed and developing countries have become too costly for public authorities to handle alone. These projects are increasingly developed by P3s, in which the private investments of companies and investors play a larger role than the public funding.

Since 1990, US$567 billion of state-owned infrastructure assets of Organisation for Economic Co-operation and Development countries have been sold to the private sector for P3 development, maintenance, and operations.[7] As of 2011, one-fifth of public infrastructure spending in the United Kingdom is managed by P3s. In Canada, P3s account for 10 to 20 percent of infrastructure. In Australia, even more is handled by P3s.[8] Although the United States lags behind Australia and Europe in privatization of infrastructure such as roads, bridges, and tunnels,[9] the global trend is affecting the United States, notwithstanding the legal, regulatory, and political barriers to this necessary direction.

Some U.S. states are moving in this direction. In Virginia, Australia's Transurban, a leading international toll road developer, teamed with the U.S.-based multinational Fluor Corporation to build 14 miles of toll express lanes on the Capital Beltway for $1.4 billion.[10] Figg Bridge Developers and Britton Hill Partners financed and built the Jordan Bridge, spanning the Elizabeth River between Chesapeake and Portsmouth. The Dulles Greenway, which opened in 1995, is a privately owned 14-mile toll road that connects Washington Dulles International Airport with Leesburg, Virginia. The greenway is the first private toll road in Virginia since 1816, and it demonstrates how the public and the private sectors can join together to supplement existing transportation infrastructure without raising taxes.

Large companies and their financial partners are responding to local demand for infrastructure to enhance city region growth as government authorities recede to a promotional and regulatory role, rather than a funding role. For example, the $3 billion construction project for Gabon's Belinga iron ore mine, which commenced in 2009, is China's largest mining operation in Africa. China Railway Construction, a Fortune Global 500 company, is building a rail system that links the Atlantic coast of Africa in Benguela, Angola, with two ports on the Indian Ocean in Tanzania and Mozambique. This is the first east-west rail link between Africa's two bordering oceans, and it is expected to boost city economies along its route. China Communications Construction is investing US$100 million in Myanmar's new capital city airport.[11]

In Europe, the Millau Bridge in France was financed with US$425 million from Eiffage, an $18 billion company with 70,000 employees, for a 78-year toll concession.[12] In 2013, The U.K. Treasury chief invited China National Nuclear and China General Nuclear Power Group to invest and play a role in the construction and operation of new nuclear reactors at Hinkley Point in southern England.[13]

The limited resources of nations for infrastructure investment have to spread their benefits across their diverse regions and cities because of political pressures. This means that each city affected by national infrastructure gets only a distributed benefit, which is not enough to give the major cities the competitive advantage they need in the race to attract investment. This is why cities throughout the world are undertaking local initiatives to attract P3 infrastructure investment, as well as industrial investment. Cities also cannot expect national governments to customize infrastructure to fit their unique industrial clusters. Local governments and local businesses have to solve their distinctive infrastructure needs with the help of nearby cities and companies.

Broadband infrastructure is a good example of this. Cities with intensive digital needs cannot depend on national or even state governments to support their service intense clusters. A port city cannot depend on national or state funds to modernize its city region ports in a global environment of port competition. The same can be said for airports and urban transportation systems.

As important as these infrastructure projects are to the undergirding of city economies, they still represent a minor percentage of total city gross domestic product (GDP) of trade, consumption, and private business investment. It's each city for itself. A nation will thrive only as a consequence of accepting the primacy of the new hierarchy: First build the cities, then build the states, and then hope that the nation will prosper.

Infrastructure is only part of the picture. Are cities capable of generating enough business to grow their wealth? The answer is yes, but only to the extent that cities can recognize and respond to the real generators of wealth. The real generators of wealth are midsize and large MNCs. In today's world, it is impossible for a city to generate a sufficient economy from small-business start-ups.

The economic expansion of world cities depends on attracting large companies to lay their eggs of global and regional HQs, R&D centers, and production and distribution facilities in the nest of city regions.

The gaming industry of Las Vegas has laid new eggs in Macau and Singapore, which are proving very successful. Rolls-Royce is investing US$550 million in a plant in Singapore, where it has started assembling engines for the A380 long-haul jets manufactured by Airbus. This investment alone represents 0.5 percent of Singapore's GDP.[14] General Electric (GE) has chosen Busan, South Korea, as its global HQ for offshore and marine business in light of the region's burgeoning maritime industry and cluster of marine-related offshore plants. Johnson & Johnson has moved its global general medicine HQ to Shanghai.

Most cities cannot generate an MNC or large business on their own. There are exceptions, such as California's Silicon Valley or São José dos Campos in São Paulo, Brazil, the HQ and major production base of Embraer aircraft. Although historically every big company started in some city, no city can plan on the accident of genius to grow a new industry and large companies. Cities need to continue to cultivate new small businesses for employment and revenue, but the major portion of their economic growth depends on attracting existing large, global enterprises to their location. City managers should think about how they can attract the right existing midsize and large MNCs to establish their presence and operations in their city.

The Growth of MNCs

Most businesses start out as small local enterprises in a town or city to serve citizens' food, clothing, shelter, and other needs. Businesses that do a good job of satisfying the needs of their customers earn a profit and use it to finance further growth. The successful small company might open a factory or another shop in the same city or in another city that it can use to produce and sell the same goods. By now, we can call this company a small or midsize enterprise (SME). SMEs make up most of the businesses in a nation. They create the largest number of jobs and revenue. As midsize companies with innovative and valued offerings begin to trade and then produce internationally, they may become MNCs.

In the United States, a small business is officially defined as having fewer than 250 employees for manufacturing businesses and less than $7 million in annual receipts for most nonmanufacturing businesses.[15] Midsize businesses have in excess of 250 employees and range in revenue from $10 million to $1 billion. Large businesses exceed $1 billion in annual revenue and are invariably multinational in their trade, production, investment, and procurement. As of 2010, 8,000 companies worldwide had reached the multinational benchmark.[16]

As companies enlarge, they often move their HQs and production centers to other cities in domestic and international markets for greater advantages in expansion and efficiency. For example, Boeing moved its corporate HQ to Chicago from Seattle. ADM (Archer Daniels Midland Company) has also made the decision to move to Chicago from Decatur, Illinois.[17] Cities compete for corporate and divisional HQs for all sorts of reasons, which are not always rational. It is dubious that Chicago will gain more than a return equal to the $60 million in incentives it offered to Boeing.[18] By contrast, Singapore has positioned itself to attract MNC subsidiaries as its core economic development strategy and has done very well. It has been announced that General Motors (GM) will move its international division HQ from Shanghai to Singapore in 2014.[19]

Foreign importers hear of foreign products and want them in their own market. After successful import, it becomes more profitable for large companies to move operations into import cities. Mercedes-Benz exported luxury vehicles to the United States long before it established production in Tuscaloosa, Alabama. Michelin exported French radial tires to the United States well before it acquired U.S. tire company facilities from Uniroyal and Goodrich and moved its North American HQ from New York City to Greenville, South Carolina, along with expanded production facilities in the Greenville region. There are often political incentives for offshore production. In the case of Michelin, the family-owned company had a fear of being nationalized and had to protect its private brand in a strong foreign market, such as the United States.

Large businesses grow by scale production and market share dominance. As exporting companies build their brand strength offshore, they soon figure out the economic advantage of foreign production. A business is likely to favor moving into another country that is close by its existing facilities, is at the same level of economic development, or speaks the same language. After a while, this company may have entered two or more countries offering its products and services. That qualifies this company to be called an international company.

As it expands further and operates on more than one continent, the company begins taking on the name MNC. Think of McDonald's, Starbucks, Nike, Coca-Cola, GE, GM, and other U.S. businesses that started locally, saturated their domestic market, and now reach throughout the world, deriving in many cases their largest profits from foreign operations.

Look at the path of GM: The automobile manufacturer started in 1908 and grew by brand acquisitions in the U.S. market for many years before it went overseas. In 1925, GM bought Vauxhall Motors of England, and then in 1929, it acquired an 80 percent stake in German auto manufacturer Adam Opel. Since then, GM has acquired many additional foreign brands and produced its domestic brands in foreign markets. Today, 70 percent of GM vehicles are produced outside of the United States. GM has a 2013 U.S. auto market share of around 17.9 percent.[20]

Think similarly of Toyota Motor and Panasonic in Japan or Samsung and Hyundai Motor in South Korea, not to mention the luxury fashion brands of France and Italy. To do business in another country, a company first chooses a base city from which to run its expansion activities. This may be a regional corporate HQ for Europe, Asia, Latin America, or other regions. For Europe, the company may place its regional corporate HQ in London, Dublin, Paris, or Frankfurt. For Asia, it will probably locate its HQ in Singapore or Hong Kong.

MNCs may also set up global HQs for their strategic business units (SBUs) in key cities that are central to the global network of the SBUs. Philips moved its global domestic appliances HQ from Amsterdam to Shanghai. In 2011, Rolls-Royce moved its global marine business HQ from London to Singapore, and Bayer relocated its general medicine SBU to China. GE moved its x-ray equipment HQ from Wisconsin to Beijing in 2011, and it moved its global marine business to Korea in 2013. In 2012, Procter & Gamble (P&G) moved its global beauty care SBU from Ohio to Singapore.

As early as 2007, Dell set up its global logistics and supply chain center in Singapore. In 2010, it made Bangalore, India, its global servicing hub. In 2006, IBM chose Shenzhen as its global sourcing HQ and created a global research center in Beijing. From modest beginnings in 2003, Microsoft has built many major advanced technology centers in Beijing.

You can begin to see the changing configuration of MNC growth and its economic impact on foreign cities as MNCs face the robust growth of developing-city market economies and the greater opportunities for profit in developing city regions than in stagnant developed regions. This movement is a tremendous boost to the economies of major cities in developing regions, such as Singapore, Beijing, Bangalore, Shanghai, Mumbai, Dubai, Istanbul, Kuala Lumpur,

Lagos, São Paulo, and Mexico City, but it also presents an economic challenge to major cities of historic commercial and industrial centers in North America and Europe.

The developing world is also generating new MNCs in familiar and unfamiliar cities. Huawei of Shenzhen, China, is already the largest telecommunications equipment producer in the world and has branched its divisions and global regional HQs into major cities of both the developing and the developed world. The same can be said for Lenovo, which has now surpassed rival Hewlett-Packard (HP) as the largest personal computer manufacturer in the world. As the market power of developing regions grows, it immensely affects the economy of city regions in the developing world and causes decline in former HQ cities in the developed world.

As if the movement of MNC SBUs from developed Western cities to developing Eastern cities is not enough cause for alarm for the city economies of the developed world, a starker trend is at hand for Western cities. An alarming number of MNCs are moving their corporate domiciles abroad. Eaton, a 101-year-old Cleveland-based maker of components and electrical equipment (with a market capitalization of $32.5 billion), announced in May 2012 that it would acquire Cooper Industries, another electrical-equipment maker that had moved to Bermuda in 2002 and then to Ireland in 2009. Eaton plans to maintain factories, offices, and other operations in the United States while moving its place of incorporation to Ireland, where it plans to save $168 million a year in taxes by 2016.[21] Cleveland and the U.S. lose the corporate tax.

Perrigo, the largest maker of private-label over-the-counter medicines in the United States (with a market capitalization of $12.4 billion), is moving its corporate legal domicile in 2013 from Allegan, Michigan, to Ireland as part of its $8.6 acquisition of Irish-based Elan. This move will reduce its corporate tax rate from 23.2 percent to 17 percent, and the company will gain $150 million in tax and expense savings.[22] For now, management remains in Allegan, but it will likely follow the company on the heels of personal income tax advantages. Apropos, Richard Branson has moved his personal legal residence from the United Kingdom to a Caribbean island, although he has not moved his Virgin Group's corporate HQ—yet. Many other corporate chief executives and celebrities have done this, as we describe in more detail later. As of the writing of this book, Pfizer, the world's largest research-based pharmaceutical company, headquartered in New York City, is offering to move its domicile to the United Kingdom in its bid for the acquisition of Astra Zeneca.[23]

Like Perrigo, Illinois pharmaceutical and generic drug maker Activis plans to make a similar move to Ireland when it acquires Warner Chilcott, a former Rockaway, New Jersey, company now headquartered in Dublin. Jazz Pharmaceuticals of Palo Alto, California, moved to Ireland after purchasing Irish specialty drug maker Azur Pharma in 2011. Insurance broker and consulting company Aon (with a market capitalization of $23.8 billion) moved from Chicago to London to be closer the global insurance market, as well as to benefit from a tax system where worldwide income is not taxed.[24]

Ireland is a favorite corporate HQ destination today, just like Bermuda was in the 1990s, when Tyco and Ingersoll-Rand moved there. Their move caused a congressional stir, and some minor difficulties were put in place to curb the ease of exit for American companies from the United States. But companies have circumvented these difficulties and now generally exit through devices like foreign acquisitions.

The United Kingdom and Switzerland are also favored corporate destinations for American companies in certain industries. Ensco, the world's second-largest offshore oil and gas well drilling company with more than 7,000 employees, annual revenue of around $2.3 billion, and a market capitalization of $12.8 billion, moved from Dallas to the United Kingdom in 2009,[25] following rivals such as Transocean, one of the world's largest offshore drilling contractors with a $16 billion market capitalization, which moved from Alabama to Geneva, Switzerland.[26] Offshore drilling contractors Noble (with a market capitalization of US$9.6 billion) and Rowan (with a market capitalization of $4.55 billion) moved from Switzerland and Houston, respectively, to London.[27] These companies move to achieve a low tax rate comparable to that of their global competitors, as well as to acquire ample technical talent, a pleasant lifestyle environment for management, and better alignment with the worldwide network of their industry.

We have to carefully distinguish these strategic market-based MNC management, R&D, and production moves from thousands of corporate domicile moves to tax and nondisclosure havens, such as the Cayman Islands, Mauritius, and Bermuda. These are fiscally motivated, not management or production, moves that the G20, a group of 20 countries, is trying to curb. HQ division and affiliate moves from west to east and west to south will increase in the coming decades as developing markets grow in consumption, trade, investment, and talent that match and even exceed developed market growth.

Several large companies are already giving up the idea of a single global HQ and have established dual global HQs. For example, the HQ of BHP Billiton Limited and the global HQ of the combined BHP Billiton Group are located in Melbourne, Australia. BHP Billiton Plc, however, is located in London.

In 2010, 73 percent of the world's 8,000 MNCs (defined as companies with US$1 billion or more in annual revenue) were located in cities of the developed world, and only 27 percent were in developing regions. Twenty cities, almost all in the developed world, hosted almost 40 percent of the combined revenues of all large companies. Of their revenue, 47 percent came from their global HQs, the rest—and majority—came from business subsidiaries, production centers, sales centers, and research centers in the four corners of the world.[28]

By 2025, McKinsey Global Institute projects an increase of 7,000 additional MNCs in developing regions, which will likely spread across 180 cities. In the developing world, 280 up-and-coming cities are expected to host a large company for the first time.[29] Forty-five percent of the Fortune Global 500 companies could be based in cities of developing regions.[30] Many Western cities will lose their MNC power, and many new developing-region cities will gain MNC economic power.

This trend of the movement of MNCs and Fortune 500 companies to the East and other developing regions has a profound impact on the ability of legacy large-company cities to hold on to what they have. The challenge to new cities, primarily in developing regions, is to accommodate the growth of new company giants.

In 2007, 600 cities with one-fifth of the world's population generated 50 percent of the gross world product (GWP); 380 developed city regions accounted for 50 percent of this total. Twenty percent of this total came from 190 American cities.[31] By 2025, 600 cities will likely make up 60 percent of the GWP, but the cities will not be the same. One out of three developed market cities is no longer expected to be in the top 600 cities. Instead, 136 new cities are predicted to enter the top 600 list, and they are all expected to be in the developing region—100 cities alone in China. Only New York, Los Angeles, Chicago, Dallas, Houston, Philadelphia, Boston, San Francisco, and Washington, DC, are expected to make the grade among the top 25 GDP cities because of the economic power of their MNCs. Only New York and Los Angeles will likely be among the top 25 in GDP growth, population, and total households. Only New York, Los Angeles, and Chicago will likely be among the top 25 in households with annual income above $20,000. None of these cities are anticipated to be in the top 25 cities in per capita income. U.S. displacement parallels an even steeper decline in Europe.[32] This changing landscape mainly results from the shifting landscape of MNC growth from West to East.

The United States is already seeing the writing on the wall. The *Financial Times* reported that

> In 2000, the US held 37 per cent of worldwide inward stock of foreign investment but by 2112, that share had dwindled to just 17 per cent. The US brought in $166bn [billion] in foreign direct investment in 2012, a 28 per cent decline compared with 2011 and slightly below 2010 levels. . . . In the first six months of 2013, the US brought in $66bn in foreign investment, well behind the $84bn of the first half of 2012.[33]

Foreign direct investment (FDI) tracks the growth of large companies in developing regions, which are not pumping dollars into the dormant U.S. economy. Notwithstanding the media hype about U.S. economic recovery, few U.S. cities are attracting FDI, or for that matter U.S. corporate investment. The United States is at an investment crossroads, and the road ahead looks bleak.

Large companies choose booming city regions around the world in which to operate by looking at a number of factors. Is the national government and political regime of the city region suitable for business operations? Companies do not move to nations or cities with high tax rates, regulatory hurdles, inadequate infrastructure, high corruption, relatively high wages, and lack of industry clusters and logistical supply chains. They move to growing city regions; in most cases, the cities to which they newly locate have a higher GDP than that of their countries.

MNCs ask these questions: What is the size of the potential buying population for the company's products? What is the income level of the average buyer? Is its middle class growing? Can the buyers be reached by advertising? What laws and regulations would have to be observed? What are the acceptable business practices? Is the economy growing or at least fairly stable? Which city in a country should the company first choose to settle its operations?

The Size and Power of Today's MNCs

Among the 100 largest economies in the world, more than 53 are countries, 34 are cities, and 13 are MNCs. The 10 top MNCs in sales are Walmart, Exxon Mobil, Royal Dutch Shell, Chevron, BP, Toyota, ING Group, Total, GE, and Allianz.[34] MNCs such as Walmart not only exceed the revenues of their HQ cities but also have more money than most national governments in the countries in which they operate. Such MNCs must be approached as civic partners. Walmart is bigger than Norway; Exxon Mobil is bigger than Thailand; Chevron is bigger than the Czech Republic; and GE is bigger than New Zealand.[35] And so the story of MNCs' scale goes and grows. City jobs and public revenues may be sustained by flourishing small businesses, but their economic power grows to the degree that they breed and attract MNCs and their affiliates.

According to the Fortune Global 500 listing of 2010, the top 50 MNCs employed nearly 22 million people worldwide in 2009. Extend this out further to the other 7,500 large companies earning US$1 billion or more in annual revenue, and we reach a significant percentage of the total global urban population of 1.5 billion people.[36]

The top 50 U.S. Fortune 500 companies in 2010 employed roughly 12 million workers out of the 55 million American people working for companies with more than 500 employees. Any U.S.-based company with at least 500 employees is international. Since the total U.S. workforce in 2010 was 157 million people, U.S. international companies account for at least one-third of U.S. employment. The extraordinary scale of these large companies is best revealed in their consolidated revenue in 2010 of $57 trillion, which is equivalent to 90 percent of the GWP of US$63 trillion.[37]

The public's attitude toward MNCs has varied over time. In the 1960s, some people saw MNCs as predatory companies carrying too much power and ready to dictate too many national economies. This view is still vented today by many on the left, such as Canadian author and commentator Naomi Klein, and antiglobalization groups. Some people are angry that MNCs are mostly from the West and bring Western values and culture to their countries. Yet we are also seeing the emergence of MNCs from developing countries, which are bringing their influence into developed countries.

We espouse a contrary view: The presence of large global companies and their affiliates determines the wealth of cities and the well-being of their citizens. MNCs have been the greatest cause of growing the middle classes of global cities. National, state, and local governments can alleviate the distress of their impoverished citizens, but MNCs build the middle class throughout the world. As much as we may talk about the importance of small business in the growth of national economies, the presence of MNC HQs and subsidiaries is vital to the economic growth of cities within a nation.

Thus, we have the paradoxical situation in which national governments endeavor to promote small business to generate employment, while cities compete to attract midsize and large MNC HQs, business divisions, and regional subsidiaries.

Cities Need to Watch MNCs Growth Plans

MNCs are always thinking about where they should locate their next operations. For example, suppose that the South Korean auto company Hyundai is planning to locate new plants to China, as well as elsewhere, that serve Asia, South America, and Africa. Hyundai has to decide which cities to select for new production plants. It has chosen Chonqing in China.[38] It also has to decide from which suppliers it will procure needed equipment and supplies. Hyundai also has to decide in which foreign cities to locate dealerships and how many dealerships to open in each city. The company's final decisions will make a big difference to the cities that Hyundai selects. Hyundai and other MNCs have the power to generate new wealth for cities.

Clearly, many cities will hear about Hyundai's expansion plans. Cities will line up for this opportunity, hoping to be one of the chosen few, whether it is for a new factory, a branch office, or dealerships. Hyundai planners will canvas candidate cities to assess their growth plans, the quality and skills of their workforce, and the city's quality of life. Each city will try to make its best case for attracting Hyundai. But the keys to successfully marketing a city are twofold: (1) to deeply understand what Hyundai is looking for and the weights that Hyundai places on different city attributes and (2) whether their city provides a good fit—because if it does not, the city is wasting its time chasing Hyundai.

We see that the real sovereigns are not the cities but the MNCs. These organizations have the wealth and capacity to choose locations, and their choices ultimately determine which cities grow and prosper. Chicago, Miami, London, Rhein-Ruhr, Amsterdam, Mumbai, Shanghai, and other major cities are reaching out to attract businesses. Business is the agent that produces growth. Cities are the vessels of growth.

Conclusions

Here are some points to remember from this chapter:

- Most nations today lack the resources to assist their cities in their effort to grow and prosper.
- The future of nations lies in the initiatives that their cities take to grow and prosper.
- MNCs are the global generators of city wealth.
- Cities have to deeply understand the opportunities available through attracting MNCs.

- Cities need to organize their leadership groups to be effective in wining and dining their prospects and in negotiating successful terms.

- Cities need to bypass opportunities in which the bidding is so intense that it leaves the winner profitless (the winner's curse).

Questions for Discussion

1. Which MNCs does it make sense to attract to your city? What are your criteria for choosing them?

2. How well is your city organized to attract MNCs? Have your business leaders formed a group to entertain and negotiate with prospective MNCs?

3. What incentives is your city ready to offer, such as tax remissions, subsidies, or free land?

4. How do you calculate the cost of attracting a specific MNC against the potential revenue and benefits in successfully attracting that business?

4 How Multinational Companies Target Global City Markets for Expansion

Given that multinational companies (MNCs) are the true powers affecting the rate at which major cities grow, we have to examine how these companies decide where to expand to and what characteristics they look for in a potential metropolitan (metro) area.

MNCs that hope to do well must look far ahead into the future to determine which areas they will enter and grow. Take for example, General Motors (GM). GM is strong in the United States and Canada, has operations in Latin America, and has one of its strongest positions in China, but has been weakening in Europe.[1] Clearly GM faces this question: Should it put even more resources into the areas where it is strong or into areas where it is present but weak, or should it put resources into new areas to start its presence there?

GM will expect its regional and country managers to make a best case for more money to be given to each of their operations. GM's chief officers will have to determine which opportunities have the best chance of yielding an acceptable return on investment. These GM officers will need to compile a lot of information to make their final decisions. In the end, GM will be giving more money to some of its regions and less money to other regions.

Suppose GM is trying to decide whether to allocate funds for increasing its number of dealerships in different cities. What does GM need to know about these cities? GM would want to know, among other things, the following:

- Projected economic growth of city regions
- Population growth
- Per capita ownership of vehicles
- Projected size of the middle class
- Plans for the city's transportation infrastructure investment
- Availability of experienced car dealerships and salespeople
- Social policies and environmental policies
- Quality of local banking and automobile financing systems

Auto demand is so great in China that both Shanghai and Beijing have restricted per family auto ownership, as well as permissible driving days per week per license plate number. Auto dealers are shifting distribution and dealerships to second- and third-tier cities, which have no restrictions, thereby growing those new midsize city regions.[2]

India is experiencing the opposite problem. The auto industry, which in the past contributed 7 percent of India's gross domestic product (GDP), has been hit by the collapse of the rupee, a rapid decline in a GDP growth rate to only 4.4 percent in 2013, and sluggish domestic demand.[3]

Domestic production has been hard hit by the rising costs of imported auto components, which rise further with the rupee's depreciation. This is a hard blow to major Indian auto manufacturing cities such as Chennai and Pune. Car sales in India fell monthly from November 2012 to July 2013. This is the first time India's auto industry has seen a decline since the global financial crisis.[4]

How MNCs Make Their Choices

Businesses are becoming increasingly professional in searching for and selecting the right location. To fulfill demand for the perfect city, an increasing number of consulting companies offer their services to companies seeking to invest. Banks, real estate brokers, and real estate developers also offer services to investors. Expatriate communities, such as foreign chambers of commerce, organize specialized location-advisory services. Services include location strategy development, labor market evaluations, operating cost and conditions comparisons, business tax comparisons, real estate searches, incentives evaluation, negotiation, and relocation project management. Evidence of this quickly rising volume of knowledge is the increasing number of city-ranking lists that have appeared in recent years. City regions are ranked by all possible—and improbable—dimensions one can imagine.

Many factors, often complex, influence the evaluation of a new city region for entry or expansion. Businesses call these indicators *attraction factors,* and they can be divided into hard and soft categories. Hard factors can be measured in more or less objective terms. Soft factors are not so easily measured and represent the more subjective characteristics of a city region.

Hard Attraction Factors

- Economic stability and growth
- Productivity
- Costs
- Property concept
- Local support services and networks
- Communication infrastructure
- Strategic location
- Incentive schemes and programs

Soft Attraction Factors

- Niche development

- Quality of life

- Professional and workforce competencies

- Culture

- Personal relationships

- Management style

- Flexibility and dynamism

- Professionalism in contact with the market

- Entrepreneurship

Different companies place different weights on the various factors. Many place most of the weight on hard factors related to minimizing their costs of operation. However, an increasing number of companies are shifting some weight to soft factors representing quality of life. The 2014 Mercer Quality of Life Survey[5] of 212 cities ranked the top cities in the following order: Vienna, Zurich, Auckland, Munich, Vancouver, Dusseldorf, Frankfort, Geneva, Copenhagen, Bern, and Sydney. The United States followed these international cities, with Honolulu in twenty-eighth place and San Francisco and Chicago tied in forty-second place. In Asia, Singapore (twenty-fifth place) beat San Francisco but Tokyo (forty-fourth place) trailed Chicago. Public transportation, including airports, and clean environments are among the top lifestyle considerations. Executives must find the right combination of such factors to emphasize.

Soft factors such as ethnic diasporas are also powerful attractions for investment. The Industrial Credit and Investment Corporation of India opened branches in Middle East cities and had a high density of Indian guest workers to provide a less expensive way to transmit remittances back to families in India. It has extended this strategy to many foreign cities in the United Kingdom, Russia, Canada, and elsewhere where there are large numbers of Indian workers. Corona beer established itself as the largest U.S. beer importer by following the vast Mexican diaspora that crossed the Mexican border into the United States.[6]

Executives thus have a number of high priorities influencing their location choices. Usually a group, rather than a single person, makes the decision using a mix of criteria. To complicate matters further, the criteria undergo constant revision as business, industries, consumers, investors, and other circumstances change.

Few cities do a decent job of anticipating midsize and large MNC location priorities and understanding their decision processes. Instead, there is a rush to offer competitive incentives to reduce the costs of doing business for potential investors. This form of national discounting marginalizes the benefits of investment in many important respects. Cities should instead examine their soft factors, such as ethnicity, and reach out to attract foreign suppliers rather than waiting for them to come. For example, Boston, Chicago, and U.S. cities with large Indian populations should take the initiative to approach Reliance MediaWorks of India to open theaters in their city for Bollywood films, which do not normally get distributed through the major U.S. cinema chains. Reliance could integrate the sale of Indian goods into a media mall concept.

This chapter addresses three questions:[7]

1. What are the main factors influencing midsize and large MNC location and expansion decisions, and what are the steps in the decision-making process?

2. What additional factors influence business, investor, and professional talent decision making?

3. How influential are published ratings of cities in the company location-seeking process?

Steps in the City Location Process

Companies and their executives always go through a location decision process irrespective of whether they are a business company or institution planning expansion, a financial organization planning commercial or industrial investment, or professionals planning their career. Cities must anticipate the steps in that decision process and develop a practical strategy to meet the needs and demands they represent. We first examine the geographical dimension of the decision process, followed by the administrative dimension.

The Geographical Dimension

Consider a company going through a site-selection process. The company is considering locating a factory somewhere in the Latin American region (LAR). The potential steps and considerations in choosing a site are described next.

The first step addresses the question, the LAR or not the LAR? Considering that the LAR is one of the fastest-growing markets in the world, every MNC wants to grow with this vast market. With a 2012 regional economy of approximately US$5.3 trillion and an annual growth of 5 percent or more, Latin America is a market to which MNCs have to pay close attention.[8] By 2025, 198 cities in the LAR with a population of 50 million will generate 65% of the LAR GDP at $3.8 trillion, with a per capita income of $23,000.[9] The highest number of high-net-worth individuals is anticipated in Brazil.[10] Within the past five years, more than 60 million consumers rose from poverty into the consumer class, half of whom were from Brazil.[11] Brazil is likely to become the top world-class country in Latin America, with São Paulo as the fifth-wealthiest global city by 2025.

The second-largest country in the region, Mexico, is part of the North American Free Trade Agreement (NAFTA) and is a gateway to the Central American and Caribbean markets. Mexico and Brazil comprise more than 60 percent of the regional economy and have large domestic demand potential. Chile has one of the highest GDP per capita rates in the region and is a model for attracting foreign direct investment (FDI) through international economic agreements from global manufacturers, retailers, commodity producers, and financial service firms. These countries have produced global giants in industries ranging from mining to food and beverages. Even Colombia has surpassed its safety issues and is becoming one of the most attractive countries in the region. Companies are expanding their footprint with deeper penetration in the maturing midsize markets of Colombia, Argentina, Venezuela, and Peru, in addition to investment-friendly destinations such as Panama.[12]

São Paulo and Mexico City are megacities, but they are not the fastest-growing cities in the LAR for sustainable growth. The best economic prospects in this region lie in Santiago, Chile, and Campinas, Brazil, a growing smaller city—with 3 million residents—that lies outside the congested São Paulo region.[13] Although most people recognize the magnitude and fortunes of the São Paulo and Rio de Janeiro city regions, the emerging cities of Belo Horizonte, Salvador da Bahia, Recife, Fortaleza, Curitiba, and Porto Alegre are determining Brazil's economic development. MNCs including Volvo, HSBC Holdings, Kraft Foods, Deloitte, Ernst & Young, Nokia, Electrolux, Toyota Motor, Exxon Mobil, IBM, KPMG, PricewaterhouseCoopers, Siemens, and Wipro Infotech are all located in Curitiba, in addition to large Brazilian and LAR companies.

Most Americans think of Mexico in terms of tourism. They are not aware of the industrial powerhouses of Guadalajara, Mexico's second-largest city and a major industrial and commercial center. Monterrey is also an important industrial center and the chief city of northern Mexico. Puebla (Puebla de Zaragoza), formerly known primarily for its textiles, now produces cars, petrochemicals, iron, and steel. These industrial and commercial cities of Mexico, Brazil,

Chile, and Colombia are growing their countries, not the other way around.

Once a company has decided to move into or expand existing operations in the LAR, management considers their best city options in the region. In the search for new business locations, companies are seldom interested in claims such as "best in Latin America" or "best in the Caribbean;" instead, they respond to functional arguments, such as those of a city that offers companies access to the internal LAR market. Miami continues to be known as a major gateway to Latin America, despite several LAR locations, including São Paulo, Brazil, and Panama City, claiming such status.[14]

During the next step, companies look for a comprehensive basket of city region offerings in all LAR nations. Most major LAR cities have established agencies for inward investments. This step is crowded with offerings, some unique and many not. Companies normally inform a number of LAR cities in different countries that a site-selection process has started with the obvious intent of boosting competition among the cities. The paradox, however, is that while LAR nations struggle to move toward harmonization of their individual economies, as well as balance with the economies of neighboring countries, city regions compete among one another to win midsize and large MNC centers and facilities for management, production, research and development, and distribution. Country economic development plans conflict with the various cities competing to attract midsize and large MNCs. The country may want to develop their second- and third-tier cities, but the major cities may be able to overcome the small cities for foreign investment.

Because of NAFTA, Mexican cities close to the U.S. border—Tijuana, Juarez, Monterrey, and others—offer unique advantages to North American business investment over other regional countries, such as Colombia, Brazil, and Argentina to the south, as well as even U.S. cities to the north. U.S. manufacturers considering off-shore manufacture think that Mexico is the most attractive nearby location from which to operate, despite drug war violence. Approximately 43 percent of companies with offshore manufacture prefer Mexico, with China in second place with a 30 percent preference.[15]

Even within Mexico, Monterrey and Guadalajara compete with different trade incentives for business attraction and foreign investment. Because of Mexico's spectacular inbound investment, other regions of the LAR have formed free trade zones to create a competitive balance in FDI. For example, Venezuela formed a Bolivarian trade region with Bolivia and Cuba to compete with NAFTA. Argentina, Brazil, Paraguay, and Uruguay founded Mercosur in 1991 and have attracted associate members including Chile, Ecuador, Colombia, and Peru.[16] Still, many countries and their competing cities work independently with worldwide cities, outside of the Mercosur framework. Brazil is proceeding to build a bilateral relationship with the European Union.

There are other regional trade groups in the LAR, such as the Latin American Integration Association (formerly the Latin American Free Trade Association), Central America Free Trade Agreement, and the South American Community of Nations. Still, the multinational LAR trade zones have not been effective instruments for inbound FDI. Mexico, Brazil, and Chile do better on their own than in combination with competing nations.

The investment attraction strength of Mexico, Brazil, Chile, and Colombia rests on the active investment attraction of major cities such as Rio De Janeiro, São Paulo, Monterrey, Bogota, Mexico City, Lima, and Santiago and other industrial and commercial metro centers. With a 2025 projected per capita of $23,000 and a projected population of 315 million people living in 198 cities in Latin America, generating US$3.8 trillion in GDP (65 percent of the total LAR GDP),[17] no MNC has the choice of omitting Latin America from its company market profile.

A decade ago, it was conventional company practice to start the international location selection process with a global region and then consider a nation within the region, followed by a region within the nation, a city within the national region, and finally, actual real estate property sites for facilities. Today, the steps are reversed. The global region is a given, and the nations are less consequential than the powerful industrial and commercial city regions within the nation. Market growth takes place at the city region level, and companies look to a city's regional district governments and national governments to see how supportive they are to city region investment initiatives. The steps look something like those in Figure 4.1.

There is a great deal of competitive intelligence data available to companies to determine into which of Latin America's 198 growing city region markets to extend their business. In general, MNCs have barely scratched the surface of Latin America's rapid urban growth. It seems paradoxical to say that the LAR is growing faster than

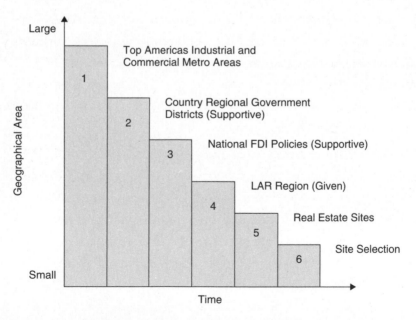

Figure 4.1   Six-Step Company Location Selection Decisions.

the MNCs, but some MNCs are aggressive and pervasive in urban markets, while others are laggard and indecisive in making their choices. A decade ago, a company simply located in the country's capital city. That is not the case today. Midsize and large cities beyond the capital city are growing faster than the capital city and the country GDP. Monterrey, Mexico, has a higher GDP growth rate than Mexico City and even Mexico. It is home to many MNCs, including as Sony, Toshiba, Carrier, Whirlpool, Samsung, Toyota, Daewoo, Ericsson, Nokia, Dell, Boeing, HTC, General Electric, Gamesa, LG, SAS Institute, Grundfos, Danfoss, and Teleperformance. And more MNCs will be coming.[18]

At the city or metro region level, MNCs meet the local economic power brokers, assess the facts of growth and competitive opportunity, and make their location decisions. Precise hard and soft factors, as described earlier, are evaluated. Many soft factors become highly relevant. Foreign companies quickly discover whether cities are living up to initial marketing messages and promises and whether local representatives are acting professionally.

The political influence of the city should carry weight in decision making, but it doesn't always play a leading role. For example, Chinese companies generally give too little weight to political influence in trying to establish their presence in the United States. Huawei is the largest telecommunications equipment maker in the world, but it cannot get a foothold in the United States because of political fears. Every effort to acquire significant assets or contracts is thwarted by politicians and regulatory agencies in Washington, DC.[19]

As a condition for its acquisition of Sprint, Softbank had to assure the Committee on Foreign Investment in the United States (CIFIUS) that it would limit its use of telecommunication equipment made by Huawei. CIFIUS views Huawei as a security risk, because of alleged ties to the Chinese military. Softbank uses Huawei equipment in its Japanese network.[20] Why did Huawei USA place its headquarters in

Plano, Texas, when it needs to make friends in Washington, DC? The company headquarters should be in Washington, DC, for the not-so-soft factor of politics. Instead, Huawei chose the hard factor of technology when it decided to locate in Texas, where it was unable to influence federal politicians.

After a company decides to enter a city metro market, it has to select appropriate real estate for its operations location. Consider the example of Chicago: Downtown Chicago is primarily an attractive headquarters location for companies in the financial services industry and media, not those in manufacturing, engineering and construction, logistics, telecommunication, energy, and other industries that cannot effectively operate in the congested and expensive real estate of the center. Large international and national companies, such as foreign-owned Takeda Pharmaceuticals, Siemens (engineering), and Aldi (food supermarkets), are located in the Chicago metro region but not in the municipality of Chicago. Takeda is in Deerfield, Siemens is in West Chicago (near St. Charles and Geneva in DuPage County, not within Chicago or Cook County), and Aldi is in Naperville. Even major U.S. companies are not in Chicago but in more suitable suburban locations: Grainger Industrial Supply, America's largest distribution company,[21] has its headquarters in Lake Forest; Beam, the maker of Jim Beam and other spirits, is in Deerfield; and Abt Electronics is in Glenview.

On Chicago's far northwest side, the O'Hare airport has opened the western suburbs of Chicago to domestic and foreign companies. Traffic from the airport to downtown Chicago can take 1.5 hours during rush hour. Companies and workers have settled in the suburban towns and cities of the metro region for decades to have accessible travel to and from work. Like many international cities, core city municipal centers in Chicago have become business locations for financial and medical services, cultural institutions, tourism centers, and residential areas for the rich, while heavy production and middle-income residential property workers locate in suburban towns and cities surrounding the primary regional city. Chicago tabulates its GDP growth not by its municipal boundary but by its standard metropolitan area.[22] Chicago competes feverishly with the towns and cities in its metro area for company location and company expansion.

Expanding from the United States outward, there are many surprises in the international location of great companies and institutions. It was a surprise to the international musical community that Juilliard School decided to open a performing arts campus in Tianjin, China, instead of in Beijing or Shanghai. But Tianjin's new financial district took the initiative to make this world-class cultural capture a high priority. Juilliard fell through the cracks of booming Beijing and Shanghai.[23]

It is not unusual for contradictory and internally competing solutions to threaten the most carefully developed decisions. A climate of local confusion often surfaces at the eleventh hour. The knowledge that a company has made a location choice spreads quickly among competing cities. For example, once ADM (Archer Daniels Midland Company) made the decision to move from Decatur, Illinois, Chicago, Atlanta, and other U.S. cities made a rash of incentive offers to attract the company. ADM finally chose Chicago and is seeking a Chicago downtown location.[24]

Monetary incentives are by no means sufficient for company attraction. A city region also has to have a reputation for being a good partner. Cities are wise to demonstrate aftercare for their new arrivals to ensure that a good reputation is communicated to others. Exhibit 4.1 in the next section discusses the roles of information exchange.

The Administrative Dimension

When an organization faces a problem with its current location, it must find a mechanism to retrieve information to make a wise decision. A company may feel that its present location is no longer favorable, or a recruiter may attempt to interest a company in seeing the advantage of a move. Although different members of an organization may play a variety of location selection roles, the person or group that is identifying the current location problem and is exploring new location opportunities may not be the one that makes the ultimate decision. Exhibit 4.1 discusses some of the roles in this process.

Exhibit 4.1 Six Buyer Roles

We can distinguish six company roles for new location decisions:

- *Initiator*: A person who has the responsibility to investigate the business climate of different city region markets may initiate the new location process. The impetus might be, for example, "Mexico City is a fast-growing market, with plenty of untapped opportunities. Although it will take many years to reach its full potential, we cannot afford to be left behind and ought to consider entering the Mexico City market despite the obvious hurdles." Walmart saw the long-term potential of its global growth and opened its first global outlet—Sam's Club—in Mexico City in 1991. By 2012, Walmart has 2,037 retail outlets in Mexico, and it is now the largest private-sector employer in Mexico with more than 200,000 employees.[a]

- *Influencer*: Influencers could be colleagues of the initiator. They may provide support, reflection, or ideas. It is important to be cognizant of who influences decision makers. Making a major effort to identify and sway the influencers is a wise strategy in a large investment project. Self-made billionaire Warren Buffett is probably the greatest influencer of enterprise acquisition and expansion in the

United States and offshore. Kohlberg Kravis Roberts (KKR) and Goldman Sachs play a similar role.

- *Decision maker*: Here, we meet the representative who has the formal authority to make decisions. Lots of unnecessary work—and wishful thinking—can be avoided if the city tries to ascertain the real intentions of the company decision maker. To understand the decision maker, the city has to be sensitive to intercultural differences. For example, a refusal to say *no* may not mean an eventual *yes*. Microsoft founder Bill Gates took the software company to China in 1992, where it bumbled its way for years before it finally got its footing. Ultimately, it took Microsoft 15 years and billions of dollars to learn how to do business in China, but Gates was convinced that China would become its biggest market and Beijing its key research center.[b]

- *Approver*: This is a person or group that can approve or reverse a decision. It can be, for example, the company's board of directors or even majority shareholders, such as when a group of shareholders with almost one-quarter of all shares in videoconferencing company Tandberg rejected Cisco Systems' $3 billion buyout offer in 2009.[c]

  The approver must be convinced that the decision is based on hard evidence to avoid backlashes later in the process. A specific investment project backed by financial incentives from a city can experience problems later if, say, questionable incentive payments are discovered. It is important to get a sense of whether the individuals negotiating an arrangement have the confidence and support of the approver.

(continued)

(continued)

Mergers always affect headquarters and staff relocation. Paulson & Co., the biggest investor in MetroPCS Communications, initially opposed its merger with Deutsche Telekom's T-Mobile USA because the combined company would hold too much debt. The merger later went through, and it will shift management and service resources to a better location than their former independent headquarter cities. MetroPCS is based in Richardson, Texas, outside of Dallas, and T-Mobile is based in Bellevue, Washington. Each city is competing to gain the benefit or reduce the loss of the merger.[d]

- *Buyer*: The company buyer is the person or team that implements the final decision. The buyer has an important role as the one to share with others experiences from the implementation. If the buyer becomes dissatisfied, a city can risk acquiring a negative image. Negatively reported experiences are dangerous to a city's reputation. During the political turmoil in Egypt in 2011, Nestlé suspended operations of its three factories in Egypt. Coca-Cola, Daimler, and Nissan Motor also suspended operations, and overall domestic investment declined drastically. However, by 2013, enough order had been restored that MNCs renewed investment in major cities of the country. Nestlé has invested in the expansion of an ice cream factory 30 kilometers (18.6 miles) from Cairo.[e]

Domestic investment is also increasing in Egypt's major cities. Egyptian billionaire Naguib Sawiris announced his plan to increase his investment in his country after the July coup that removed President Mohammed Morsi from power. Sawiris controls many large companies in Egypt, such as Orascom Group, Egypt's largest conglomerate. He also has deep financial interests in construction, telecom, hotels, and technology and employs more than 100,000 people.[f] As another example, Ford Motor was in China in the 1920s. After suspending operations after the Communist victory in the 1949, it took Ford 50 years to return to China for production.[g]

- *User*: The users of the company location decision include employees, suppliers, distributors, consumers and investors. These users are undoubtedly the best marketing ambassadors for a city.

Sources:

[a]Santiago Gutierrez, "Wal-Mart Is Latin America's Top Employer," PR Newswire, July 9, 2013, http://www.prnewswire.com/news-releases/wal-mart-is-latin-americas-top-employer-214797561.html

[b]David Kirkpatrick, "How Microsoft Conquered China," *CNN Money/Fortune*, July 17, 2007, http://money.cnn.com/magazines/fortune/fortune_archive/2007/07/23/100134488/.

[c]Steve Goldstein and Benjamin Pimentel, "Tandberg Holders of Over 24% Reject Cisco Bid," MarketWatch, October 15, 2009, http://www.marketwatch.com/story/tandberg-holders-reject-3-billion-cisco-bid-2009-10-15

[d]Chris Welch, "T-Mobile and MetroPCS Merger Finalized, Company To Begin Trading as 'T-Mobile US'," The Verge, May 1, 2013, http://www.theverge.com/2013/5/1/4286622/t-mobile-us-metropcs-merger-complete-tmus.

[e]Sara Aggour, "Euromoney: Nestle Egypt CEO: We've Invested About LE1 Billion Over the Past Three Years," Daily News Egypt, November 10, 2013, http://www.dailynewsegypt.com/2013/11/10/euromoney-nestle-egypt-ceo-weve-invested-about-le1-billion-in-investments-over-the-past-three-years/.

[f]Mfonobong Nsehe, "Billionaire Naguib Sawiris Says He'll Increase His Investment in Egypt," *Forbes*, July 17, 2013, http://www.forbes.com/sites/mfonobongnsehe/2013/07/17/billionaire-naguib-sawiris-says-hell-increase-his-investment-in-egypt/.

[g]Keith Bradsheer, "After Nearly 90 Years, Ford Wants China to Give It a Second Chance," *New York Times*, October 20, 2013, http://www.nytimes.com/2013/10/21/business/international/after-89-years-ford-wants-a-second-chance-in-china.html.

To illustrate the six buyer roles, imagine that a company based in California's Silicon Valley and specializing in Internet exchanges and software development wants to locate a branch in San Jose, Costa Rica. Costa Rica, small as it is, contends with Chile and Brazil in the fight to become the San Jose, California, equivalent in Latin America. It is already home to Intel, IBM, and Oracle.

The process begins after the Americas Conference on Information Systems in Dallas, Texas. One of the company's employees participated in the event and was impressed with the number of speakers who mentioned opportunities for information and communications technology (ICT) development in Latin America, notably mentioning the research centers and enterprises of San Jose and Santiago, Chile. She was so inspired by these city regions' market potential and the promising forecasts for San Jose and Santiago that on her way home, she wrote a memo to her colleagues (initiator). The market manager was interested and started to gather some general information on Latin American and Caribbean market developments and the particular alternative locations of San Jose and Santiago. The market manager also prepared for the chief executive officer (CEO) a list of additional potential cities: Mexico City, Buenos Aires, and São Paulo (influencer).

The CEO and the marketing manager decided to conduct a fact-finding mission. They traveled to both San Jose and Santiago (decision maker). Returning to Silicon Valley, the CEO presented to the board of directors a plan for establishing the company's first LAR office in San Jose. The board of directors approved the plan (approver).

To facilitate the implementation in San Jose, the CEO hired a well-known Costa Rican, who is given complete responsibility to establish the San Jose office (buyer). After six months, the original initiator moves to San Jose, takes over as business manager, and hires six additional employees (user).

Cities need to understand the structure of company location decision making. By understanding the different roles played by different people, destination marketers can implement a proactive strategy instead of responding reactively. Understanding the steps those decision makers will take is equally important for city managers.

The Four Steps in the Company Location Decision Process

The major steps in a company location decision process are (1) information search, (2) evaluation of alternatives, (3) purchase decision, and (4) postpurchase behavior. We describe each in turn.

Information Search

Location strategists use different levels of information searching. A minimum information search implies that the company's buyer already favors a city highly and needs confirmation. Basically, the buyer wants to make the best possible deal with the city and may talk about alternative cities merely to improve the company's negotiating position. The actual information search goes quickly and may not reveal the buyer's true intentions. The city's job is to find out what type of information search is taking place in each particular case.

A medium-level information search indicates a limited number of city options on the buyer's shopping list. An authentic situation of choice exists. The company buyer needs information to acquire an understanding of available opportunities but may already have a basic knowledge of the cities being considered.

A maximum information search requires a total analysis of potential city regions. If the project is a large one, consultants are often invited to conduct the information search. With the increasing number of Latin American cities competing for foreign and domestic investment and frequently presenting similar offerings, there is a need for maximum information searches in the LAR.

Maximum information searches are equally common in other parts of the world. With rising labor costs in Guangdong Province, China, industrial cities such as Shenzhen, Guangzhou, Foshan, Dongguan, Huizhou, and Shantou, many of the province's apparel, toy, and consumer electronics makers are moving operations to cities in Vietnam and Cambodia. Each of these countries has advantages and disadvantages. Vietnam and China have historic animosities that can backfire on a Chinese company. Cambodia has always had a more benign relationship to China, but the skills of its labor force are generally lower than those of Vietnamese workers.

In the United States, Austin, Texas, is racing ahead in its ICT industry. For new ICT companies, Texas offers cost-savings advantages over Silicon Valley in California. However, it does not have the intensive presence of venture capital funds that is found in Silicon Valley. It takes a careful information search to reach a location decision.

Buyer information sources fall into four categories:

- *Commercial sources*: advertising, destination-marketing materials, city economic planners, local business leaders, industry experts, and the Internet
- *Public sources*: mass media, trade publications, city ratings, and public reports
- *Personal sources*: family, friends, neighbors, acquaintances, and work colleagues
- *Experiential sources*: visits to proposed cities

The importance of these sources varies with the decision situation. Figure 4.2 shows how these sources relate to the steps that a company goes through in making a new city region location choice. In the first step (the total set), the company recognizes that many eligible cities exist, including many of which its executives may not be aware. In the second step (the awareness set), the buyer views commercial and public sources of information and becomes aware of certain potential details that are important to the company's needs. In the third step, a further search narrows the field to a consideration set based on certain

1. Total Set

Most cities that might be relevant for an IT company (could be hundreds)

2. Awareness Set

Assunción, Belo Horizonte, Bogotá, Buenos Aires, Caracas, Guadalajara, Guatemala City, Kingston, La Paz, Lima, Managua, Mexico City, Monterrey, Panama City, Porto Alegre, Quito, San Josè, Santiago, Montevidèo, São Paulo, Rio de Janeiro, Santo Domingo, Tegucigalpa, and Valparaiso

3. Consideration Set

Buenos Aires, Monterrey, San José, Santiago, and São Paulo

4. Choice Set

Monterrey, Santiago, São Paulo

5. Decision

São Paulo

Figure 4.2   Successive Sets Involved in Company Location Decision Making.

important criteria influenced by more personal and experiential sources of information. In the fourth step (the choice set), only the main competitors remain. Experiential sources now become crucial. The final choice set is often formed after intensive negotiations and is more or less guided by the exact fulfillment of the search criteria.

The real value for the city seeking company investment comes from recognizing the stages of the company decision process overall and the information search sets in particular. Knowing this, the city can undertake appropriate measures to meet the company's information needs. Exhibit 4.2 examines how a buyer gathers information.

Exhibit 4.2 How Buyers Choose

The decision to select a site has traditionally been surrounded by mystery and speculation, much like the selection of the Pope or the next site for the Summer Olympics. Andrew Levine, of Development Counselors International, polled 1,000 U.S. companies in an attempt to get into buyers' heads. The results are surprising and demonstrate that most cities make investments that companies consider to be of low priority:

- The number-one source of buyer information was the corporate grapevine, followed by news stories and corporate travel.

- Direct mail, meetings with economic development agencies, and print advertising were seen as less valuable.

- Buyers found that the most important support services were specific rather than general. For example, help in getting permits, information about relocating, and accessing training programs were highly rated. The speed of response was also important.

- Less crucial to buyers were general site information, nonrequested mailings, phone calls, and lavish parties.

The results are important. They imply that cities must listen carefully to what the company wants, be precise in answering requests, improve the various city operational service skills that meet investor needs, communicate clearly and effectively, and try not to confuse or dazzle the client.

Although Levine only surveyed U.S. companies, these results have implications for investment practices in the LAR.

Source: Andrew T. Levine, "Getting Inside the Site Selector's Brain," *Commentary,* Fall 1997, 20–26.

Evaluation of Alternatives

The alternatives to the choice of a location are evaluated by combining subjective and objective factors. The role of subjective factors should not be underestimated, as illustrated in Exhibit 4.3 by the site location process that led to the establishment of a Mercedes-Benz assembly line in Juiz de Fora, Brazil.

Exhibit 4.3 Subjective Evaluation

Daimler-Benz's decision to locate a new assembly facility in Juiz de Fora, in the Brazilian state of Minas Gerais, was made not only by assessing the objective attributes of prospective cities but also by comparing their performances on soft factors. Given the intangible nature of some of these factors, such as quality of life, numerical indexes were created. This methodology allowed dispassionate comparisons among contenders.

In the site selection process, Daimler-Benz's management team also took into account impressions formed during both official and unofficial visits to the cities. These visits rendered distinct benefits for the company. Official visits, for example, helped managers form an opinion about the accessibility, performance, commitment, and response time of state agents. By contrast, unofficial visits allowed nonintrusive observation of the day-by-day dynamics of the cities.

One of these impromptu visits led to the elimination of the Espírito Santo state, which had initially been one of the strongest contenders. The São Paulo state was tarnished by its negative image regarding its quality of life, union and labor relations, and safety. In addition, the widespread perception of urban violence in Rio de Janeiro negatively affected the evaluation of the city

(continued)

(continued)

in terms of safety and the effectiveness of state agents to solve problems.

Hence, individuals' perceptions, not necessarily substantiated by hard facts, deeply influenced the Daimler-Benz site decision process. In addition to fulfilling requirements set by company objectives, city leaders must do their best to correct inaccurate images of their cities and strive to provide company managers and officers with the best possible experience possible during their visits.

Source: Valeska Godói Gadelha, "Análise do Processo de Compra de Localidade: Estudo de Caso das Empresas Mercedes Benz, Volkswagen e General Motors no Brasil," [Analyzing Place Buying Behavior: Mercedes Benz, Volkswagen, and General Motors in Brazil] (master's thesis, COPPEAD, Federal University of Rio de Janeiro, Brazil, September 1998).

Despite subjective considerations, certain basic concepts can help us understand a company's new location evaluation processes. First, the buyer sees each contender city as a collection of attraction factors. Such factors vary with the type of decision:

- *Cities to live in*: job opportunities for family members, educational system, cost of living, and quality of life
- *Production sites*: relevant labor skills, labor relations, taxes, land costs, and energy
- *Suppliers*: necessary suppliers of resources, parts, components, and systems for efficient production
- *Service sites*: purchasing power and retail channels of the local and regional market, relevant labor skills, information-technology (IT) standards, and network of available competencies
- *Logistics*: storage and transport capacity for domestic sales and export

- *Convention sites*: service facilities, capacity, accessibility, service, and costs

Second, companies differ over which attractions they find salient and important for choosing a location. Each company decides which attraction factors are important and assigns importance weights to the relevant factors.

Third, the company is likely to develop a set of beliefs about where each city it is considering stands in regard to each attraction factor. The total set of beliefs that the company holds about a particular city forms the company's image of the city region. There may be a discrepancy between this image and the true standings of the city. A negative image of Colombia, largely because of drug trafficking, does not necessarily reflect the true situation of investment, trade, and consumption in that country. For example, in describing the successful launch of global bonds by Chile and Mexico in 2003, *EuroWeek* considered Colombia "one of the better plays in the Latin bond markets this year."[25] Thus, although competition in the investment attraction market is often a battle between perception and image, the Colombian example shows that perceptions among specific sectors may vary considerably from the general perception of a city.

Fourth, companies have a utility function for each attraction factor. Cities need to estimate the utility function of company decision makers to adapt their offerings and arguments.

Fifth, company leaders arrive at attitudes and judgments about choices of location through various evaluation procedures. Buyers may apply different evaluation procedures to make a choice between alternatives.

Purchase Decision

In the evaluation stage, the company forms preferences among the cities in the choice set and begins to lean toward a particular city.

However, at least four factors can intervene during investment, intention, and decision.

One factor is the attitudes of others. Suppose that the CEO of a Silicon Valley–based company is warned by a colleague about Brazil's erratic electric power supply. In August 2013, Brazil had a power shortage and transmission problem. There were many power outages affecting manufacture, as well as civil life. Recent improvements in infrastructure have mitigated this problem. Factors such as this can influence the ultimate purchase decision.

Another factor concerns the company's perception of the credibility of the people involved in the purchase process. A company decision's preference increases if the executives greatly respect the city official's opinion. As a result, it is important for cities to build credibility. One of the best ways to project credibility is to raise the public profile of local personalities by placing regular, well-written opinion pieces in major publications. Former Mayor Michael R. Bloomberg of New York City made his fortune in business and finance before becoming mayor of a great city. He thus had the professional respect of foreign businesses and investors and brought a lot of FDI to New York City during his two terms of office. He was not just a politician.

A third factor influencing a purchaser's intentions could be unanticipated situational factors that can emerge and alter the buyer's perception of costs and benefits. A Silicon Valley company's CEO, for example, may learn from news reports that Monterrey-based IT companies are having trouble finding enough IT workers and that the shortage is expected to grow as a result of the availability of more technical visas to the United States. That information could change the CEO's assessment of Monterrey. This is especially the case when the evaluations of one or more cities are close.

A fourth factor is that of perceived risk. New investment, especially if it is costly, involves risk. Risks of natural disaster like Hurricane Katrina affect location and investment in New Orleans to this day.

Typhoon Haiyan affects industrial investment in the Philippines. The political turmoil in Thailand has put a damper on investment expansion in Bangkok. Companies also face many risks in Latin American investment expansion. A new tax situation in Argentina, danger of expropriation in Bolivia, kidnappings in Colombia, or currency devaluations in Venezuela can occur suddenly. Different companies develop different routines for reducing risk, such as postponing a decision, gathering further information, and establishing preferences for safe situations. Cities must understand the factors that create a feeling of risk and provide information and support to counter them.

Postpurchase Behavior

After purchasing premises and operating in the chosen city, a company experiences some level of satisfaction or dissatisfaction. The city's job, therefore, does not end when the purchase is made but continues into the postpurchase period. This phase can be called the aftercare period. Indeed, in some LAR cities, such aftercare has been used as one of the main attractions, as well as one of the investment retention factors. Unfortunately, some cities have only belatedly recognized the impact of aftercare on reinvestment after years of neglect and the transfer of investors to more accommodating locales.

Postinvestment Satisfaction

What determines whether a company is highly satisfied, somewhat satisfied, or dissatisfied with their location decision? A company's satisfaction is greatly influenced by how closely the city's perceived performance matches the company's prior expectations. Companies base their expectations on information received from the seller, colleagues, friends, and other sources. If the seller exaggerated attraction factors, the buyer experiences disconfirmed expectations, leading to dissatisfaction. The larger the gap is between expectations and performance, the greater the buyer's dissatisfaction.

Chile and its major cities have met investor expectations for more than a decade. Chile is currently reaching a record level of FDI. In 2012, inbound investment reached US$30.3 million, which is 32.2 percent over 2011. This spectacular growth places the country in eleventh place among leading FDI host economies, according to UNCTAD's World Investment Report. Chile is now regarded as the most business-friendly country in Latin America.[26]

Since 1992, Chile's Foreign Investment Committee has tracked foreign investment satisfaction views. For each company that it lists in it tracking survey, there is a testimonial from a top executive about doing business in Chile. This gives confidence to business investors.[27] See Figure 4.3.

Figure 4.3   Testimonials for Chile's Business Quality.

Postinvestment Actions

The company's level of satisfaction or dissatisfaction influences its subsequent behavior. A satisfied company is more likely to say good things to others about the city it has chosen. Many cities actively use their satisfied companies as investment ambassadors.

The Organisation for Economic Co-operation and Development (OECD) gathers from a large sample of companies' perspectives on the ease of doing business in 189 economies throughout the world. In 2013 and 2014, companies expressed their satisfaction with Singapore and named it the number-one country for ease of doing business in the East Asia and Pacific region.[28] High ease of doing business ratings by the World Bank, and other international agencies like the OECD, influence companies in their selection of new locations for regional offices and operations. Reuters reports that "Singapore will dethrone Switzerland in the next two years as the world's top center for managing international funds . . . as a global tax crackdown and tighter regulation weaken the Alpine nation's appeal to investors." The prognosis was derived from a survey of financial experts in 51 countries.[29]

Dissatisfied investors often make their bad experiences in certain countries known through surveys. In the case of Mozambique, KPMG's annual Business Environment Index indicated that many businesses are dissatisfied with the quality of public services there. Only 2 percent of businesses were "very satisfied" with public services, while 37 percent were just "satisfied," and 26 percent were "dissatisfied." Corruption is one of the biggest barriers to improving the business environment of Mozambique. Corruption reduces economic growth.[30]

The Influence of City-Rating Information

Companies typically search for comparative data on the attractiveness of different cities, including GDP per capita adjusted to purchasing power parity, inflation rate, interest rate, and unemployment level. During the last decade, many new indicators have emerged, leaving almost no aspect of a nation, region, or city's attractiveness untouched.

City ratings, which have long played an active role in the United States, have become a common tool in Latin American countries as a result of the intensified competition between its top-ranking cities.

KPMG's Global Cities Investment Monitor ranks global cities according to different criteria, including three major groupings: political and economic context (consisting of political stability, market accessibility and size, and economic growth), workforce and cost criteria (consisting of skilled human resources, infrastructure, living costs, quality of education, and real estate availability), and quality of life and research (consisting of quality of innovation and research and of life). In 2013, São Paulo was the first Latin American city to enter the top six global cities in economic growth, market accessibility and size, and availability of real estate. This is a great breakthrough for São Paulo in the first instance, for Brazil in the second instance, and for Latin America in the third instance. The city now has to retain its current standing and show greater strength in the other criteria.[31]

Immediately after city rankings are published, winners usually exploit their positions in their city marketing promotions. For instance, São Paulo has extensively publicized in presentations, websites, brochures, and other promotional materials its outstanding positions in numerous international rankings. These ratings play an important role in the country's efforts to project itself as an attractive investment destination.

The struggle for FDI and other forms of investment is intensifying competition among LAR cities for international recognition. Thus, more emphasis is given to rankings, and the conclusions demand more attention. This is a worldwide competitive issue. An introduction to an Asian survey on best cities reads, "In an increasingly complex world, cities need to be run more like corporations, with an emphasis on planning and competent management."[32]

Today, company managers and leaders can access city region profiles on the Internet. These websites, easily found with the help of search engines such as Google, Baidu, Bing, and Yahoo, provide information on city geography, demographics, economies, communications, transportation, and military. Some websites allow viewers to compare hundreds of cities in several countries at once by listing similar information on different cities side by side. This feature helps company managers compare city regions in a practical way. The U.S. Central Intelligence Agency's *World Factbook,* the World Bank, the International Monetary Fund, the Economic Commission for Latin America and the Caribbean, and the Inter-American Development Bank are other principal sources of city data.

How Reliable Are City Rankings and Ratings?

City ratings are seen as having several questionable characteristics. First, different rating services often produce inconsistent rankings for the same city region. Confusion may occur when a city receives the highest rating in one survey and then, a month later, another survey using similar criteria reveals that the same city has fallen into third position.

The second problem is that the same rating service can change the city's position in line with new definitions and methods of collecting data. This can generate frustration and, if methods undergo significant change, undermine general trust in the rating.

The third problem is the difficulty of rating hundreds of global city regions. There are so much data available that companies have difficulty extracting meaningful information.

A fourth problem is that, because most city rating surveys are conducted in English, results may be skewed toward expatriate sectors of regional communities and the Western MNCs within those communities. It is difficult to get data on the economic growth of midsize cities in emerging economies and the growth performance of midsize companies. For example, the strong growth rates of many second- and third-tier cities in China and India are hard to identify. Rating surveys do not drive down enough to strongly growing cities but tend to focus on first-tier cities that may have less growth opportunity than emerging cities. Professional analysis is necessary to find the truly best hot spots for business investment. It takes intensive investigation to get beyond the first-tier cities of China and India to discover the opportunities of Wuhan in China or Pune in India.

A final problem is particularly nettlesome. In their competitive battle for investment ratings, cities continuously expand the scale of their metro region to absorb the new economic growth of outlying districts, which often masks the declining growth of central cities. For example, Chicago data show growth, but the real growth of the metro regions is in the outlying towns and cities of Joliet, Geneva, Naperville, and Schaumburg and in other intrametro municipalities. The logistic and industrial hub of Chicago reaches far beyond the municipality of Chicago. Is Chicago growing, or is the growth in outlying towns and cities? Should a company locate in Chicago or in Naperville?

For a company seeking a new market location, city rankings and ratings should basically be seen as scanning tools supplying initial data. It would be foolish to rely on these alone. The company needs additional facts and needs to put customized values on these attributes.

Conclusions

Cities that want to be more effective in attracting new company investment need to know the steps used by different companies in choosing a location. We described the steps in the company evaluation process. We illustrated the steps in relation to choosing city regions with opportunities in Latin America and other worldwide regions. We also emphasized the importance of chosen cities fulfilling the buyer's expectations so that they can credibly attract further investment.

All principles of identifying the best city locations, evaluating them, and choosing the top one can be applied to choosing any location.

The global city selection process is becoming increasingly complex. To discover the most attractive locations, companies need to be more systematic in their searches.

The information given in this chapter can help city marketers organize their understanding of what many companies go through in making a city decision for new market location. Despite being useful, the examples given here may not account for how all city decisions are made. Some companies may even shortcut the decision-making process for a variety of reasons. Still, anticipating buyer decision-making processes can aid cities in anticipating what companies think and do when making their global city location choices. The next chapter focuses on how city managers and leaders can develop a strategic plan to attract new and expand existing company investment.

Questions for Discussion

1. As a company executive looking for new market location, what is your procedure for identifying and choosing city regions to invest in? What are the major improvements that you can make in your process of identifying and choosing target cities?

2. What city selection mistakes have you made in the past, and what could you learn from this experience?

3. Do you have a long-term vision of city market growth on different continents and which cities are the best places for new investment?

4. Do you make it a practice to announce your intention to several target cities to get them to compete more carefully and be more generous in their terms?

5. How well do you audit chosen cities for your level of satisfaction and the level of satisfaction felt by the citizens of those cities?

5 How Cities Compete to Attract Midsize and Large Multinational Companies

In the last chapter, we described the processes that midsize and large multinational companies (MNCs) use to identify, evaluate, and choose locations to invest in. Now we need to turn to the place sellers: cities and metropolitan government organizations that use their understanding of the place buyers to prepare the best case for becoming the preferred and chosen urban location.

A city needs to organize a leadership group to work out plans for attracting companies, investors, and skilled workers to the city. The leadership group needs, with the help of community leaders, to define what kind of city they want it to be and determine what would satisfy the citizens and deliver growth, prosperity, and the good life.

The city must examine its main strengths and weaknesses, as well as its main opportunities and threats. Above this, it must be honest

109

with itself and only pursue what is reasonable and feasible. This will help it choose worthwhile company targets and not waste its time and resources in pursuing improbable ones.

Consider the case of Chicago. Chicago wasted a great deal of time, money, and reputation going after the 2016 Summers Olympics. After the Wall Street financial crisis of 2008, the United States had lost a lot of its glamour as a global hot spot for the world's biggest city event. President Barack Obama was a Chicagoan, which did not help matters. It probably was a negative factor in an increasingly multipolar world. But on facts alone, Chicago is not a suitable place for a multibillion-dollar constructed event. The city's Millennium Park was completed four years behind schedule and at three times the anticipated budget.[1] The Dan Ryan Expressway went twice over budget.[2] Chicago is notorious for its infrastructure and event budget overruns. Many trade and professional conventions avoid Chicago because everything is unionized, which means slow work and high costs.

There was a Chicago leadership controversy over the ambitious financial commitment that Chicago would offer for the Olympics. Then-Mayor Richard M. Daley tried to avoid signing the host city bidding agreement. He finally did, but probably not without notice of his reluctance by International Olympic Committee (IOC) members. Finally, everyone asked: Did the Chicago public want this event? "A *Chicago Tribune* poll . . . showed that only 47 percent of Chicagoans supported bringing the Games to Chicago while 45 percent opposed it," according to NBC Chicago's website. Add to this the IOC bribery scandal at the previous U.S. Olympics in Salt Lake City and a string of Illinois governors, mayors, and legislators serving time for crime, and there is little case for sustaining the reputation of the Olympics in the city. What may be good for Chicago is not necessarily good for the Olympics.[3]

However, it pays to study other cities that have had great success in attracting business, residents, and events. Successful cities include

Shanghai, Beijing, Mexico City, São Paulo, London, Hong Kong, Istanbul, Seoul, Milan, New York, Los Angeles, Seattle, Tokyo, and Paris.

One of the great location business attraction stories is the success of Suzhou Industrial Park. Suzhou is a classical Chinese city of great cultural heritage. But it needed to industrialize in the 1980s, so Suzhou's municipal and provincial leadership turned to one of the Asian tigers, Singapore, to lend its name and industrial development experience to build a vast modern and global industrial center in a cultural city. Singapore is highly respected by Western MNCs as a good place to do business. In 1994, Suzhou leased 80 square kilometers (30.9 square miles) to Singapore for the development of an industrial park. A US$20 billion investment agreement was penned by the legendary founder of modern Singapore, Lee Kuan Yew. The project has had its ups and down over the years, but it is now an industrial behemoth, renamed Suzhou Industrial Park.[4]

MNCs in Singapore had confidence in the development in Suzhou and located there, and Suzhou overcame early obstacles. Two decades later, Suzhou Industrial Park has grown to 288 square kilometers (111.2 square miles). As of 2010, there were 15,000 foreign-invested companies in Suzhou Industrial Park. The Park planners developed a higher education zone within the park, which included Siemens, Emerson, Bosch, Panasonic, General Electric (GE), Bayer, Johnson & Johnson, Nokia, and Hydro, as well as leading Chinese companies. Today, 40 Chinese and international universities are established within the education zone and supply tremendous talent to the companies within the park.[5] This is smart company attraction planning.

If we follow today's global press, there is a clear observation to be made: Cities are increasingly competing with one another to attract domestic and global companies and investment. New York spent $5 million for global advertising 2007.[6] We estimate that between 5 and 10 percent of today's advertising space in newspapers, in magazines, and on the Internet are devoted to marketing city places and countries. In addition, detailed surveys describing city regions are published regularly.

In this chapter, we focus on four questions:

1. What can a city do to improve its attractiveness?
2. Who are the major actors in marketing the city to midsize and large MNCs?
3. Which target markets does the city need to attract?
4. How do city marketers go about marketing their community?

What Can a City Do to Improve Its Attractiveness?

Before a city can get serious about attracting companies, it must undertake a solid assessment of its strengths and weaknesses. Does the city have enough physical and social infrastructure to absorb an inflow of new midsize and large MNC facilities and operations? Infrastructure means the basics of running water, waste management, electric power, police and firefighters, health facilities, schools, and a number of other things. Without any of these to a sufficient degree, the city can't hope to attract midsize and large MNCs.

One major deterrent to industrial development in India is the uncertainty of the electric power supply. In July 2012, India had the largest power outage in history that recurred over several days and affected more than 620 million people, or 50 percent of India's population and 9 percent of the world's population. Aside from colossal blackouts like this, outages are common in the industrial zones of Delhi, Mumbai, Chennai, Pune, and many of India's large metropolitan manufacturing centers. Although India has the world's fifth-largest electrical system and has made policy reforms since the 1990s, there has been little management follow-through. The grid is antiquated, and neither the gas nor the coal that powers 70 percent of India's electricity is a native resource. There is an ever-widening gap of electricity demand and supply throughout the industrial and commercial cities of India. Unless this problem is solved, India's major manufacturing cities will be hard-pressed to attract global manufacturers or domestic investment in manufacturing. Although labor is competitively cheap, energy is competitively dear. This is not a good prospect for export production.[7]

Besides infrastructure, other questions arise. Does the city have a skilled and unskilled labor force willing to work? Does it have well-trained technicians, doctors, lawyers, managers, and other professionals? Cities such as Boston, Monterrey, Mexico, Austin, Texas, San Francisco, and Shanghai have great pools of talent for high-tech business development. But that is not the case in some locations. Although land, facility construction, and unskilled labor costs are cheap in Eastern Kentucky, for example, there is a woeful lack of technical, professional, and management talent to transition from a declining coal-mining and steel-making based economy and attract high-tech investment.[8]

Beyond the existing workforce the company may want to draw on, does the city have some attractive features to interest the managers and high-tech professionals that come with every movement of a company into a new city region? Do the company's talented people want to live there? Does it have a good environment and educational system for new families? Does it have the amenities of parks, sports teams, good restaurants, festivals, museums, and performing arts?

The Maracanã in Rio de Janeiro, Brazil, originally built for the 1950 World Cup, is an example of a great sport attraction. It seats up to 125,000 people. Rio de Janeiro, as well as Sydney, Buenos Aires, and Xiamen, China, also have a desirable climate and amenities for middle- and high-income families and singles that come with global companies. In contrast, Zhengzhou, China, however ancient, logistically well located, and heavily populated for low-wage labor, lacks contemporary amenities to attract young high-tech talent. But Wuhan, despite being miserably hot in the summer, has several of China's top universities and an abundance of talent for invested businesses.[9]

The Sydney Opera House is a signature landmark venue that has become the symbol of the city as a modern, ambitious, entrepreneurial, and global urban center. When the United States needed immigrants for its growth, the Statue of Liberty became a universally known welcome mat for millions of new American workers. By contrast, a century later, the border fences and security of Texas and Arizona are telling Latin Americans to keep out.

The next attractiveness question concern access. Is it easy to get from A to B in the city using good roads for driving or good public transportation? Is it easy to get licenses to buy land and open a business? Many cities have simplified their regulations for new business start-ups. In 2013, the top five city regions in the United States for small-business growth based on company age were Houston, Tampa–St. Petersburg, Denver, Seattle, and Dallas–Fort Worth, according to business loan marketplace Biz2Credit. Even expanding to the top 10 cities for small-business growth, its list had no cities in the Northeast and only St. Louis in the Midwest. New York, Philadelphia, Boston, and Chicago were considered to have missed the boat for new business growth.[10] They are too highly regulated, too unionized, too expensive, and too heavily taxed.

Our main point is that if the city is lacking some basics or attractions, it has to undertake adding them before it can venture into the national and global arena to attract target companies.

Who Are the Major Actors in Marketing the City?

The marketers of a city for company investment can sometimes be difficult to identify. City marketing is a continuous process that involves all citizens. However, the groups listed here constitute the most active city marketers.

Local Actors: Public-Sector Actors

- City and state politicians and government managers
- City economic development agency
- Metropolitan government organization
- City region planning departments
- Public information bureaus

Local Actors: Private-Sector Actors

- Civic leaders
- City and metropolitan business councils
- Leading enterprises
- Real estate developers and agents and legal support
- Financial institutions (banks and insurance companies)
- Chambers of commerce and other local business organizations
- Labor market organizations
- Universities and training institutions
- Media (newspaper, radio, and television)

Regional Actors

- Intracountry and regional economic development agencies
- County, state, and province governments

National Actors

- Executive and congressional leaders
- Regulatory agencies
- MNCs and midsize businesses
- Legal and lobbying support

- Media relations groups
- Inbound investment business councils and organizations

International Actors

- Embassies and consulates
- International organizations and agreements with an economic development focus (e.g., the United Nations, Organisation for Economic Co-operation and Development, Association of Southeast Asian Nations, and North American Free Trade Agreement)
- Top global consulting companies that track and facilitate global investment (McKinsey & Company, Goldman Sachs, PricewaterhouseCoopers, Bain & Company, etc.)

We focus on the local actors. Place marketing strategy frequently emerges as a process in which the local actors provide the driving force. One could say: Think globally with the city marketing strategy—but work it out locally.

Public-Sector Actors

In cities where unemployment, underemployment, and weak economic performance are perceived as primary problems, citizens often expect their elected officials to improve the climate for local growth. Unfortunately, public-sector actors often do not know what to do when taking office, despite their campaign promises. They have a long tradition of focusing resources on redistributing wealth but often lack competence in generating wealth. Public-sector actors enjoy a proud tradition of social engineering rather than economic growth engineering.

A new generation of U.S. city mayors is trying to govern cities like economic growth enterprises. Voters are crying out for jobs, and these mayors are responding in a variety of ways. Former Mayor Michael R. Bloomberg of New York City, who built a business fortune from scratch, ran his office like a trading floor, "paying homage to business in almost everything he does," wrote an *Economist* blogger in 2013.[11] Bloomberg used business methods to improve everything from city services to long-term planning. He attracted great investment to the city after the 2008 financial crisis and began work to develop a new high-tech zone within Manhattan through the collaboration of Cornell University and Technion of Israel. As the *Economist* put it in 2013, "He sees New York as a corporation, city workers as talent, and the public as customers—and by and large New Yorkers love him for it."[12]

Bloomberg was not alone in his approach. Other U.S. cities are following Bloomberg's high-tech business attraction policy. The Mayor of Houston created a concierge service for companies, while San Francisco's Mayor organized a Tech Chamber of Commerce. The former mayor of Portland, Sam Adams, sought to double the city's exports. Mayors are stepping up to the plate of economic development because they cannot depend on national or state government investment initiatives. As the *Economist* reported, "Bloomberg argues that cities are being forced to 'tackle our economic problems largely on our own. Local elected officials are responsible for doing, not debating. For innovating, not arguing. For pragmatism, not partisanship.'"[13]

U.S. mayors are actively seeking Chinese investment in their cities.[14] Other cities around the world are doing the same. Tel Aviv Mayor Ron Huildai is wooing international business investment for the Tel Aviv's Tech Hub.[15] Chinese mayors take investment road shows to London, New York, Frankfort, Tokyo, São Paulo, and other business centers around the world.[16] City leadership initiatives are paying off. Google has opened offices at King's Cross in London[17] and Chelsea Market in Manhattan rather than in the cheaper suburbs. Zappos, an online shoe shop, has moved its 2,000 workers from the Las Vegas suburbs to the city's downtown.[18]

The trend of competitive city initiatives for economic growth and the business responsibilities of mayors and local officials will continue as the proportion of the world's population that lives in cities reaches an anticipated 75 percent in 2050 in the developing world. Experts at the think tank New America Foundation say that two-thirds of global economic output and an even higher proportion of innovations worldwide are being produced by just 40 global city regions.[19]

In Argentina, the financial crisis in 2001 and 2002 acted as a strong force, driving public-sector actors to deal with economic growth engineering. At that time, Buenos Aires fell from being the most expensive to the cheapest city in Latin America. Jobs were gone; pensions were gone. People took to the streets in violent protest, leading to the resignation of the president of Argentina, Fernando de la Rua, and the nation's economic minister, Domingo Cavallo. Argentina and Buenos Aires soon recovered its economic footing and grew up to 9 percent annual GDP by 2011, only to fall to 1.9 percent in 2012. Growth increases to 3 percent by 2013.[20] The Buenos Aires urban region contributes 36 percent of the country's gross domestic product (GDP) and produces 50 percent of the country's products but holds only 11 percent of its population.

At the local level, Buenos Aires officials and political party leaders, as well as business and civic leaders, are pressing for a new approach to growth. They have witnessed how new strategies implemented in some regions and communities have produced impressive results. The local media widely distribute cross-border success stories. The members of one community visit other successful communities to learn strategic city marketing.[21] When a sufficient number of local public-sector actors adopt a growth orientation, a climate for change is felt at the city level and presses upward to the national level.

In the 1960s, Brazil built a new capital city to emphasize the importance of leadership coming from a city. The new city of Brasilia was inaugurated in April 1960 by Brazilian President Juscelino Kubitschek. President Dwight D. Eisenhower and Queen Elizabeth II were among the 150,000 guests who attended the inauguration.[22]

Brazilian architects Lúcio Costa and Oscar Niemeyer, influenced by French modernist architect Le Corbusier, designed the city. Brasília was created to symbolize Brazil's aspiration to become a modern and leading economy in the world, and as "an emblem of the future."[23] The city is located in Brazil's central plateau, a fairly uninhabited location in the center of the national territory. The location choice aimed to make the city equally accessible to the various regions to integrate them into a new era of progress in the continent-sized country.

Leadership, talent, and a capacity to work out long-term strategies are the necessary characteristics of effective public-sector actors. These characteristics drive forward the climate for change. City mayors, city managers, and other public executives can act as important catalysts for creating a new local business climate. Exhibit 5.1 is an example of this.

Exhibit 5.1 Case Example: Mayor Bloomberg

Former New York City mayor Mike Bloomberg presents an example of the most comprehensive innovation in city policy and operations that affect the attraction of business investment. We focus for a moment on his pantoscopic vision and how he has become a model for city mayors all over the world.

Bloomberg served for 11 years, and during that time he oversaw reform in every department and agency of the city. One area of reform was education. Companies look seriously at the quality of local education, because their investment must be sustained by a continuing supply of talent. The talent challenge of cities starts at the primary and secondary school levels. Bloomberg appointed Joel Klein as chancellor of the new Department of Education, which succeeded the Board of

(continued)

(continued)

Education in 2000. Working with Klein, Bloomberg's strong mayoral control of education increased test scores and raised the high school graduation rate to 60 percent. This was the highest graduation rate since 1986. Bloomberg fought and later compromised with the teacher unions for greater productivity enhancement and took the controversial step of banning cell phones in schools.[a]

In social policy, Bloomberg led the legalization of same-sex marriage. This is no small matter for business. In the high-tech state of Washington, 17 percent of marriages in 2013 were same-sex marriages. There is a lot of talent in this segment of the U.S. population.[b]

In public health, Bloomberg appointed Dr. Thomas R. Frieden, an activist epidemiologist, and made HIV, diabetes, and hypertension top priorities. He extended New York City's smoking ban to all commercial establishments, including bars and nightclubs. This move was considered trendsetting, and many municipalities in North America and Europe have subsequently enacted similar bans. In May 2012, Bloomberg announced a plan to restrict the sale of sugary soft drinks in venues, restaurants, and sidewalk carts to 16 ounces (473 milliliters). This was supported by health authorities, but was widely criticized and eventually overturned by the courts.[c]

In environmental safety, Bloomberg proposed a traffic congestion fee to alleviate traffic jams in Manhattan. A fee of $8 would be charged for cars entering Manhattan congestion zones at peak hours to alleviate some congestion south of 60th street. The plan failed in the State Assembly. Bloomberg's ill-fated plan was based on systems in place in London and Singapore, which have been successful in reducing congestion, as well as pollution. Bloomberg also called for a ban on Styrofoam food packaging and began encouraging recycling of more plastics and food waste.[d]

In crime and security, Bloomberg continued the reduction of crime that began during the tenure of Rudolph Giuliani, the city's prior mayor. Bloomberg was a strong advocate of gun control, and many sting operations on illegal gun sales were conducted during his term of office.[e]

In fiscal policy, Bloomberg helped stabilize New York's finances by introducing and overseeing the passage of a $3 billion tax increase in the middle of fiscal year 2003. With the city's financial recovery in 2006, he unilaterally set aside $2 billion for a health fund for retirees formerly employed by the city. He was criticized by many for not cutting bloated city payrolls and for making New York City one of the highest tax-rate cities in the United States. Still, by strengthening the pension and health fund, he maintained the city's credit rating for bond financing even as many other U.S. cities were downgraded for perilous unfunded pension and health liabilities. New York City remains a rich city that managed to grow during Mayor Bloomberg's final term with no new taxes and no major public job layoffs.[f]

In economic development, Bloomberg focused on making New York's economy more diverse. One of his final development initiatives was the Cornell New York City Tech Campus on Roosevelt Island, which has attracted more than $500 million in private funds and is expected to strengthen New York City as an information and communications technology (ICT) and biotechnology innovation center. Israel's Technion, which has a graduate value output of $21 billion, has joined

(continued)

(continued)

the effort. From 2003 to 2012, information technology (IT) jobs in New York City climbed 60 percent, and venture capital deals rose 32 percent in the city despite falling 11 percent across the nation. More than 1,000 technology companies were hiring in New York City in 2012 and Bloomberg may have set in motion a new Silicon Valley on the East Coast.[g]

As these actions illustrate, Bloomberg is the kind of mayor who sustains and enhances a great city.

Sources:

[a]Ben Chapman, "Mayor Bloomberg's Education Reforms Yielded Mixed Results," *New York Daily News*, December 19, 2013.

[b]Michael Barbaro, "Bloomberg States Case, Emphatically and Personally, for Same-Sex Marriage," *New York Times*, May 26, 2011.

[c]Michael M. Grynbaum, "Health Panel Approves Restriction on Sale of Large Sugary Drinks," New York Tims, September 13, 2012.

[d]Esmé E. Deprez, "Plastic-Foam Container Ban Approved by New York City Council," Bloomberg, December 20, 2013.

[e]www.MikeBloomberg.com.

[f]David Chen, "As Fiscal Cloud Lifts, Mayor Offers a Budget Free of Tax Increases or Broad Layoffs," *New York Times*, February 2, 2012.

[g]Nikki Chung, "Putting New York City's Tech Jobs on the Map," *New York Times*, May 18, 2012.

Private-Sector Actors

Without the consent and active participation of private organizations and individual citizens, little growth engineering in a city is possible. Pride building is a primary element in a city marketing strategy, and it can apply to government, political, business, media, and community support for domestic and global business attraction to the city and its metropolitan region.

San Francisco has a dedicated agency, ChinaSF, for attracting business investment and Chinese companies to its city. San Francisco has had 150 years of ties with China from the tea-trading days of the past to the tech-trading days of the present, as well as a domestic service business presence in China. One-quarter San Francisco's population is ethnic Chinese, and many American Chinese populate the financial, engineering, architecture, and IT firms of the city, as well as its famed universities.

The San Francisco Bay Area is a metropolis of choice for Chinese companies seeking to establish North American headquarters and business operations, as well as for Chinese real estate investors, who are pouring into the city and driving up real estate prices. ChinaSF works closely with the San Francisco Center for Economic Development to attract Chinese companies to the city, as well as to attract private inbound investment.[24]

In addition to public/private investment attraction agencies like ChinaSF, great events in any large city build its brand strength to companies. The Olympics, the Formula One Grand Prix, the World Cup, New Orleans's Mardi Gras, and Rio de Janeiro's Carnavale have worldwide coverage that adds a lot of business value to host cities. But general pride among community members must go beyond the occasional megaevent. Pride must inhere in local universities with their unique profiles, science and high-tech parks with their entrepreneurial companies, a new high-speed railway, prominent companies and new start-ups with an exciting success story, and affordable housing and comparatively low taxes.

Global companies also want to know how dedicated a city is to improving services to its citizen and building pride in city communities. They are impressed by progressive services improvement. Foreign companies must have confidence that the citizens of the cites they are examining for selective investment are building civic confidence and household economic opportunity. They do not want to invest in an angry city or passive city.

One example of services improvement in India comes from Reliance Industries. The company offers mobile wireless in local loop services, which connect outlying subscribers to the common carrier. Reliance offers financing options for low-cost handsets and free calls for a low monthly flat rate, provided a subscriber signs up for the services for a couple of years. Reliance has made mobile telephony available to millions of low-income families that could not otherwise afford mobile service.

In Ethiopia, the monopoly telecommunications Ethio-Telecom structured its mobile network and introduced mobile products and services in 2011 to achieve equitable access to all income groups. This step-by-step business model allows low-income people to benefit from modern services. Ethiopia, like India and other developing economies, is interconnecting its people for greater consumption, knowledge exchange, and enterprise assistance. These local loops, enabled by advanced foreign technology, make people in outlying areas feel they are a dynamic participant in the life of their metropolitan city and its economic growth.[25] This can be rephrased in a more fundamental way: The city's marketable value proposition for new domestic and global businesses must be widely known and accepted by its citizens.

One important type of private-sector city marketers is the leading enterprises. These enterprises recognize the advantage they will accrue by helping to improve the city's image. It is good for their employees, it attracts suppliers, and it is good for their domestic and international trade. Business provides an enhanced image for a city and an identity that can be used in the national and international arenas. Such business could be the automotive industries in Kuala Lumpur, the software industry of Silicon Valley, the regional jets made by Brazil's Embraer aircraft company in San Jose dos Campos, or the fashion industry of Paris.

Among other private-sector actors, real estate developers and agents, insurance and financial institutions, retailers, and universities all recognize the importance of local identification for their future enterprise growth. Hartford, Connecticut, is well known for the number of insurance companies operating there. Columbus, Ohio, and Charlotte, North Carolina, spawned a number of new banks that went national. Houston, Texas, is well known as an oil and natural gas city because of the large number of energy companies headquartered there.

Real estate developers and agents have played critical roles in city marketing. Real estate developers are very active in economic development efforts, and they will continue to play an important role as place competition accelerates. Real estate developers and agents not only sell and develop property but also participate in larger efforts to raise the profile of an entire city. Real estate developers often have a good understanding of how potential place buyers make their decisions based on the attractiveness of a given place.

The local government of Shaanxi Province's capital city of Xi'an, the former eastern terminus of the Silk Road and site of the Qin dynasty imperial burial city of thousands of warriors, is spending $2 billion opening new ancient treasures to increase its tourist attraction and extend the duration of visits.[26] Private developers have renovated the classic architecture of the entire walled city into a stunning cultural and aesthetic destination for hospitality and consumption of Chinese cultural artifacts. Xi'an has also leveraged its Tang dynasty treasures into the industrial development sphere and has one of the largest high-tech industrial zones in China. Xi'an is now China's leading city in aviation technology and development. Kotler China helped plan the restoration of Xi'an's Tang dynasty summer palace, as well as its national commercial aviation base.

In another part of the country, property developers and global hospitality management brands have turned Sanya, Hainan, into the Miami Beach of China. By 2013, Sanya tourism reach 150 million visitors and a revenue of $3.6 billion U.S.[27] Approximately one-third of this revenue derives from international visitors.[28]

Like real estate developers, financial institutions such as banks and insurance companies participate vigorously in local and regional economic development. Financial institutions are expected to serve their market for a long period. If these companies are to grow, the local market must grow as well. Therefore, an active presence becomes a natural aspect of business strategy for banks and insurance companies.

In one example, global banks are moving to Nigeria. Lagos has become a city of 21 million people and has attracted foreign banks, including Citibank, Standard Chartered Bank, and Barclays, to participate in the growth of the city region.[29] Indonesia's Jakarta, a city region of 12 million, also has attracted many foreign banks, including Bangkok Bank, Bank of America, Bank of China, Bank of Tokyo Mitsubishi, Citibank, Deutsche Bank, HSBC, and Standard Chartered Bank. But in 2013, domestic Indonesian banks were outperforming the foreign banks. It takes time for foreign banks to establish trusted relationships that domestic financial institutions have developed over decades.

Beginning in 2000, Spain's two big banks, Banco Bilbao Vizcaya Argentaria (BBVA) and Grupo Santander, were invested heavily in operations in Latin America. With the 2008 global financial crisis, the desiccation of Spain's economy, and nearly zero growth in Europe, Spanish banking investment has increased heavily. "Santander's and BBVA's investment in Latin America, in terms of GNP [gross national product] scale, represents the biggest transfer of currency across the Atlantic since Spanish galleons crossed the other way laden with treasure from the New World."[30] Santander has banks in Mexico City, São Paulo, Rio de Janeiro, Buenos Aires, Santiago, and other large cities in Latin America.

Chambers of commerce and other local business organizations also can play a great role in city development. They are a great source of information and consultation. These types of organizations offer considerable support by establishing dialogue and partnership with local business organizations.

Every major city has a tourism and convention board. The Singapore Tourism Board has done an outstanding job attracting global conventions and meetings to the city's Suntech convention center. Singapore is building a new and larger convention center. The most aggressive boards globally after Singapore are Hong Kong; Brussels, Belgium; Seoul, South Korea; Toronto, Canada; and Orlando, Florida. The American industry of trade and professional associations, represented by the American Society of Association Executives, is moving beyond it historical base in Washington, DC, and has set up offices in Singapore, Seoul, and Shanghai.[31]

Among actors in the private sector, hospitality and retail industries (hotels, restaurants, department stores, other retailers, and entertainment centers) recognize that their success rests on the local image. The global apparel and fashion industry turns largely on the images of Paris, Milan, and New York City. ICT companies depend on the images of Silicon Valley, Austin, Seattle, and other cities where they are located. The American auto industry is rapidly repositioning itself away from Detroit. Once the bearer of a powerful image, Detroit is now saddled with an image of bankruptcy.

Xin Tian Di in Shanghai, which paradoxically was the location of the site of the first Congress of the Communist Party of China, is now a premier upscale entertainment site with fine restaurants and high-end shops. It is a cosmopolitan neighborhood for young Chinese and expatriate entrepreneurs, professionals, and executives. Manhattan and its theater district constitute one of the largest tourist attractions in the United States, and its Fifth Avenue, Chelsea, and Soho neighborhoods are fashion destinations. Every major luxury hotel chain is located in the midtown Manhattan.[32]

Labor market organizations have a different yet still high impact on a city's business attractiveness and its labor retention. While local universities and private industrial schools generate talent and skilled labor, union organizations often restrict talent and labor flow to sustain high wage levels for current members. Unions often oppose immigration that threatens a city market search for talent and skill, especially in periods of high unemployment. They are called upon to play a constructive role in negotiating with a manufacturing plant or business that is threatening to move out of the area. Chicago, Philadelphia, and New York leaders are among those in a constant struggle with construction and services unions to keep down the cost of labor for new business entry.

Architects, in contrast, can help create and promote a sense of place. Architectural style and design can reflect a city's ambition for growth in a direct and powerful sense. The skyscape is a symbol of economic growth. There is no question that the Petronas Towers announce Kuala Lumpur as a dynamic city. The Burj Khalifa in Dubai is the tallest building in the world. Dubai, only 8 hours away from two-thirds of the world's population, has laid its stake as a top global commercial city. Shanghai Tower is billed as the talent building in China. It epitomizes China's unstoppable growth and the centrality of Shanghai to China's economy. The failure to match these heights in Manhattan, Chicago, London, and Paris raises skepticism about Western economic growth.[33]

As a final example of private-sector actors, the media (newspapers, radio, and television) can help or hurt a city's image. If the media focuses on negative stories—bankruptcy, crime, poor schools, breakdown of infrastructure, resident flight, or pollution—it hurts a city's image. Detroit is caught in a media death trap. After years of receiving negative press for its defaults, crime, and now bankruptcy, businesses, investors, and visitors steer clear of Motor City. The city is trying to fight back, and there may be a comeback story in Detroit's downtown district that the media has yet to tell convincingly. Even in bankruptcy, Detroit is making a comeback in its limited downtown area. Campus Martius in downtown Detroit is seeing a resurgence of housing demand. Companies like Twitter and Quicken Loans are opening new offices in redeveloped historic buildings. Quicken Loans has moved thousands of employees from the suburbs to downtown Detroit. CEO Dan Gilbert has confidence in Detroit's renewal and is investing heavily in downtown properties, but he will need a lot of help from media, public relations, and the local politicians if Detroit is to be reborn.

In another media example, Beijing has been struggling to improve its air quality. It does have a pollution problem. The international media has magnified this problem with horror stories of respiratory calamities and mothers not letting their children outside to play.[34] One of the authors of this book lived part-time in Beijing for 14 years and finds these stories exaggerated, except possibly for people with asthma and special respiratory problems. But it is hard for the media to get off a sensational campaign, and there is no question that Beijing's pollution is a salient negative for business location, albeit arrayed against its positives.

City marketers must work closely with the media to communicate how city agencies are dealing positively with such negatives. Success markers have to be communicated to the media. Cities need regular dialogue with journalists and other media agents and should be straightforward with them.

The main point is that many features of a city affect how insiders and outsiders feel about it. The planning group must take all of these features into account in assessing the city's strong points and weaknesses. The planning group then selects the strong features to promote in trying to attract a particular company or target group and has ready answers to questions about weak factors and how work is going on to improve these weaknesses.

Which Target Markets Does the City Need to Attract?

A city needs to focus on three target markets in its search for growth and prosperity:

1. Business and industry
2. Cultural and educational institutions
3. Residents and employees

Attracting Business and Industry

We have asserted that a city needs to attract midsize and large MNCs to bring their business into the city. The city must decide which businesses and industries to attract. Attracting business and industry is the hottest market today because of a low global-growth rate following the financial crisis. Although cities in the developing world have fared better than developed cities, which are struggling with declining growth rates, business attraction to reduce worldwide unemployment in cities is a global imperative.

Too often, places fail to define what kind of businesses they should try to attract. The United Nations Conference on Trade and Development and the World Association of Investment Promotion Agencies have promoted workshops on investor targeting in an effort to help Latin American economies in this matter. There are many global business forums, such as those held in Davos, Switzerland, that city leaders should routinely attend and use to promote their cities as business and investment destinations. The *Financial Times, Forbes,* and the *Wall Street Journal* also have annual business forums. These are attended by public officials or civic advocates of cities. Companies attend to promote their business, not their place of business.

Cities need impressive official agents, business leaders, and celebrities. We are struck by the generally low caliber of bureaucratic officials that cities and higher levels of government send to business events and even allow to manage city attraction offices in top global cities. Lower-level bureaucrats are no match for the highly experienced business executives they meet. Too often, these bureaucrats know nothing about real business and speak superficially about abstract win-win policies to business leaders who live in a competitive win-lose business environment. Upgrading the caliber of city commercial representatives should be a high priority for most cities.

Most large cities use promotion agencies that offer investor services and develop marketing efforts to attract new businesses.

For example, after the stabilization of Brazil's economy in the late 1990s, automobile manufacturers such as Renault, Honda Motor, Volkswagen, Ford Motor, and General Motors announced massive investments in new assembly lines in Brazil.[35] Several metropolitan city regions competed intensively to attract the business.

Consider the challenges that Chile faced in trying to attract foreign investment. The Chilean Economic Development Agency (CORFO) invested a great deal to energize its High Technology Investment Promotion Program. The program was promoted online as invest@chile. Its main purpose has been to attract foreign IT investment to the country. In efforts to achieve this goal, the agency promotes an ever-greater amount of cooperation between the public and the private sectors. The main thrust behind the effort is the desire to launch new economy sectors in Chile.

CORFO is located in Santiago but is a national agency, and it has a wide berth of promoting business attraction to numerous Chilean cities. Businesses, however, want to drive down to a specific best place. The city of Santiago should add a ministry of economies to its makeup. Santiago cannot rely on CORFO to do its bidding.[36] It has to put forward its city leaders and specific opportunities it provides to foreign businesses as a city.

National promotion efforts are less effective than city promotions. Santiago is known for its economic stability and prosperity, perceived low-risk business climate, access to Latin American markets, and quality of life. It is also one of a new generation of *smart cities* that use software networks for sustainable operation and development. Such cities are also emerging in Europe's small countries, such as Oulu, Tempere, and Turku in Finland and Aalborg, Aarhus, and Odense in Denmark.

As a smart city, Santiago constantly emphasizes its commitment to support new IT endeavors.[37] It has first-class infrastructure that has already attracted MNCs such as Abbott Laboratories, AES Gener, Amazon, Apple, Alcoa, Caterpillar, and Chevron. Santiago is also

Chile's retail capital. Foreign consumer brands—Louis Vuitton, Hermès, Emporio Armani, Salvatore Ferragamo, Ermenegildo Zegna, Swarovski, MaxMara, Longchamp, and others—have opened retail outlets to make Santiago a Latin American fashion center.

Santiago has a partnership with Ciudad Empresarial, which is a high-tech business park in the Northeastern part of Santiago. They collaborated to develop a high-tech integrated smart city pilot project called Smartcity Santiago. The top private utility in Santiago, Chilectra, is partnering on a project to pilot technologies of the future.[38] Buenos Aires, Bogota, and Medellin, Colombia, have also been Latin American regional leaders in the smart city movement.[39]

Santiago is recognized as a top location in Latin America for its business-oriented infrastructure, healthy environment, quality education, and intellectual capital, labor efficiency, innovation, and financial institutions.[40] Santiago is the Silicon Valley of Latin America and competes for investment with other global high-tech intellectual locations, such as Kuala Lumpur's Multimedia Super Corridor, Tel Aviv, and Bangalore, India.

Despite Santiago's concerted efforts, competition for IT companies will constantly grow. Santiago and other Latin American city regions, such as Mexico City, aim to develop their IT sectors. Santiago must intensify its efforts every step of the way. Global market cities have to outpace one another for IT business attraction, because their competitive field is the globe.

At this point, let us turn to considering the types of industries and businesses it makes sense for a city to try to build or attract. We distinguish three broad categories:

1. Heavy industry (steel, cars, and refineries)

2. Clean industry (assembly, high-tech, and service companies)

3. Entrepreneurs

Attracting Heavy Industry It used to be the goal of a large city to attract heavy industry such as a steel plant, automobile factory, food-processing factory, or glass, paper, or chemical manufacturer. These businesses provided a lot of jobs. Pittsburgh at one time was an excellent example of a heavy-industry city. The main negative was that many of these factories bellowed out smoke all day and the city of Pittsburgh ended up having bad air pollution. A citywide movement was started to regulate pollution, and in the end these companies had to bear extra costs in operating their plants.[41] Several great companies moved most of their operations out of Pittsburgh: Heinz, U.S. Steel, Gulf Oil, and (in 2013) U.S. Airways, which merged with American Airlines.

Pittsburgh settled for replacing these heavy industries with cleaner industries. Turning to its major higher education institutions, such as the University of Pittsburgh, Carnegie Mellon University, and Duquesne University, Pittsburgh shifted its economy to health care, biotechnology, robotic engineering, and finance. The University of Pittsburgh Medical Center is the largest university hospital system in the United States, with hospitals in Ireland, the United Kingdom, Italy, and now moving with one of the authors to open research hospitals in China. Carnegie Mellon has spawned new robotic companies in Pittsburgh, and Pittsburgh is now home to PNC Financial Services, one of the fastest-growing banking systems in the United States.[42]

The Pittsburgh story reminds us that companies often choose to leave their location for a better location. Every day, businesses leave or threaten to leave one place for another. Cities that are looking for new businesses need to be alert to which companies in their city are unhappy and to try to retain them; likewise, they must be alert to which companies are unhappy with their current cities and try to attract them.

Consider an example. In December 2001, Euzkadi, a German tire manufacturer, closed its manufacturing facility in Jalisco, Mexico.

The company's decision was attributed to Mexico's labor laws. According to the company, the laws failed to consider the employer's needs.[43] Other cities need to know about this and about other unhappy companies they might pursue.

Heavy industry has primarily migrated to Asia. Chinese cities such as Wuhan, Changsha, Shenyang, and Changzhou are the new heavy-industry cities of the world.[44] Ulsan is the major heavy-industry city of South Korea. Visakhapatnam, India, is home to several state-owned heavy industries and a steel plant; it is also one of India's largest seaports.

Attracting Clean Industry   Instead of heavy industry, many cities today prefer to attract clean companies, such as software companies, advertising agencies, design companies, corporate headquarters, and retail businesses. Dalian, China, once a heavy-industry city, has become a high-tech city and the location of Davos Asia.[45] India's leading software cities are Bangalore, Chennai, Pune, Ahmedabad, Bhubaneswar, Kolkata, Ajitgarh, and Chandigarh.

Even small cities seek to attract strategically relevant clean development projects. Such projects often create side contacts with commercial advantages. Consider the example of Itajubá, Brazil, in Exhibit 5.2.

Exhibit 5.2 High-Tech Small Cities

Itajubá is a city of nearly 90,000 people in the Brazilian state of Minas Gerais. It is the home of Helibrás, the only helicopter manufacturer in Latin America, and has set a high bar for technology attraction.[a]

Itajubá aims to become a Technopolis—a community that values education and culture, and makes use of science and technology as a differential to promote a well-distributed and balanced comprehensive development.[b] To begin with, it has established a zero illiteracy rate objective. The strategy to use education, culture, and technology to foster development has led to the development of Incubadora de Empresas de Base Tecnológica de Itajubá (INCIT), an incubator park for technology enterprises supported by a number of local, state, and national organizations, including universities, small-business services, and governmental agencies. INCIT offers office space, computer networking, professional software, Internet connections, phone and fax lines, meeting places, laboratories, and consulting services to entrepreneurs who are willing to establish research and businesses within the city. Preferential sectors to receive INCIT's support include electronics, technology, information, automation, biotechnology, new materials, precision instruments, and the environment.

Despite its small size, Itajubá is already achieving prominence in the Brazilian marketplace. In the period between 1970 and 1996, Itajubá experienced the second-highest economic growth among all Brazilian cities.[c] According to the United Nations Development Programme, Itajubá's social indicators such as life expectancy, education, and per capita income have given the city the highest score on the Human Development Index in the state of Minas Gerais. Itajubá's educational system has probably helped it achieve this. Noteworthy is Itajubá's density of researchers—1,200 doctorate holders per million people—which is five times the national average.

Itajubá's holistic approach to economic growth, which emphasizes education and interorganizational cooperation, provides insight into the necessary steps toward bettering a place.

(continued)

(continued)

Itajubá is an example of a community that has separated itself from its competitors through a combination of inherited and accidental strengths, coupled with a determined improvement campaign.

Sources:

*a*Helihub, "Helibras Signs Partnership Agreement with Federal University of Itajubá," November 26, 2013.

*b*INCIT (Technology Incubator of Itajubá) and CEGEITt (Itajubá Generating Center of Companies), 2006, http://www.incit.com.br/en/news55.html.

*c*Nahara Bauchwitz, Liége Fuentes, and Neide Oliveira, "Salto Industrial: Cidades Médias Estão Mais Ricas: O Desafio Agora É Melhorar a Vida da População," *Revista VEJA*, March 7, 2001, http://veja.abril.com.br/070301/p_082.html.

Moving from clean energy initiatives to the performance of small cities in manufacture, we have the notable example of the Mittelstand SME companies of Germany. Seventy percent of German GDP derives from thousands of small and midsize enterprises (SMEs) in hundreds of small and midsize cities in the country.[46] Medion (electronics) is in Essen; Sellner (automotive) is in Heilbronn; EMAG (machinery) is in Salach; KSM (automotive) is in Hildesheim; Format Tresorbau (industrial) is in Hessisch Lichtenau; Gustrower Warmepumpen (machinery) is in Gustrow; and Preh GmbH (automotive) is in Bad Neustadt.

This is a good place to mention McKinsey Global Institute's regional forecast of urban economic growth rates. McKinsey predicts midsize-city GDP growth will exceed megacity GDP growth in the period of 2012–2015. This is true of Germany, which has no megacity of 10 million or more people.[47]

Another category of businesses to attract are successful exporters. A strong export industry makes it more likely that a city will develop a global orientation and a global income. To expand exports, cities can employ a number of tools:

- Public- and private-sector actors can cooperate to develop strategies for strengthening export opportunities for local businesses.
- The local government can establish export advisory offices.
- The local government can provide financial incentives to stimulate export-oriented activities, such as participation in trade shows.
- The local government can assist export-interested businesses in recruiting personnel with relevant experience. Training in intercultural relations and languages are two increasingly important steps.

Thinking about exporting, the small port town of Puerto Montt in southern Chile, developed a salmon farming industry. In the 1990s, Chile's salmon industry received about US$4 billion in investments, and 35,000 jobs were created. Chile's salmon exports exceeded $1 billion in 2000, compared to approximately $160 million in 1991.[48] By 2012, salmon export grew to roughly $2 billion. Norway is the only country in the world that rivals Chile's export of salmon. The success of Chilean salmon has transformed the product from an infrequent and expensive delicacy into a common dish on consumers' tables. Chile is now adding value to the product by packaging it smoked with spices and by promoting new and unique recipes.

Nine of the largest global export cities are in Asia. Seven of these leading port cities are in China: Shanghai, Ningbo, Tianjin, Guangzhou, Qinhuangdao, Qingdao, and Hong Kong. Pusan, South Korea and Singapore fill out the Asia list. The only Western port in the top 10 is Rotterdam.[49] This one fact tells the story of how global manufacturing has shifted from Europe and the United States to Asia over the past four decades. There is no single U.S. port of this magnitude. The total 2011 cargo tonnage of the three ports of South Louisiana,

Houston, and New York was 623.5 tons.[50] Compare this to Shanghai's 2012 cargo tonnage of 736 million tons. Six Chinese ports handled more cargo tonnage than all U.S. ports in 2012. Although ports are central to the economies of dozens of Chinese cities, there is no U.S. city, with the exception of Houston, whose economy rests primarily on its port business. Rotterdam, which deals with a great portion of European exports and imports, handled 411 tons in 2012, nearly 50 tons less than the port of Tianjin, which is not even China's largest port. Export traffic is not in the cards as a major economic driver for cities in the developed world.

Attracting Entrepreneurs Cities should not limit their economic development thinking only to attracting existing MNCs and SMEs. A city should also extend welcoming support to entrepreneurs. California's Silicon Valley is testimony to this point. Many cities have laid plans for entrepreneurial growth. See Exhibit 5.3 for the example set by Chicago.

Exhibit 5.3 Building an Innovative City in Chicago

How does a city go about encouraging and attracting entrepreneurial talent? Here are six major initiatives occurring in Chicago:

- Chicago's new mayor, Rahm Emanuel, has given great support to innovation initiatives. In 2011, Emanuel announced ChicagoNEXT, a council on innovation and technology aimed at promoting entrepreneurship, attracting investment, and creating jobs.

- Excelerate Labs is run by proven entrepreneurs, Sam Yagan and Troy Henikoff. They manage an intensive summer accelerator for start-up entrepreneurs. Many entrepreneurs apply for the program, but only about 10 to 15 individuals are selected. Those selected work with scores of mentors from around the country in direct, one-on-one meetings. The aim is to help each entrepreneur to fine-tune ideas and present a polished 10-minute presentation. The program culminates in an Investor Demo Day at the end of August, where each entrepreneur makes a presentation and pitch for money to an audience of more than 500 investors, praying that enough investors in the audience will support the proposed project. Excelerate Labs has been running its program for four years.

- The Chicago Innovation Awards, established in 2002, draw attention and celebrate each year the most significant new products and services created and launched in the Chicago area. Chicago-based companies nominate successful innovations that their company has launched within the past three years. Each year, the 10 best innovations are selected. The sponsors of the event include such companies as Hyatt, Disney Institute, PricewaterhouseCoopers, Comcast Business Class, Grant Thornton, and Wintrust Financial. One of the celebrated winning innovations in recent years was Groupon, which raised $700 million in 2011—the largest initial public offering (IPO) by a U.S. Internet company since Google raised $1.7 billion in 2004.

- The initiative 1871 is a coworking center for digital start-ups. Located in the famous Merchandise Mart, 50,000 square feet of space was set aside to provide Chicago start-ups with affordable workspace and access to mentors, programming, educational resources, potential investors,

(continued)

(continued)

and a community of likeminded entrepreneurs. The 1871 center is buzzing with vitality and action and could be the springboard for intriguing innovations.

- In May 2013, Chicago's mayor announced the launch of the Supply-Chain Innovation Network to focus on increasing the city's competitive edge in supply chain, transportation, and logistics. This program was launched with DHL's $35 million Global Forwarding facility at the Chicago O'Hare International Airport.

- Two major Chicago business schools—the University of Chicago's Booth School of Business and Northwestern University's Kellogg School of Management (in conjunction with Northwestern's School of Engineering)—have launched major research and teaching programs on innovation. Their students are busy designing and developing innovative products and services to propose to businesses and investors.

Source: Philip Kotler conducted interviews with these groups and wrote this memo.

Representatives of many domestic and global cities have visited Chicago to examine its exemplary support for small businesses and start-ups. In view of China's 2013 Plenum support for greater government assistance to the private sector of large and small enterprises, Chinese cities should visit Chicago. China has 40.6 million private businesses, which contribute 60 percent of China's GDP.[51] This sector has been constrained by the government's primary support for state-owned enterprises and needs greater credit and regulatory assistance.

Growing numbers of cities in Latin America and South Asia are also introducing aggressive entrepreneurial support programs. These programs train and advise entrepreneurs, encourage local banks to advance microfinancing programs, establish incubators, and provide incentives to starts-ups.

Attracting Residents and Employees

A city seeking growth needs to attract the right number and types of people who could settle in the city and aid its growth. We can recognize four types of people to attract:

1. Wealthy individuals and investors

2. Skilled workers and creative artists

3. Skilled business managers and professionals

4. Skilled educators and educational institutions

Let's examine each group.

Attracting Wealthy Individuals   Many great cities owe a great deal to individuals who built a great business. Andrew Carnegie was important to the growth of Pittsburgh; Andrew W. Mellon influenced the growth of New York, as well as Pittsburgh; John D. Rockefeller built great institutions in New York City; Walter Annenberg built his publishing empire in Philadelphia and contributed generously to public school reform in his city and elsewhere in the United States[52]; Edward Bronfman and his Seagram company brought a new prosperity to Montreal, Canada; Mark Zuckerberg of Facebook gave $100 million to upgrade the public schools of Newark, New Jersey[53]; and where would Seattle be today without William Boeing and Howard Shultz of Starbucks or neighboring Redmond without Bill Gates of Microsoft?

Many nations have emigration policies that expedite visas and citizenships to wealthy individuals. More than 50 percent of Canadian millionaires are immigrants. Australia has followed Canada's initiative and has launched its golden ticket visa program for foreign millionaires willing to invest $5 million in the country's economy. The United States has an EB-5 investor visa program that involves an investment of either $500,000 or $1 million and the creation of at least 10 jobs for U.S. workers over a two-year period.[54] U.S. cities join with developers to create EB-5 regional centers, largely for real estate development construction. Wealthy Chinese people seeking visas to the United States for their families invest in these projects. A $450 million commercial construction project, generating 7,540 jobs, can yield 775 visas or 1 visa per 10 jobs. One author of this book is involved in such a program. Wealthy foreign individuals coming to a U.S. city have a multiplier effect on retail, tax revenues, and further business investment.

An excellent example of attracting both an MNC headquarters and its high-earning executives is provided by the story of how Chicago lured the Boeing Corporation to move from Seattle, Washington. Phil Condit, Boeing's chief executive officer (CEO), reflected on his move of Boeing headquarters from Seattle to Chicago in 2001:

> Chicago has a cohesiveness of the Chicago business community, where CEOs frequently gather to nail down civic goals ranging from landing new companies to building world-class parks.... A meeting in which Starbucks, Microsoft, Costco, Boeing and Weyerhaeuser and a bunch of small businesses are all in the same place hardly ever happens in Seattle. It happens all the time in Chicago.[55]

As Boeing spread its wings from commercial to military aircraft, and reaped its profit more from global than from U.S. sales, Seattle began to seem limited. Condit went on:

> Headquarters is supposed to be thinking longer-term: Where are markets going, have we positioned the company correctly, are we

developing the right people, what's the compensation structure that we have, how do you run this big corporation, how do you avoid getting deeply engaged in the day-to-day activity, and ignoring those strategic things?[56]

Finally, Condit was impressed with former Chicago Mayor Richard J. Daley, "Chicago presented a single united front, and I give Rich Daley a lot of credit for this."[57]

Attracting Skilled Workers and Creative Artists Every city needs skilled craftspeople, electricians, plumbers, carpenters, computer programmers, systems analysts, medical professionals, educators, and many other product and service workers. If the city has an automobile plant, for example, it needs skilled welders, casters, and other specialized skilled people. If it wants to improve its restaurants and food services, it needs to attract certified chefs.

If a city wants to provide good entertainment, it needs to attract musicians, actors, actresses, and others in the entertainment arts. A city like New York has these people in abundance—more people than there are jobs. Many of these talented artists should be recruited by other cities to build their cultural districts. Unfortunately, too many unemployed actors would rather stay in New York than give their attention to Buffalo or Rochester. Still, Washington, DC, and Chicago are becoming top-rate theater towns. Beijing is a magnet for contemporary fine artists throughout China. Lahore is the cultural capital of Pakistan and a venue for new art and music. Paris has been the art capital of Europe for 150 years and has revamped Palais de Tokyo, the largest contemporary arts center in Europe.[58]

Attracting Skilled Business Managers and Professionals A city needs business managers to run its product and service businesses. And it needs the surrounding skilled people—lawyers, accountants, software designers, finance experts, management specialists, human resource experts, statisticians, and researchers—a group that we can call *business knowledge workers*. These people are found in midsize and large cities and are in short supply in the smaller cities. It takes a lot of allure to attract talented business professionals to the smaller cities. The smart city movement, mentioned earlier in this chapter in relation to Santiago, Chile, is a key driver of growth for small cities around the world, especially in the West. These small cities are attracting software talent and new urban management specialists.

Attracting Skilled Educators and Educational Institutions A city hoping to attract professionals needs a strong university. The university trains operations and software engineers, financial and marketing professionals, lawyers, consultants, and accountants, among others. Consider the city of Monterrey, Mexico. Monterrey is home to more than 13,000 companies,[59] including national giants such as Cemex, the third-largest cement company in the world, and global corporations such as GE, which has several manufacturing plants in Monterrey's vicinity.[60] A significant part of Monterrey's success is attributed to one of its most prized assets—the Technological Institute of Monterrey (ITESM). The institution's reputation is greatly responsible for the attraction of many global companies to Monterrey.[61] ITESM doctoral graduates hold up to 80 percent of the executive positions in the most prominent companies in the Monterrey area.[62] The availability of a skilled labor force, a high quality of life, and educational and work opportunities continues to propel Monterrey's growth and investments. ITESM has expanded and offers programs across 32 campuses in Mexico, as well as in other Latin American nations such as Colombia, Venezuela, Ecuador, and Panama. A successful distance education program, its virtual university, also helps ITESM reach students in locations where it does not have a physical presence.

Talent attraction requires great investment in bright, young people looking for a topnotch education, which cities and their universities can make by offering qualified student scholarships in local institutions. Many times, there are no strings attached other than the hope that the student will grow attached to the place and decide to stay after graduation. If a place does not possess the appropriate educational infrastructure, it can still sponsor the education of locals in reputable institutions elsewhere, requiring or hoping that they will return after they complete their training.

The Central American Institute of Business Administration (INCAE), a business education institution founded in San Jose, Costa Rica, in 1964 by Central American governments and business communities, attracts students from 15 countries.[63] No more than 20 percent of a given class comes from the same country. Since its inception, INCAE has maintained close ties and collaboration with Harvard Business School. INCAE's success has created opportunities for geographical expansion. Today INCAE also offers executive education in a number of Central and South American locations.[64]

Two Brazilian governmental agencies, Coordination for the Improvement of Higher Education Personnel[65] and the National Council for Scientific and Technological Development,[66] illustrate efforts to develop and maintain highly skilled workers. For decades, they have granted scholarships that can cover as much as full tuition and paid living expenses for qualified people, both in top Brazilian and in foreign higher education institutions. Support has been granted primarily to educators and researchers, with the expectation that they will resume their activities in their institution of origin after they have completed training.

In other instances, countries are working to win back citizens who are studying or working overseas. According to the Institute of International Education, there were 820,000 international students attending U.S. colleges and universities in 2012.[67] By 2014, Chinese student enrollment in American universities reached 287,260, or 29 percent of all foreign students in U.S universities.[68] In 2014, international students contributed $24.7 billion to the U.S. econ-omy.[69] Foreign students help keep colleges and universities afloat with full-tuition payments.

The strategies for winning back citizens who have moved to other regions of the world can be complex. In 2012, The Chinese Ministry of Education reported that 272,900 Chinese students who studied abroad returned to China.[70] Although the number of Asian students studying in the United States is growing, they are not staying and contribut-ing to the U.S. economy to the degree that they used to. Tough U.S. immigration restrictions for educated foreign professionals and grow-ing economic opportunity in their home countries are increasing the number of skilled returnees. "It's only really come to light in the last year or two, but we're noticing a pattern of highly skilled children of foreign-born U.S. immigrants leaving the U.S. for the countries where their parents were born," said Madeleine Sumption, a policy analyst at the Migration Policy Institute.[71]

Sumption says the trend is strong in China, India, and Brazil where dramatic economic growth over the last decade has opened up oppor-tunities for entrepreneurship and led global MNCs to hire overseas employees with Western educations. This is causing a pronounced skill shortage in Silicon Valley, Austin, Boston, and other high-tech cities in the United States.[72] With the United States facing a shortage of skilled workers, the wave of skilled professionals who are either turning their backs on or are turned back by America is foreboding.

Most Latin American students studying abroad pursue degrees in both technology- and business-related fields. Latin American nations have consistently failed to offer attractive conditions and competi-tive salaries to their citizens once they have graduated from a foreign university. For example, more than two-thirds of Peruvian doctoral can-didates in American universities reportedly do not plan to go home.[73] These and other well-trained and highly skilled Latin American professionals have ended up assuming positions in foreign hospitals, universities, research centers, and corporations.

In the United States, small and midsize cities are competing with large cities for this talent. An American guide to the selling points of small towns sums up the main message by asking, "Are you fed up with big-city living? Would you like to start a new life in a place with clean air, safe streets, good schools and friendly neighbors? If so, here are one hundred all-American small towns where you can find your dream!"[74] This type of place marketing is spreading across many international regions. The accessibility of a good home has been a major selling point in some marketing campaigns.

However, the tables are turning for Latin America. The rapid economic growth of Latin American cities in the past decade, such as Monterrey, Mexico City, São Paulo, Rio de Janeiro, Lima, and Bogota, are beginning to draw back large numbers of high-tech professionals who have studied and worked in the United States. Latin American economies are also racing to get a head start in the high-technology fields by luring bright young people to local incubators. In addition, target groups are offered venture capital funding and special incentives to establish businesses at home.

To attract families, city marketers should be aware of several subgroups:

- Families without children
- Families with small children
- Families with preteenage and teenage children
- Families with children who have moved out of the house (empty nesters)

Each target group has specific characteristics and needs. For example, Educational quality appeals to families with young children and teenagers but it is less appealing to empty nesters.

Some communities that want to attract child-centered families build and emphasize fine schools. As of 2014, there were 570,000 Asians living in the Washington, DC metro area. Chinese are most prevalent in Montgomery County, Maryland, where public education is superior to that in DC. Koreans in particular flock to Virginia's public schools and are the largest group in Centerville.[75]

Many private secondary boarding schools in the United States are marketing to foreign students. Some schools manage this new market segment with special housing, dining, and cultural options to make these students feel comfortable in their U.S. setting. Like many U.S. universities, these secondary boarding schools depend financially on the full-tuition payments of foreign families.

Several public high schools are joining the act. A bill that was introduced in the U.S. House of Representatives in 2012 would let foreign exchange students stay at public schools for more than one year of study. The Strengthening America's Public Schools Through Promoting Foreign Investment Act would be a great opportunity for top-rated city school districts such as those in Raleigh, Colorado Springs, Pittsburgh, Tampa, San Francisco, San Jose, and Portland, Oregon, to offset substantial cuts in state and local government revenues. As of 2014, the bill has not been enacted by Congress.[76]

If a community wants to attract specific professional groups, it can also offer and promote its cultural institutions and activities. For example, Washington, DC, is the center of the association industry in the United States and is home to most U.S. trade, professional, and charitable associations.

How Do City Marketers Go About Marketing Their Community?

The fundamental takeaway for city marketers is that businesses and investors are looking to the top 250 global-growth cities, from midsize to large cities and even megacities, for location of their enterprises. Small cities and towns stand little chance in this competition.

They may succeed in tourist attraction but not in midsize and large MNC attraction. Large city regions must ferociously compete for business attraction, investment, and talent. Small cities are wise to scale their efforts and to try to become sustainable. If you are small, it is foolish to be too ambitious; instead, look for some unique destination value for visitors.

Even if a large city is declining in growth, it is often better to scale back than to rush forward. No business wants to be identified with a deadbeat city. Detroit, for example, could reduce its size and focus on a revitalized central business district and residential areas instead of pretending it can revitalize its 138 square miles. The creative problem for many legacy industrial cities is to plan to downsize rather than to purport to grow again.

There is another creative alternative that one of the authors has advanced. Detroit might consider selling or leasing several square miles of its unused land to a Chinese special economic zone (SEZ), either Shenzhen SEZ or TEDA SEZ in Tianjin, to create a Chinese industrial park, bringing perhaps 500 Chinese companies to Detroit to access the U.S. market. Detroit has industrial and logistic assets that would be attractive to Chinese companies.

Other U.S. cities are thinking about this. Former Mayor Michael Bell of Toledo, Ohio, embraced Chinese investors from the Dashing Pacific Group, who purchased the Docks restaurant complex and offered $3.8 million to purchase 69 acres of the Marina District for residential and commercial development.[77] Mayor Michael Bell worked tirelessly to shift Chinese focus on top U.S. cities and see the merits of Toledo for investment. After many trips to China and visits from Chinese groups to Toledo, Bell succeeded. "They looked on a map, figured out where we were sitting and saw the benefit," said Mayor Bell. He added, "They could see that this town needed to be helped a little bit and that it could be on the upswing—that there was potential, that they could do something, that it could be incredible and it would not probably take a whole lot to do."[78] Chinese companies are eager to build in the United States, and they would respond to a bold offer of land for a SEZ. China SEZs have spread to numerous countries in the developing and developed regions of the world.[79]

This brings us to the next point. The impetus of global city growth is Asian investment. This is true for the United States, Latin America, Europe, and Africa. Talk to Ethiopians about their country, and they will tell you the Chinese are there building infrastructure and enterprise. Singapore is a master of industrial organization. American and European cities should covet its leaders' advice and investment in industrial renewal. They should welcome the Chinese, who are eager to invest in American and European city assets. After all, money is money, and money is economic growth and jobs.

The smartest message to all cities in the West and the East is do it yourself. Do not depend on national and state or provincial governments for new and sustainable investment. The nations are broke, and the markets are in cities.

National policy is important, however, because it can block city growth. It rests upon the political, business, and civic leadership of cities to circumvent national obstacles and market their locations. This kind of marketing has to be smart, because you cannot market nothing. Cities need growth plans that fit and extend their capabilities and reputation. If a city cannot grow on its merits, then it should downsize for sustainability.

The message of sustainability has great currency today in the West, and its message is downsizing rather than growing. This is the fate of many older, once-rich Western cities that no longer have the hardworking culture and demographic population of the East. Cities may mouth the nice words of sustainability, but their better course is global economic growth.

Regrettably, the West reviles economic and population growth. Its leaders claim that their welfare systems cannot support greater populations, and their unemployed citizens revile immigrants, who threaten their job opportunities and wage levels. This is a fatal attitude for the well-being of Western cities. They cannot renew themselves. They need fresh blood and money to sustain their glory. Otherwise, they will fall into the decay of highly principled ancient Rome and lose their empire to the developing world of Asia.

In a nutshell, there is no way for the United States to compete for growth, with a population of 320 million, against China and India's 2.5 billion people, many of whom are as educated as Westerners and more energetic and ambitious. If the United States were smart, it would open its door and double its population. At the same time, Asia has to be cautious and humble. Economic fluctuation is merciless. Look at the growth decline of resource countries, where the growth rate has been halved but is still far ahead of that in the West.

In the urbanized world of the twenty-first century and forward, urban markets will tell the tale. Midsize and large MNCs will go to strong cities and lobby their way around the obstacles of national and state regulations and politicians. Local political, business, and civic leaders, and the vast markets they oversee, will be the constructive force of business attraction and economic growth all over the world. The West must fight for business power. There are plenty of emerging urban markets to which global businesses can turn. Western cities must be up to the challenge. They must carefully plan and implement their moves to succeed in coming decades.

We are in a new age of talented urbanization and global business reach. The global reach of MNCs to the great city regions of the world are our best surety for world peace and prosperity. Politics divides assets; business aggregates assets. Business coalesces friendship; politics divides friends. While global business may consolidate mutual interests, politics is always there to upset the apple cart. But business must persist in its mission of prosperity, notwithstanding the fate of nations.

Cities must expand their political influence and business acumen. Businesses must carefully choose their city region locations for enterprise and growth. In a strange way, we are reaching back and pulling forward in a new way the mercantile genius of city-states. World peace and prosperity depend on how we reconcile the rebirth of city-states with the caprices of national politicians and heroes.

Conclusions

In this world of global competition for investment by cities all over the world, some will succeed and grow; others will fail and decline. Successful cities have to do five things:

1. Honestly and systematically analyze their strengths and weaknesses for investment attraction. Every midsize and large city has some opportunity for a global midsize or large MNC. The trick is to find the city's genuine strength and target the right company for whom the strength is appropriate.

2. Correct the city's weaknesses and improve its attractiveness to companies in matters that are important to them, such as available talent, good educational quality, an exciting cultural life, a good family living environment, high environmental quality; and civil order and safety.

3. Enlist the active participation and cooperation of universities, cultural institutions, and political, civic, and business leaders in the investment attraction campaign.

4. Attract wealthy foreign residents to the city, as well as intellectual, professional, and technical talent.

5. Organize investment attraction efforts into a systematic marketing and promotion program with realistic objectives and professional marketing analysis, and good management execution.

Questions for Discussion

1. What is your city's strategy to attract businesses? What industries and companies is it pursuing? Assess this strategy and suggest improvements.

2. What is your city's strategy to attract new residents? What types of residents is it trying to attract? Assess this strategy and suggest improvements.

3. What is your city's strategy to attract business visitors and conventions? What steps should it take to make their experience in the city gratifying? Assess this strategy and suggest improvements.

4. What is your city's strategy to attract tourists and travelers? What are its major attractions? What other attractions should be added? Assess this strategy and suggest improvements.

6 How a Nation Can Help Its City Economies

In stressing the growing importance of cities and metropolitan (metro) centers undertaking more responsibility for self-development and self-improvement, we don't mean to understate the role that the nation has to play in aiding city development. Government units on the federal or state level can either aid or stall cities in accomplishing their objectives.

Consider the current situation with Detroit, which declared itself bankrupt in July 2013. This may be the biggest American city to declare bankruptcy, but it is not the last. The common notion is that a city like Detroit is too big to fail and must be rescued. If Detroit doesn't pay its bills to suppliers and investors, they won't lend more money, and Detroit may become a city without adequate electricity, water, infrastructure maintenance, and public workers. The pensions of Detroit government workers may have to be reduced, not to mention other drastic adjustments.

Should Detroit's fate be left in the hands of the state of Michigan, a state that also lacks money and has a number of other cities that might object to their budgets being cut to help Detroit survive? Or should the U.S. government adopt the role of savior, and with what conditions? The U.S. government has given relief for locations afflicted with a natural disaster, but it has not aided a fiscal disaster. Is Detroit entitled to emergency funds from the U.S. Treasury? Should this also apply to other already-bankrupt cities, such as Stockton, California; Jefferson County, Alabama; San Bernardino, California; Harrisburg, Pennsylvania; and Central Falls, Rhode Island,[1] as well as numerous others on the verge of bankruptcy, such as Fresno, California; Irvington, New Jersey; Newburgh, New York; Oakland, California; and Providence, Rhode Island?[2] If substantial federal aid is forthcoming, rest assured that other cities teetering with pension liabilities will move more readily to restructuring. If they do, how far and long can federal aid extend, and what federal policies and programs can get Detroit and other cities out of their mess?

Detroit is a case at one extreme. At the other extreme are U.S. cities that are healthy and prosperous, such as Boulder, Colorado; San Diego; and Washington, DC. We might conclude that these cities need little assistance from their state or federal governments, but we would be wrong.

Boulder gets great economic support from the U.S. Air Force Academy, the North American Command Headquarters, and other military facilities. Naval Base San Diego is the largest U.S. naval base on the West Coast and has 40,000 military and civilian personnel. It is the cornerstone of San Diego's economy.[3]

Other U.S. cities prosper from federal support. Spirit AeroSystems, a major manufacturer of military aircraft that employs nearly 11,000 people, as well as McConnell Air Force Base, employing 6,000 people, are among the top three employers in Wichita, Kansas.[4] Lockheed Martin employs 14,500 people in Fort Worth for military aircraft construction.[5] Finally, it would be no surprise that the federal government presence in Washington, DC, along with its contractors, has made the city the top per capita income urban metro region in the country. There are 297,305 federal civilian personnel living in Washington, DC.[6]

Part of the reason these cities thrive is because of direct and indirect help that they get from higher government levels. They may receive state government subsidies connected with some of their industries. Florida, like many states, offers businesses that it wishes to attract to its cities a menu of incentives, such as tax refunds for target industries, capital investment tax credits, high-impact performance incentive grants, and training programs. The state of Washington offered Boeing a multiyear incentive package of $8.7 billion to build its 777X plant in Bellevue.[7] The state of Missouri entered the bidding war with an offer $1.7 billion in tax breaks to Boeing to bring 777X production to its state, but lost out to the state of Washington.

Federal-level import duties help cities sustain their industries. The current U.S. duty on imported tires has helped Akron, Ohio, and its principal manufacturing facility of Goodyear Tire and Rubber and of Bridgestone (formerly Firestone), founded in Akron.[8] With several hundred polymer-based material companies in the city, the University of Akron in 2010 organized the country's first College of Polymer Science and Polymer Engineering and the National Polymer Innovation Center. This operation receives funding from the federal government and the state of Ohio.

Many countries protect their unique industrial advantages by excluding foreign entry into their urban markets. Japan is notorious for resistance to foreign cars; so is South Korea. China excludes or severely curtails foreign companies from entering into its seven national security and economic industries. U.S. financial institutions are prevented from commercial entry into Shanghai, Beijing, and large financial cities.

India is notorious for its exclusion of foreign multinational company (MNC) retail chains from entry into its city region markets.

After losing its battle for a fully owned foreign investment, Walmart had to joint venture with Bharti Enterprises in 2007 to gain entry into Mumbai and other major Indian cities. That joint venture dissolved in 2013, with each company going its separate way. Walmart is having great difficulty sustaining its 20 independent megastores under the weight of regulatory restriction on supplier requirements.[9] There are also innumerable cases of national governments saving domestic city industries from foreign competition. It is fair to say that free trade works—if, when, and where it is allowed to work by national politicians.

No one is saying that the cities in a state or nation are likely to do better if the state or nation didn't exist. There were great city-states in ancient Greece and later in Europe in the Middle Ages (such as Venice, Genoa, and the cities of the Hanseatic League), but few thought leaders are arguing today for the elimination of the nation and all cities being left on their own. However, several "city-states" in today's world prosper, including Singapore, Dubai, Liechtenstein, and Hong Kong. Milton Kotler argued in 1969 for the breakup of U.S. cities and the devolution of governing powers to the neighborhoods as constitutional units of state governments. Only a few luminaries at the time, such as economist Kenneth Boulding, Oregon Senator Mark Hatfield, and political theorist Hannah Arendt, supported his radical position. It may ironically be the only solution for Detroit in 2014.[10]

The task in this chapter is to consider how nations can aid and encourage their cities to do a better job and reach for a higher ambition. We consider the following questions:

1. What functions should the nation be expected to perform?

2. In what ways can the central government help weaker cities get on their feet?

3. In what ways can the central government assist stronger cities to climb even higher?

What Functions Should the Nation Be Expected to Perform?

There is a long history of debate about the size and role of the national government in contributing to the economic and social performance of the various cities and groups in a nation. One side favors a strong role for the nation in dealing with the problems facing the country. China represents this end of the spectrum. The other side wants the nation to play a limited role and even accuses it of causing some problems that otherwise wouldn't exist. Major political parties span both extremes. Our job is not to plea for one side or the other but instead to describe the six main roles that most people agree that the national government should carry out. They are:

1. Infrastructure development
2. Defense
3. Education
4. Public safety and health
5. Emergencies
6. National directives

Infrastructure Development Roles

Although anyone can start a business, it probably won't go far unless some level of government makes certain investments in infrastructure. For example, it is not enough for McDonald's to choose a contractor to build another restaurant. McDonald's needs a license and various permits to be sure that its restaurants fit with the surrounding area. McDonald's needs electricity, running water, waste disposal, streets and sidewalks, and other facilitating factors that source from public infrastructure.

Citizens expect the government to build streets, roads, bridges, sewage systems, airports, and marine ports because the private sector lacks the profit motive incentive. The reality today throughout the world is that most new infrastructure is developed by public-private partnerships, in which governments concede management and user fees to private investor partners for a period in exchange for their private capital investment.

Some new businesses need foreign investment to supply the necessary funds. Much of the American railroad system was paid for by foreign capital flowing from England. The U.S. government played a role in letting this capital flow into the country and setting the conditions that had to be met.

Foreign investment in infrastructure construction and management can be politically sensitive for national security reasons. For example, the 2006 attempted sale of the port management businesses in six major U.S. seaports by British-owned P&O to DP World was stopped. DP is a company based in the United Arab Emirates (UAE). Strong congressional opposition blocked it even though it had White House approval.[11]

State and local governments often work with private investors to build, operate, and transfer roads. They grant private rights to operate roads with tolls at a regulated rate for a period of years until the road ownership is transferred back to the government. We have even seen local governments sell back public property to the private sector to raise enough money to cover current government operating and debt costs. For example, the city of Chicago decided to sell the city-owned parking meters to a private firm for a lump sum payment that represented the present value of the future income stream going to the private sector buyer.[12]

There is little controversy surrounding the government's infrastructure responsibilities. Business complaints usually occur when roads are not maintained, there are an insufficient number of roads, traffic congestion is high, or waste removal has slowed and caused a health hazard.

In the United States, the major difficulty in adding or improving local infrastructure—schools, bridges, roads, and urban transit—is that voters must approve bond issues for the infrastructure and that the voters often vote no because the financing increases their property taxes. They consistently vote against school bond issues because most voters do not have children in school. The same can be said for bridges because most voters do not use the same bridge. This is why it usually takes leadership and persuasion to get bond issues through.

Defense Roles

An equally uncontroversial debate surrounds the role of government in protecting its citizens and their property against civil violence or foreign powers that might wage war. Every country hires police and firefighters and maintains an army, navy, and air force to protect the lives and property of its citizens. We hope that most of the time the armed services will be idle and their cost will be borne by grateful citizens.

Defense requires military bases, and these are spread across cities throughout the United States. The top 10 U.S. military cities with the largest concentration of active and retired military are Fayetteville, North Carolina; Hampton Roads, Virginia; Jacksonville, Florida; Jacksonville, North Carolina; Centerville, Georgia; San Antonio, Texas; Clarksville, Tennessee; Oak Harbor, Washington; Tacoma, Washington; and Fort Riley, Kansas. The cities would perish if their military bases were closed. Members of Congress fight doggedly to keep these bases open for the survival of cities in their districts.[13]

Military manufacturers lobby intensely for their $225 billion in arms production every year. Contractors such as Northrop Grumman ($28 billion), Raytheon ($23 billion), General Dynamics ($23 billion), Boeing ($35 billion), Lockheed Martin ($35.7 billion), Honeywell ($5.4 billion), and Pratt & Whitney ($4 billion) employ hundreds of thousands of workers in many city regions in the United States. A radical reduction of defense and security spending would imperil many large cities, including Washington, DC; Orlando and Tampa,

Florida; Huntsville, Alabama; Dallas–Fort Worth, Texas; Colorado Springs, Colorado; Tucson and Phoenix, Arizona; and San Diego and Los Angeles, California, and it would spell doom for smaller city locations.[14]

U.S. defense spending and international security assistance is being gradually reduced. As of 2013, this spending of $643 billion represented 19 percent of the federal budget of $3.5 trillion, but it still costs nearly 5 percent of the nation's gross domestic product (GDP).[15] Any serious increase in base closings and reduction in defense production would have to be offset by substitute economic investment to spare these cities. Displacing defense costs onto national social programs would not save cities with bases and production facilities.

While Western governments are slowing the growth of their defense spending, countries in Asia, Africa, and the Middle East are increasing their defense spending and growing the city economies of major defense manufacturers and deployment. In China, the People's Liberation Army Navy (PLAN) is the second-largest naval service in the world, behind only the U.S. Navy. With personnel strength of more than 250,000, PLAN also includes the 35,000-strong Coastal Defense Force and the 56,000-strong Marine Corps, headquartered in Shanghai, with strong naval installations along China's eastern seaboard in the cities of Qingdao, Yulin, Beihai, Donghai, Ningbo, and Zhanjiang. These already-powerful commercial and industrial cities are strengthened further by the defense industry. China built a nuclear submarine base at Hainan Island in 2008.[16]

Saudi Arabia and the UAE continue to grow their military and naval bases in Bahrain and other cities, including Riyadh. King Khalid Military City is a special city in northeastern Saudi Arabia and about 60 kilometers (37.3 miles) north of Hafar Al-Batin. The city was built to provide lodging for several brigades of Saudi troops, with a target population of 65,000 people.[17]

Education Roles

Citizens broadly accept the view that some level of government needs to supply education—at least at the elementary, high school, community college, and state university level—if the country is to improve its human capital to fit the needed jobs. The private sector normally cannot supply elementary and high school education because too many citizens wouldn't have the money to pay for its high price. So it falls to the government to set up public education and citizens to pay for free primary and secondary education through taxes and for higher levels of education through tuition fees that are moderate compared to those at private higher education institutions.

However, some parents still opt to send their children to private schools that can charge enough to provide superior teaching, a religious education, or both. The worse public education becomes, the more parents decide to send their children to private schools. For example, the public school system in Washington, DC, is so bad that many upper-middle-income families send their children to private schools. Eminent economist Milton Friedman argued in the 1950s that parents should receive public vouchers to send their children to any school of their choice, which would stimulate competition among schools and raise the quality of public education.[18] Important advances have been made in the charter school movement that embeds competition within the public education system.

Many cities promote their real estate on the basis of superior public education. *U.S. News & World Report* does an annual ranking of the best public high schools in the country. The 2013 top 10 leaders were the School for the Talented and Gifted in Dallas; Basis Tucson; Gwinnett School of Mathematics, Science and Technology in Lawrenceville, Georgia; Thomas Jefferson High School of Science and Technology in Alexandria; Basis Scottsdale; Pine View School in Osprey, Florida; Loveless Academic Magnet Program High School in Montgomery, Alabama; Biotechnology High School in Freehold, New Jersey; International School in Bellevue, Washington; and Academic Magnet High School in Charleston, South Carolina. Aspiring families with talented children who can make the grade flock to jobs in these cities to get into these schools.[19] Even within cities, such as within the Washington, DC, city region, aspiring families move to neighborhoods with high-ranking schools, like the top schools in Montgomery County, Maryland, and in Fairfax, Virginia. They avoid Washington, DC, public high schools.

It is notable that the high-ranking public schools in the once-thriving Northeast, East, and Midwest of the United States have shifted to the South, Southwest, and West Coast in concert with the growing prosperity of these once-backward cities, and the corresponding decline of formerly thriving cities.

The question remains about the provision of higher education and who should bear the cost. The immediate beneficiaries of higher education are the cities where major universities are located. They are often the largest employers in these cities, and many companies move to these cities for their university-educated talent pool. This talent pool also contributes to the high-value sector of new business start-ups. But few cities can financially support their universities except with indirect land and zoning favors and some tax benefits. Instead, state governments and the federal government financially support higher education through research grants, contracts, and direct loans for tuition.

The University of California and its campus cities of Berkeley, Los Angeles, San Francisco, Irvine, Davis, Santa Cruz, and elsewhere derived roughly 80 percent of a 2010–2012 budget of $2.5 billion from federal and state government sources, whether direct grants, student loans, federal medical fees, or other benefits.[20] The University of California employs 121,000 faculty and staff members through its state campuses. In Pennsylvania, the University of Pittsburgh and its affiliated University of Pittsburgh Medical Center are the largest employers in Pittsburgh. The University of Pittsburgh is scrambling to offset the commonwealth's appropriation, which fell from $184.9 million in fiscal year (FY) 2011 to $144.5 million in FY 2012. This takes the university back to its lowest level of state support since FY 1995. The university had to eliminate 1,000 jobs.[21]

The federal and Massachusetts state government support to Harvard University, Massachusetts Institute of Technology, Boston College, Tufts University, Boston University, and other colleges and universities help sustain the largest employment sector in Boston. In Maryland, Johns Hopkins University is the largest employer in Baltimore and contributes $10 billion to the state economy.[22] Serious reduction of federal and state government support would deeply injure the economies of both cities.

The universities and colleges of Chicago are not its largest employers; here, government takes the prize. In 2012, Chicago employed 143,553 full-time federal government, public school, city government, and Cook County government workers.[23] Although the number of public employees increased, the population of Chicago shrunk, with an exodus of more than 200,000 people during the 2000s. Chicago was only one of several of the 15 largest cities in the United States that lost population during this period. Chicago's population dropped to a level not seen since 1910. The demographic disaster extended beyond city limits. Cook County as a whole lost population during the first decade of the twenty-first century. Among America's 15 largest counties, the only other one to lose population during this period was Detroit's Wayne County. The larger Chicago metro area suffered a net loss of more than 550,000 people to other parts of the country.[24] Despite Chicago's efforts to present itself as a global city, and despite some important technology initiatives, the best way for the federal government to help Chicago is to help it untangle the knot of its devastating public finances. This means less money, not more, until the pressure on Chicago's politicians becomes so great that they have to face cutting their public pension liabilities. The state government of Illinois cannot help Chicago because its finances are even more perilous than those of the city. Supporting basic hard science and innovative technology at its leading universities and freeing children from the bondage of its futile public school system through federal vouchers are the only sensible federal government investments.

In countries such as England, France, and Germany, a college education has been free for decades. The financial crisis in Europe has changed these matters. The United Kingdom, France, Italy, and other countries in the European Union have instituted high, rather than traditional nominal, tuitions. The University and College Union, a British trade union, reported its belief that more than 15,000 posts—most academic—could disappear from the United Kingdom in the next few years.[25]

A four-year college education in the United States is expensive—even when provided to in-state students by public state universities, such as the Universities of Michigan, Wisconsin, and Illinois. The average U.S. college graduate is leaving college with a loan debt of $25,000. The debt for graduate and professional studies can reach above $100,000. The federal government carries $1 trillion of higher education loan debts, with half of this amount not being repaid. The 2013 default rate of is almost 9 percent, almost five times higher than the consumer credit default rate of 1.9 percent.[26] Graduates are without the discretionary money to buy homes or to spend heavily on consumer goods and thus grow local economies.

Those who cannot afford university tuition can go to community colleges at a more affordable cost or skip college altogether. Community colleges are supported primarily by city and county budgets. Many people agree by now that the escalation of college tuition costs will have to stop somehow; otherwise, the nation will lose its human capital. Germany is one example of an alternative. It provides a dual education system, enabling students to choose the option of a vocational instead of an academic high school education. An apprenticeship with a company is incorporated in the vocational option. The vocational students graduate with several years of experience in a company and are already positioned in the workforce when they graduate.

Governor Rick Snyder of Michigan has created the Advanced Technician Training Program for Detroit automakers. This program is modeled after the German auto apprenticeship program, which he wants to Americanize. The program costs are mostly being covered by the participating companies.[27]

It is clear that business gains from the degree to which the government develops and supports a good education system that produces citizens with quality training and skills. According to *Forbes*, the top 10 U.S. cities for high-tech jobs are Austin, Raleigh, Houston, Nashville, San Francisco, Salt Lake City, Seattle, San Antonio, Indianapolis, and Baltimore. They all have large university clusters that generate talent for high-tech employment.[28]

The major savior of higher education in the United States is foreign enrollment at full tuition. In 2013, 19.9 million students were enrolled in higher education in the United States.[29] Nearly 4 percent, or 819,000 of these students, were from foreign countries, half from Asia, primarily from China, India, and South Korea. This percentage of international students is increasing every year.[30] As principally full-tuition students, this international student contingent makes a considerable economic contribution to local college and university communities. Even public high schools are jumping on the foreign recruitment bandwagon. New York State, Maine, and Massachusetts are leaders in this trend.[31]

Globally, the real city beneficiaries of new school and university development are in China, India, Singapore, Malaysia, and elsewhere in Asia. India launched a plan in 1961 to establish 16 institutes of technology in the cities of Bhubaneswar, Chennai, Delhi, Gandhinagar, Guwahati, Hyderabad, Indore, Jodhpur, Kanpur, Kharagpur, Mandi,

Mumbai, Patna, Ropar, Roorkee, and Varanasi. These institutes have successfully built a talent base to attract investment to their cities.

China has opened new universities and expanded established universities to aid the city economies of its different regions: southeast, northeast, central, southwest, and far west. Many cities of the Guangdong province are rich in universities and good schools. Wuhan, in central China, has the leading law school in China and has other fine departments in engineering, technology, and business management. Wuhan is growing at a fast rate because of this talent resource. Nanjing University, historically famous in China for biological science, has spawned a massive biotechnology industrial development in cities of the Yangtze region. Chengdu University is a powerhouse of southwest China growth.[32]

Tuition is low in India and China. Government support and testing ensure a high turnout of capable young graduates and professionals to grow the economy of cities. Faculty salaries are moderate but still attract talent because of the high esteem of education in Chinese culture. As of 2011, 15,647 U.S. students were attending Chinese universities (including Hong Kong and Macau as well as mainland China), and increasing numbers of U.S. students are applying to Chinese universities.[33] Tuitions are high in the United States, because universities have accreted high overhead from many decades of growth. While China's government is investing heavily to expand its university system as a priority central government policy, federal and state governments in the United States are under budgetary pressure to decrease investment in higher education. Higher education is not as high a government policy priority in the United States as it is in China.

Public Safety and Health Roles

Most people want government at the local, state, and federal levels to oversee its citizens' safety and health concerns. The United States has established the Department of Agriculture, Department of Health and

Human Services, the Food and Drug Administration, the National Institutes of Health, the Centers for Disease Control and Prevention, and other agencies responsible for inspecting food and drug safety. Most city hospitals are vitally dependent upon federal Medicare payments and federal and state Medicaid payments. U.S. hospitals are overbedded, and the likelihood is that many hospitals will downsize and consolidate.

The local availability of quality health and hospital care is a major factor in business attraction. With the exception of large specialty hospitals in ophthalmology, pulmonology, and rehabilitation, 44 of America's top hospitals are located in only seven cities. The 44 hospitals contribute a large part of the economies of Houston, New York City, Cleveland, Baltimore, Boston, Los Angeles, and Rochester, Minnesota.[34]

New global medical destinations are emerging in Asia to compete with high-price elective surgery in the United States and long-wait surgery in the public health systems of Europe. Singapore has earned a reputation as one of the hottest medical tourist destinations in Asia for orthopedic surgery. High-quality hip and knee replacement facilities await those arriving from around the world to benefit from expert physicians and surgeons in Singapore.[35]

The global destination of choice for cosmetic surgery is Bangkok, the capital of Thailand. Thousands of foreigners come to Bangkok Hospital for cosmetic surgery. It has a number of highly accredited hospitals, which practice varieties of cosmetic surgery, including facelift, breast augmentation and reduction, eyelid surgery, tummy tucks, hair transplants, and many other beauty enhancements. Prices are often half of Western home country surgery, and the environment of the city is conducive to effective and inexpensive recovery. There are some terrible hospitals as well, so medical tourists have to be very careful to research published standards and rankings.[36] In Latin America, Bogota, San Jose, Costa Rico, and Mexico City are becoming major destinations for medical tourism, bringing in hundreds of millions of dollars to these cities.[37]

Regarding food safety, many federal health agencies were established as a result of early scandals in the U.S. meatpacking industry and shoddy or dangerous products claiming health and other benefits. If the U.S. government were to provide absolute levels of protection, there would be so many things to watch and evaluate that the public probably would rebel. Federal agencies are subject to tight budgetary control and often have to focus solely on the most critical health and safety issues. Taxpayers want the government to protect health and safety—but only to a certain limit.

Under a broader idea of health and safety, should the government provide a safety net for those who are disadvantaged by age, disability, unemployment, or poverty? The United States does this through Social Security, Medicare and Medicaid, unemployment compensation, and welfare programs. Each government needs to consider how far it will go in this direction. The newly enacted Affordable Care Act (ACA), commonly and somewhat derisively called Obamacare, has involved a gruesome political fight. Despite great initial difficulties in implementation and swirling controversy, the ACA had enrolled 8 million people by April 2014 and had met its initial enrollment objectives. It is still a political hot potato and its future is uncertain.[38] Its thousands of pages of regulations are still being drafted, and 2014 will be the crucial year for universal enrollment, the financial cornerstone of the act. The implementation of the act is uncertain, as politicians and civic groups crusade on both sides of the issue. Opponents of the act point out its perils for small-business growth and the insurance cost affects on consumer sales. Even supporters, including the International Brotherhood of Teamsters union, fear that companies will rush to reduce full-time employment to part-time to evade the mandates of the act.[39]

The largest-growing agency of the federal government is the Department of Homeland Security. With its growth, along with the growth of the National Security Agency and its ever-widening surveillance activities, the city of Washington, DC, continues in the top ranks of city GDPs.[40]

Despite increased funding for national security, after the fiscal crisis of 2008, many state and local governments cut back their police and fire services. But these were partly offset by President Barack Obama's first fiscal stimulus effort. Whether this federal input will be sustained is open to question.

Health and food safety is a major interest of cities around the world. China is struggling against great odds to reduce pollution and carbon emissions in the face of pressures for high economic growth. Beijing's livability reputation to the global business community is compromised by its chronic pollution. Chinese authorities are increasing regulatory control of food safety after terrible scandals with unsafe milk, pork, and other areas of food production.[41] Air pollution and impure water supplies are barriers to urban growth in many cities of India.[42]

Health and environmental safety programs are expensive. The Western world, particularly Europe and the United States, faces a tradeoff of environmental protection and cost of economic growth. Although clean and healthy environments may attract tourists, they repel manufacturing industries. Asia, so desperately in need of mass jobs, forsakes environment for relatively unregulated industrial growth and jobs. Even the United States, which foresees a manufacturing and resources recovery, will not sign on to a carbon tax to charge companies for carbon emissions.[43]

Businesses should support government regulations that best insure safety and health. Good competitors and entire industries suffer when a company produces fake or harmful drugs, food products that contain harmful ingredients, or toys that can harm or poison children.

Emergency Roles

All locations may experience natural disasters such as hurricanes, floods, or earthquakes—terrible events that kill people and leave the survivors devastated by the loss of their family members, homes, and possessions. Most cities expect their government to make provision for emergency aid in the case of natural disasters, whether it is Hurricane Katrina in the United States, the Sichuan earthquake in China, or the Japanese tsunami of 2011. Businesses can help in emergencies by providing material supplies for rebuilding, food and water supplies, and emergency health care and drug supplies. Individuals and nongovernmental organizations help with volunteers, monetary contributions, clothing, and a host of emergency services. They also profit from repair. S&P's depositary receipt oil and gas equipment and services exchange-traded funds follow a basket of 27 companies related to repairing, constructing, and servicing the oil and gas industry. This fund was up 20 percent in 2010, and a good deal of this came from repair sales after Hurricane Katrina. Recovery of New Orleans and other southern Louisiana cities and their industries after Hurricane Katrina were largely funded by penalties to BP and other oil producers and providers of equipment, which were responsible for insecure offshore oil rigs. The private sector has also footed a large part of New Orleans's recovery bill.

National Directive Roles

What role should the national government play in making sure that the country's economic system is productive and works in the public interest? We would generally assume that the government should act to ensure a level playing field for businesses and consumers engaged in commercial transactions. Businesses must be protected against unfair practices such as predatory pricing, rigged bidding, cartels, and other efforts that would reduce competition. The government also has to be mindful that the financial markets don't take excessive risks that would endanger the economy. Furthermore, consumers need to have a way to voice complaints of unfair business practices, which is the aim of the newly created Bureau of Consumer Protection.

Despite this highly principled dictum of national responsibility for federal investment in the economic growth of the nation, the reality of the local preferences of congressional politics has probably contributed more the growth of certain city economies important to members of the U.S. Congress and Senate than to the economic growth of the nation. China has a far different system of public investment. Although local politicians do their best to build their city economies, their borrowing practice remains fairly well monitored by the central government and Communist Party. Every Chinese mayor thinks his or her city is the best for local and national growth, but the Communist Party has its list of preferential cities for investment.

Many countries and cities in the developing and even the developed world are looking skeptically at the economic pitfalls of democratic representative government, where local economic support is a function of political tradeoffs rather than rational opportunity. The most controversial role that the government can play is to try to direct the economy to move in certain directions. Free marketers do not want the government to play favorites or influence which industries and companies should grow. They want market forces, not government edicts or money, to influence the direction economic growth. At the same time, many of them lobby for favors from the government to support their industry or company.

Another group favors guided economic development. This group wants the government to figure out which industries are needed that will provide the country with good economic growth and a sufficient number of jobs. They want to identify the industries that are likely to grow more in the future and to encourage government support for these growth candidates and the cities in which they are located.

The government may be willing to subsidize emerging industries that have great future promise and are environmentally protective. For instance, the United States, as well as other countries, subsidized renewable energy industries in solar and wind power. But the failure of

A123 batteries and of Solyndra and many other subsidized renewable energy companies in the United States raises the question of whether the federal government has the skill and objectivity power to make successful selections. There have been some success stories like Tesla Motors, but these have been offset by fruitless subsidies to Fisker Automotive and Chevrolet's Volt.[44]

The other question inherent in this approach is what the government should do about mature industries that are at a competitive disadvantage in global trade. They can be left to a slow death or offered tariff protection and public research and development (R&D) investment. An example of this is U.S. government protection of its essential tire and steel industries from foreign low-price competitors by imposing duties allowable under world trade agreements. Some of these actions are upheld by the World Trade Organization. The federal bailout of General Motors (GM) from bankruptcy has cost U.S. taxpayers $10 billion, because GM sold off its last collateral shares in the company in November 2013.[45]

Countries such as China, Japan, South Korea, and France are comfortable guiding their nation's economic development. Consider how rapidly Japan recovered after World War II by government direction in the development of automobiles, motorcycle, and electronics and how South Korea chose similar industries to grow. There is always the danger of choosing the wrong industries. But if a government works with businesses to bet on several new industries, hopefully one or more of them will be successful enough to cover mistaken choices.

Most businesses are organized into trade and professional associations that work hard to influence government economic policy, even in a free-market environment. Industries such as solar power in the United States advocate for subsidies, special tax benefits, or duty protection to carry on their work. Companies and different government agencies file thousands of antidumping claims every year to restrict foreign imports by heavy duties. It is hard to imagine companies that are not trying to improve their situation through government influence or actions. In the face of increased global competition, city governments play a growing role in lobbying the federal government for import protection for local industries, R&D funding, infrastructure grants-in-aid, and strategic trade agreements.

In What Ways Can the Government Help Weaker Cities Get on Their Feet?

The cities within a nation can be classified into four groups according to their economic condition:

- Dying or dead cities
- Sick cities
- Stable cities
- Growing and healthy cities

It does not make sense for the state or nation to give equal aid to all of these cities. We would argue that less, rather than more, state and federal money should be given to dying and sick cities. They offer little chance of being resuscitated. Beyond giving humanitarian aid to those suffering in these cities, little should be added to help these cities. They just won't bloom again. Companies in the Rust Belt have left behind empty factories, and there are no job opportunities. Riverside, California; Detroit and Flint, Michigan; Toledo and Dayton, Ohio; and Scranton, Pennsylvania, fit this class.[46]

Instead of giving resuscitation money to these first two city types, state and federal money should be used to feed further growth in the last two city types. As stable and growing cities do better, hopefully people will migrate from the sick cities to the growing cities and find jobs there.

China considers an additional class, namely, the building of new cities. Instead of spending money on dying cities, China stakes out districts where new cities can be built. This creates a double impact. First, it puts a lot of new money into a vacant area. Even accounting for the relocation of people in developing districts, building a new city is still cheaper and more promising that urban renovation. Second, the new city will hopefully draw people away from the dying areas where there is no future. China is on course to build thousands of new urban centers in the next 10 years.[47]

In What Ways Can the Government Assist Stronger Cities to Climb Even Higher?

One can argue that a strong city needs little help from its state or central government. But if such a city is already growing, then helping it grow faster makes sense. Suppose the city lacks some infrastructure that it cannot finance by itself. Suppose the city cannot borrow enough to finance its ambitious growth plans. The nation's role is to determine how to use its public finance and debt to help strong city regions plan good competitive vessels for investments and how to encourage and facilitate business investment in these places with incentives.

Conclusions

In the face of increased global competition, central governments are likely to play a growing role in helping their cities and their domestic companies improve their global competitiveness with commercial support services, R&D funding, tax advantages, strategic trade agreements, and advocacy of fair trade practices.

Questions for Discussion

1. In achieving your city's goals, name three major needs that should be supplied by the government (at federal, state, or local levels) that are missing now.

2. What improvements are needed in the functioning of your city's government to help businesses achieve their planning goals?

3. What do you think of the incentive packages that your city government is willing to extend to help your city attract its targets?

4. What can the federal government and states do to reduce red tape and facilitate quicker and less costly entry into their cities for interested companies?

7 The Responsibilities of Companies and Cities

We have encouraged metropolitan (metro) areas seeking growth to do their best to attract targeted multinational companies (MNCs). We have examined the decision-making practices of MNCs to help metro areas use this information to increase their success in attracting them. Now we want to turn to another question: How will these attracted MNCs conduct themselves in these metro areas? We also have to consider the new position of cities and metro regions as primarily agents for economic development. This is a departure from their traditional position as urban administrators of public service to the population.

We can imagine two extremes. At one extreme, the attracted businesses might act like hit-and-run businesses, squeezing out as much profit as they can, staying as long as the profit is there, and then moving to the next global city that is extending generous incentives. At the other extreme, we can imagine attracting fine industries and companies that look for a long-term position in that metro area and plan to infuse ideas and funds to help both the business and the metro area achieve their respective objectives.

Most businesses attracted to an area will do some good and some bad. Suppose the city of Mumbai manages to attract a new steel mill. The good news is that this will create needed jobs. But the bad news is that the new steel mill will add pollution to the city, especially if it is loosely regulated. The good news is that this will bring more money to the Mumbai economy. But the bad news is that it will add grime to the grist. The rapid influx into Dhaka, Bangladesh, of garment manufacturers doing contract work for MNC garment brands has done wonders for Dhaka's gross domestic product (GDP) growth, but there have been tragic factory fires, killing hundreds.[1]

The Role and Impact of MNCs in an Urban Area

We need to assume that MNCs will choose a metro area not as a charitable gesture but as a result of calculating a good return on their investment. Both the price buyer and the price seller work up numbers hoping to show that entering this metro area will produce jobs and a target rate of return. If the calculations indicate a sufficient return, then the company feels that city and its investors will be satisfied.

But many soft factors intervene to create a rough ride for MNCs in both developed and developing countries. The anti-French civil outbreak in China, following a French insult to its Olympic team, caused havoc in 2008 for Carrefour department stores, from which it has not fully recovered to this day. Chinese nationalist emotions over its island disputes with Japan have had an adverse effect on Japanese car sales in Beijing, Shanghai, and cities across China.[2] There are civil eruptions in Indian cities over the penetration of MNCs into its markets, which are seen as threatening small shopkeepers.[3] MNCs have to be vigilant in their public relations to preempt city unrest toward their operations.

A business may also enter a large city region to achieve some additional advantages, namely:

- Increase the company's market coverage and power
- Defend the company's brands against competitors and disrupters
- Seek a balance between market share growth and profit growth

From the metro area's point of view, the question is whether a particular MNC or small or medium enterprise (SME) might make a further contribution to the metro area's development. Most areas face a number of problems:

- Poverty, hunger, and slums
- Unemployment and homelessness
- Poor physical and digital infrastructure
- Traffic congestion
- Poor school attendance
- Crime, gang wars, and street violence

What responsibilities might businesses assume toward these problems? The causes of these problems go deeper than anything that business has done to contribute to these problems. But should businesses participate in addressing any of these problems? Should the metro area consider the businesses' profile before inviting them in? Should the metro area even suggest ways in which it hopes the entering businesses might aid the social and economic environment of the metro area?

Most MNCs have corporate social responsibility policies that lay out specific actions of assistance to the cities in which they operate. Japan's Sumitomo Electric stipulated basic policies of social contributions to local communities in which they operate, including monetary contributions, human resource development, and support of volunteer activities.[4] Posco, South Korea's largest steel company operating in many cities throughout the world, was named an excellent company for its corporate social responsibility management at the 2013 East Asia 30 Awards.[5] Posco contributes to the education, health, culture, and social welfare programs in many cities where it operates. Host cities urge Posco to commit more resources to corporate social responsibility to reduce opposition to its investment. In Bhuhubaneswar, India, the local Naveen Patnaik government has asked Posco to aggressively implement corporate social responsibility projects to ward off the challenge posed by the anti-industry lobby to its major industrial development and to woo the electorate.[6]

Today, cities have to turn more to business for aid in managing their social problems than to government. Government is broke, and business have resources to aid communities in distress. We can go further and suggest that citizens will increasingly put more weight on a company's corporate social responsibility profile in judging which brands to buy and support. Citizens will rate a company not only by the number of products it makes and sells but also by the ideas and values that the particular company manifests. MNCs need to turn more of their attention to purpose and reputation. Besides a company building its brand, what does the company stand for?

In this chapter, we examine the following questions:

1. What damages can a company inflict on a local economy?
2. What improvements can a company contribute to a local economy?
3. How can a metro area be sure that a prospective company will contribute more good than bad to the local economy?

What Damages Can a Company Inflict on a Local Economy?

Companies will be attracted to choose a particular local economy if it offers lower costs, all other things being equal. This could consist of lower labor cost, lower land cost, lower capital cost, and lower regulatory cost. The last cost, lower regulatory cost, often tips the scale in bringing a foreign business into a specific global city. If city X doesn't have minimum wage laws and minimum laws on working conditions, a foreign investor would have lower costs. Developing countries and their major city regions in particular are preferred by many MNCs because of weak laws to protect children or workers. Consider the following case.

In 1995 Nike subcontracted with a Pakistani firm called SAGA Sports to begin the manufacturing of its soccer balls.[7] Nike knew that there was a large-scale use of child labor in Pakistan. Nike profited from its subcontractor, which used cheap child labor to stitch the soccer balls. Nike hid the case behind its good public image for charity. In May 1996, 12-year-old girls were working 70 hours a week making Nike shoes in Indonesian sweatshops. Nike still remained silent. In June 1996, *Life* magazine published an article carrying the photograph of Tariq, a 12-year-old boy, surrounded by pieces of Nike soccer balls and paid a meager wage. Within weeks, activists across United States and Canada were protesting outside Nike stores. In May 1998, Nike developed a standard code of conduct for its Nike factories, which stipulates, among other things, that the manufacturer will not employ any person below the age of 18 years in the footwear industry. Nike promised to root out underage workers and to ensure that its subcontractors follow U.S. health and safety standards.

Another case involves the death of 1,034 textile workers in a fire in a Bangladesh garment factory in late April 2013. This raised alarms about the dangerous working conditions in Bangladesh's $20 billion garment industry that provides clothing for major retailers around the globe. The fire was blamed on shoddy construction and a disregard for safety regulations.[8]

Another potential harm of foreign companies occurs when they do not cover their *negative externalities*, by which we mean the costs that they create in the environment for which they are not charged. Foreign-owned factories can produce carbon emissions that pollute the air within their host country, or these factories can dump chemicals into streams that make the water undrinkable. It is a practice of companies in developed countries to move their operations to developing countries where environmental regulations are weak or nonexistent. Japan, for example, moved many of its toxic plants into developing countries, where government officials welcomed the job creation irrespective of the pollution.

The major need is for all countries to establish and enforce laws that respect human rights to livable wages, health, and safety.

Unions are one force that could exert pressure on government to enact minimum age limits, good working conditions, and other protections. But unions are often nonexistent, weak, or corrupt in many large cities of poor countries. Another force could be investigative reporters and independent media that publicize abuses. But in many countries, the press is weak or corrupted. One hopes that opposition parties would seek votes on the promise to improve working conditions. But opposition parties, despite their good-sounding rhetoric, often are poorly financed and poorly led.

A major hope would come when more MNCs take more responsibility for overseeing local conditions and refusing to manufacture in countries known to have immiserating working conditions. As more MNCs favor good working conditions for their brand reputation, more countries will set up the regulatory machinery to require entering businesses to observe and install better working conditions.

What Improvements Can a Company Contribute to a Local Economy?

A metro area needs to develop some attractive features that go beyond what it offers economically to potential MNCs and SMEs. In particular, it needs a good image regarding the quality of life that can be enjoyed in that area.

Some places are fortunate to have natural and lifestyle attractions. Berlin is a new lifestyle and cultural center of Europe and is attracting many companies and creative people from all over the world. The cities of Sweden and Finland are leading Europe in high-tech digital start-ups. Stockholm is the most digitally connected city in Europe and has an entrepreneurial ecosystem led by pioneering ventures such as Kazaa, Skype, MySQL, Pirate Bay, and Spotify.

Cities have to put their foot forward to build a brand for doing business. One common strategy to enhance a place's attractiveness is to build a giant convention and exhibition center. In November 2001,

Puerto Rico launched construction for the Puerto Rico Convention Center. Phase one, which included an exhibit hall, meeting space, ballroom, and support and service areas, generated $200 million in investments. The center is part of a more comprehensive project to promote tourism in the San Juan Bay waterfront area. The complex includes casinos, hotels, restaurants, and other business and entertainment spaces.[9] In Florida, the Orange County Convention Center is the country's largest convention center in the United States, with 7 million square feet and all the bells and whistles an organization could want. It plays a vital role in the economy of Orlando, Florida.[10]

The biggest challenge facing city governments and metro councils in the age of global competitive economic development is to change the agenda of local politics. Mayors understand the imperatives of competitive advantage in attracting new companies and investment. But how do city leaders convince voters that this is to everyone's advantage? Voters want their services and low taxes. Most citizens are employed and assume their jobs will continue. They do not want to make personal sacrifices for economic growth and the entry of MNCs into their communities. They worry about pollution. They worry about their property values. They worry about increased traffic. Citizens largely have a short-term view of city life.

Cities need leaders with charisma or character who tell the truth about the future and win over the reluctant minds and hearts of their citizens to support the entry of new MNCs and job growth into their city. Mayors have to convince the voters that redevelopment to attract high-tech talent to new lifestyle communities is worth their while and that bond financing for infrastructure and schools is essential to the future well-being of the city and to jobs for citizens and their children.

Just as MNCs have to advance a larger program of corporate responsibility to the cities they wish to enter, politicians and civic leaders have to convey an urgent concern among a city's citizens for new businesses and investment. The name of the game is civic sacrifice for a better or secure future.

Among other types of lifestyle redevelopments is the conversion of a downtown area into a pedestrian mall. Florida Street in Buenos Aires, Argentina, is a remarkable artery for many visitors who seek a leisurely shopping experience. Nearly 1 million people walk every day in front of the stylish stores, restaurants, and art galleries that spread along the street's 12 blocks. Its cafés, malls, and leather goods shops are definite destinations for Buenos Aires's visitors. Florida Street businesses include the traditional *El Ateneo* bookstore, the famous Harrods, and the *Galería Pacífico,* a mall where visitors can appreciate a 5,000-square-meter mural painted by celebrated Argentinean artists.

One of the authors remembers hearing the story of Olivetti, a former Italian manufacturer of typewriters and other equipment. Olivetti would enter a major city to set up a factory and make provision for improved housing and other conditions for the workers. There are several other examples of such paternalistic companies that want to establish a good quality of life for their workers. George Pullman, whose company built railway sleeping cars in the late nineteenth century, set up a planned worker community (or company town) in Pullman, Illinois, now part of Chicago, replete with worker housing and worker councils.

Companies requiring well-trained and loyal workers need to enter each new community with a good labor policy. Companies such as Coca-Cola and IBM benefit from their reputation for treating their workers well and participating in community affairs and improvement. These companies see these actions as contributing to their success in achieving their long-term objectives.

How Can a Metro Area Be Sure That a Prospective Company Will Contribute More Good Than Bad to the Local Economy?

Cities need to understand that inviting foreign businesses into their economy can bring in both good and bad developments. Usually, cities ignore the downsides because they have one thing in mind, namely, to create jobs and income in the local economy. There will always be parties who gain and who are willing to ignore any ill effects.

Hopefully, the decision to invite certain companies is done with some discussion and deliberation. Most countries and local economies have some laws preventing certain types of companies from coming in and limiting the number of other types of companies coming in (such as heavy industry and foreign media companies). Beijing, for example, has consistently moved heavy industries out of the city to reduce pollution and environmental damage.

MNCs meet many obstacles in entering major global cities. In 2009, Walmart set out to be India's top retailer by 2015.[11] Today, Walmart has barely moved. It has only succeeded in opening only 20 stores through a joint venture with Bharti Enterprises for wholesale operations in the country. There are a number of problems. In particular, small retailers politically oppose the entry of the world's largest retail chain into the cities of India and have successfully prevented Walmart's entry into direct retail sales. In 2013, Walmart suspended its investment expansion in India because it couldn't break into direct retail operations.

A second problem is India's labyrinthine process is the bureaucratic tangles and corruption involved in buying commercial real estate and opening stores. Obtaining municipal licenses is difficult and slow in India. This is true not only for Walmart but also for Indian companies. A company may need dozens of local permits and licenses from municipal agencies. Businesspeople say they commonly have to pay bribes to move projects along.

A third problem has been compliance questions raised about whether Walmart violated the U.S. Foreign Corrupt Practices Act. Walmart has had to step up its efforts to keep its partners and employees in line with both U.S. and Indian laws. Walmart has had similar problems in Mexico.[12]

A fourth problem is that the Indian government requires foreign retail companies to source 30 percent of their goods from India. Walmart argued that this can't be done and wanted the requirement to be lowered to 20 percent. Meanwhile, some Indian officials wanted to raise the requirement to 40 or 50 percent. The Indian government will be facing elections in 2014, and is hesitant to make any change in the 30 percent requirement.[13]

Today Walmart projects in India have halted. In one case, a municipal agency ordered construction to stop because of missing permits, and government officials sealed the site. In another case, Walmart opened a wholesale store without licenses for rice, lentils, fruits, and vegetables, which required separate license applications.[14] Walmart had to be vigilant being in full compliance with all Indian and U.S. laws and regulations. The procedure of entering the large cities of India went through too many difficult steps to make further expansion reasonable.

The Walmart case illustrates the irony of large cities in the developing world trying to attract world-class businesses only to find local opponents, laws, and ordinances standing in the way. Each economy must (1) determine what kinds of businesses it wants to attract and (2) how to simplify the procedures to make entry easy.

Conclusions

Cities seeking more growth are normally pleased to attract MNCs that will plant their offices, factories, and retail venues firmly into the local economy. We have suggested that this is a naive approach. Cities should be more focused on what industries and companies they want to attract to their metro area. They should seek to build strength in certain industries and with certain companies that have the best chance of being competitively successful.

In this chapter, we have argued that MNCs entering developed and developing city markets can only succeed if they have strong corporate social responsibility program that wins the hearts and mind of local leaders and citizens. Many opposing businesses can raise civil objection and unrest. MNCs have to be aware that their corporate social responsibility to the city and the goodwill it engender is as important as hard facts of investment and return on investment.

Conversely, city regions should consider which MNC targets would add the best net value to the local economy. They should ask what impact their target MNCs would have on the local economy and on the problems that the metro area is facing. Some businesses present a mixture of good and bad results. The local economy has to decide whether to insist that targeted businesses cover the cost of the bad results. Other businesses might enter and not only produce good job and income results but also become strong contributors in helping to reduce problems in the local economy. Those would be the best types of businesses to attract.

Questions for Discussion

1. Look at an industry that your metro area is attracting. What are the good things that this industry might bring into the local economy? Are there bad consequences? Will that industry address these issues, or must the local government cover the impacts? Is this a good industry to attract?

2. Can your metro area select one of the major problem areas— education, health, poverty, and corruption—and feature it as the problem that existing and new businesses in the area should focus on improving for the next three years?

3. Can your metro area set up award ceremonies that honor exemplary business behaviors that would inspire other businesses to emulate the practices?

8 How Marketers Manage the City-Centered Global Economy

We have shown how growing a business in the top global-growth cities is a two-way street between how midsize and large multinational companies (MNCs) compete with one another to position their business expansion and how global cities compete with one another for investment by top companies. Company marketers have to pick the best city regions for their headquarters and business divisions. City marketers, primarily operating through their city or metropolitan (metro) economic development agencies, have to win the competitive battle to attract top companies to their city and city region.

Two major impediments to this thinking must be overcome. On the company side, business and marketing organizations have to overcome decades of thinking that global market expansion has to proceed at a global region level and a country level. The preponderance of data and analysis of economic growth is compiled at global, regional, and national levels, not at city and city region levels. Hence, the strategic tendency of company marketers is to investigate opportunities at a national level and do business at a central government level. We call this the *diplomatic route*, and it is out of date.

Economic growth is not happening at the national level. The rate of gross domestic product (GDP) growth of many top global cities exceeds the national rate of GDP growth. Company marketers have to shift their focus from geographical regions and nations to global city growth, and they must mine city region–level economic data for company growth opportunities.

On the city marketing side, there is an obverse problem. Conventional city economic planning emphasizes support for existing local small businesses and for generation of new small-business start-ups. This small-business view is driven by the belief that small business is the prime mover of employment. Although this is true statistically, it is not how cities grow economically. Global economic growth is driven by the consumption, trade, and investment in the goods and services of midsize and large MNCs, not by small companies. MNCs acquire successful small companies and absorb them into their global location matrix. For city economies to grow to global-city status, they have to attract midsize and large MNC company headquarters and their business divisions. Support for small businesses is important, but it will not make a city great.

In short, MNCs have to understand that global-growth cities are their pivot for revenue and profit expansion. Cities have to understand that their pivot of economic growth is the capacity to attract MNCs and their business divisions.

Companies have to change their vision of growth from large (the world, region, or nation) to small (the city or city region). They must develop a city-centric view of consumption, trade, and investment. Cities have to change their vision of growth from small (small businesses) to MNCs and their business divisions. They still must support small enterprise retention and growth for employment, but this is not the scale of attention that will get them in the big leagues. They need midsize and large companies. These are major strategic challenges of MNCs and cities.

Let's first look at the company marketing side of the equation. MNCs have a critical interest in choosing the right cities in which to produce, distribute, sell, and support their products and services. This task falls to the company's business development group, consisting of its executive-level strategic marketers and location experts. Their goal is to place their company in the top global-growth cities, build effective business and marketing organizations in those cities, and network these cities into a coherent corporate structure. They have to discover opportunities and advocate support from top management.

Company marketers have to learn how to do identify, select, organize, and operate in these top growing city markets. MNCs have many business divisions. Which are the best cities for their different divisions? Which cities have the best value chain for their business divisions, both downstream for supply and upstream for consumption and trade?

Marketing investment has to be ranked by priorities. There are many great, growing global cities, but which are the best fit for the company's competitive advantage? Marketers have to learn how to rank different global city investment opportunities. They have to be demographic and economic analysts and skilled advocates in the corporate environment to win strategic investment decisions from top management. Their strategy has to fit the city opportunity, not a national policy model.

Once an MNC's marketers target a set of global cities they think are the right fit for its business growth objectives, they have to negotiate with the city for the best terms of entry. Other companies, and most likely competitors, also have their sights on these cities, so the negotiation process is usually complex.

Company marketers prepare a prospectus for the city and need to negotiate these best terms for investment. The company has to weigh the diverse benefit packages that different suitable cities may be offering to them. If agreement is reached, the company has to organize its business and marketing functions as a city-level strategic enterprise, rather than as a tactical sales unit. Marketers have to go to market in the top global-growth cities they have selected and win market share and profits.

Global marketers have to become geographers, anthropologists, demographers, sociologists, and economists, as well as business managers, to operate successfully in a culturally and economically diverse city-centric global world. They have to become urban geomarketers.

Every brand has to be localized to fit the culture of each top global-growth city. A global brand caries market weight, but it has to be adapted to local cultural meanings. MNC portfolios have to adapt to the unique needs and opportunities of different top global cities. They have to adapt their product portfolio, pricing, promotion, distribution channels, and sales management to local requirements.

The MNC headquarters and business divisions have to become a vital part of the life of the global cities in which they operate. Marketers have to devise a unique corporate social responsibility program that fits the needs, wants, culture, and ambitions of the host city region. They have to win civic welcome and goodwill.

Company marketers have to become business and civic leaders of the global cities they select, not foreign agents. They have to serve the needs and wants of the global cities in which they operate, and build personal relationships with the political, civic, and business leaders of their host cities. Companies have to assign city-centric marketing managers for a sufficient duration of time to grow these imperative relationships.

An MNC business organization has to be a bottom-up matrix of city-centric enterprises, not a top-down system of business delegation. City-centric marketers must bind their city region operations to the other city regions of the company for efficient production, cross-marketing, and cross-selling.

City region marketers need greater business responsibilities. The compensation pyramid of the corporation has to be inverted, with greater compensation to city region marketers, where the money is made, and less to regional and headquarters marketing, where money is spent. The global marketer's career path has to aim toward the matrix management of global city marketers and vertical corporate accountability and leadership. The corporate headquarters chief marketing officer has the ultimate responsibility of placing global city marketers and monitoring, measuring, evaluating their results.

Here, we summarize the actions that a company must take.

Company Opportunity in Global Cities

Imagine that a top private MNC in China, which we will call Xinhao, a conglomerate of $20 billion in annual revenue, has a large heating, ventilation, and air-conditioning (HVAC) manufacturing division, which we will call Lengri. Xinhao has an outbound investment strategy and sees opportunity for Lengri's production, sales, and servicing of high-quality, lower-cost equipment and installations in U.S. cities that are undergoing a commercial and residential condo construction boom.

Xinhao and Lengri have to decide which U.S. cities are most suitable to establish Lengri's U.S. branch headquarters for optimal sales position. Their research shows the top 20 cities in the United States with the highest commercial construction. New York City is number one, with $20.5 billion in commercial construction in 2012. This is followed by Dallas and Houston, with roughly $11.1 billion each. Washington, DC, follows with $9.6 billion, and then Los Angeles comes in with $7.9 billion and Atlanta has $7.9 billion. These are the top six U.S. markets for new HVAC commercial equipment purchase and installation.[1]

Because a large part of the new construction in Washington, DC, consists of federal government projects, the city would politically favor domestic providers. Xinhao eliminates Washington. New York is an old and established commercial economy, with well-placed legacy providers such as Carrier in nearby Farmington, Connecticut. Xinhao eliminates New York City. Lennox International is headquartered in Dallas and would present stiff competition to the entry of a foreign HVAC company in the markets of Houston and Dallas. Xinhao eliminates Houston and Dallas. Trane, a division of Ingersoll Rand (a corporation registered and maintaining global headquarters in Dublin, Ireland), is located in Davidson, North Carolina, a small city of 10,000 people in 2010 and far from the top commercial construction cities. This leaves Atlanta and Los Angeles as reasonable cities to approach. Xinhao notes that its competitor Johnson Controls, with headquarters in Milwaukee, Wisconsin, is distant from these cities, although it has a sales presence in all top commercial construction cities.

Company Profiling of Opportunity Cities

Xinhao decides to consider Atlanta and Los Angeles. Atlanta has a lot going for it. In 2012, it was ranked fourth in North American cities with the largest number of new projects, first in the best cities to start a business, fourth in entrepreneurial activity, and sixth in North American cities of the future, according to information published by the Metro Atlanta Chamber.[2]

Los Angeles is also an attractive location. The Los Angeles metro area is the second-largest megacity region in the United States, with 13 million people, only trailing New York's city region of 19 million.[3] It is also second after New York in GDP, at $792.4 billion.[4] It is the third-largest metro economic center in the world after Tokyo and New York.[5] It also has the third-largest Chinese population in the United States after New York City and San Francisco, which is a goodwill advantage to the entry of a Chinese HVAC company.[6] Finally, none of the top five U.S. HVAC companies has headquarters on the West Coast.

Company Reaching Out to Opportunity Cities

Xinhao and its Lengri HVAC division engage expert U.S. consultants in their industry who know these cities, their construction forecasts, and how top U.S. competitors penetrate the HVAC market of these cities.

They visit Atlanta and Los Angeles and meet with each economic development agency, as well as political, business, and civic leaders. They research the commercial property growth rate of these three cities, study the positions of competitors in these cities, and identify niche opportunities for their potential business.

They explore partnership potential with commercial property developers, the local and regional HVAC demand profile, the local talent supply, incentive benchmarks that these cities have offered to other companies, and finally their friendliness to Chinese business entry in their city region market. They prepare a strategic letter of interest to each of these cities. The cities respond positively, meetings are arranged, and discussion proceeds in both cities.

Actions by the City

Now let's turn to the city marketing side of the equation. Cities have a critical interest in attracting more companies to do business in their cities. This task usually falls to the mayor and his or her economic development agency, politicians, and business groups in the city to create sound company attraction plans. What actions have to take place to bring about successful city and company decisions that ultimately produce strong benefits to the city, as well as to the company?

City Core Strengths for Investment Attraction

Cities determine which companies could reasonably be attracted to do business in their city. The city recognizes that it cannot be an attractive city for all companies to invest in. As a city, it needs to be proactive in identifying which industries and companies could potentially benefit from doing business in that city.

The city must start by identifying its special skill sets and attributes. In our example, Atlanta and Los Angeles were among the top five U.S. cities in commercial construction in 2012. They know that they have an opportunity to attract a major global HVAC to their community, because they have no top U.S. HVAC headquartered in their city region. They also know from their research that top Chinese HVAC companies are interested in entering the U.S. market. They also know the advantage of attracting a major Chinese company, because other Chinese investment will follow in cities where initial Chinese investors have a satisfactory business experience. Chinese investment in a city begets more Chinese investment.

Reaching Out to Potential Investors

Atlanta and Los Angeles reach out to top Chinese HVAC companies, including Xinhao's Lengri division. They do this through representative offices in China, as well as through their local business leaders who are already doing business in China. The mayor in each city reaches out through private and public channels to get the attention of Xinhao. They get a response of interest from the company.

Each of these cities also leverages the interest of Xinhao to approach top U.S. HVAC providers to deepen their investment in the city and thus shield their sales against the entry of a new global player. Carrier, Johnson Controls, Trane, and Lennox have sales organizations in their cities, but a foreign HVAC headquarters could be stiff competition. The U.S. providers may want to fortify their positions in these cities with greater investment to cut any Chinese company out of the game.

Each of the contending cities knows that Chinese Xinhao and its Lengri division have several other options in the United States and many other opportunities for investment throughout the developing world. Playing legacy companies against them in a bidding war may not win Chinese goodwill and focused interest. One of the two prospective cities decides on a bidding war. The other decides to focus on the Chinese company and negotiate a deal. The Chinese may take this city seriously.

The Negotiation Process

A long process ensues in which strategy and tactical details are discussed. If discussions achieve a level of trust and mutual benefit, the parties will take the next step to draft a time-dated memorandum of understanding (MOU), with underlying conditions of exclusivity.

This MOU gives each side the time for due diligence and to prepare a proposal. On the Chinese side, this is a draft offer proposal; on the U.S. city side, it is a draft incentives offer. There is an exchange of proposals. The discussion of interest and counterproposals involves many support agents, including engineers, industry specialists, lawyers, financial institutions, marketing specialists, public relations agents, both U.S. and Chinese government commercial offices, partners, and political, business, and civic leaders. This long process of negotiation may result in an agreement to close the deal, continue negotiation on an options basis, or terminate talks. If the parties reach a decision to close, there may still be a long way to final closure.

Conclusions

We have developed this example to show the dance that usually takes place between a city and a company searching to maximize their respective opportunities and advantages. Both sides are drawing on the marketing power they might have in relation to the other side. If the company is well known and respected, and if the city is one of many sites being considered, then the balance of power lies with the company to get better terms, even if it diminishes the value which the city seeks. However, the opposite might be the case: The city may be vastly superior to other competing cities, and the company may have little choice and need to locate there. Each situation calls for negotiation experience, hard data, and good judgment formed from many previous city-company attraction experiences.

We remain conscious that the thousands of episodes of this kind that take place will make a huge difference in the rate of economic growth of competing cities on the one hand and the profitability and growth of competing companies on the other hand. To a great extent, the difference will be determined by the degree of sophistication in the modern marketing and negotiation skills of the parties on the city side and the company side. These episodes reflect the unending and inescapable drama of business-to-business decision making that is taking place everywhere in the world and determining the future of cities and companies.

Questions for Discussion

1. Is your company organized at an executive level to make strategic selections of new global city regions of business opportunity?

2. What kind of team does your company have for this purpose? And to whom does the team report?

3. Which MNCs, in your view, are best at this city-centric global investment process?

4. Does your city have an economic development agency with sufficient resources, talent, and authority to identify global MNCs that

are suitable for your business environment and that can benefit by their investment in your city?

5. Is your process of identification, profiling, communication, and negotiation systematic or is it ad hoc?

6. Which cities, in your view, are best at this MNC global investment attraction process?

NOTES

Chapter 1   The Economic Power of Global Cities

1. World Urbanization Prospects, 2007 revision (online data), and Japan Statistics Bureau-Keihin'yō Major Metropolitan Area, www.stat.go.jp/data/kokusei/2000/final/zuhyou/092.xls.

2. "India Still Second Fastest Growing Economy," *The Hindu*, July 27, 3013, http://m.thehindu.com/business/Economy/india-still-second-fastest-growing-economy-chidambaram/article4959820.ece/?maneref=http%3A%2F%2Fwww.google.co.in%2Fsearch%3Fhl%3Den%26q%3Dindia%2520is%25202nd%2520fastest%2520growing%2520economy%26spell%3D1%26sa%3DX.

3. Michael Barbaro, "Bloomberg Focuses on Rest (as in Rest of World)," *New York Times*, December 15, 2013, p. 1.

4. "President Reaches Out to Mayors," *Herald Tribune*, December 15, 2013, p. 5A.

5. Nirmalya Kumar and Jan-Benedict Steenhamp, *Brand Breakout: How Emerging Market Brands Will Go Global* (New York, NY: Palgrave Macmillan, 2013).

6. *Cities* refer to standard metropolitan areas (SMAs) of municipalities. *City regions* extend beyond the SMAs. Megacities exceed 10 million in population; large cities range from 5 million to 10 million people. Midsize cities range from below 5 million to 150,000 people.

7. Yiqin Fu, "Half of China's GDP Comes From Major Cities," Tea Leaf Nation, http://www.tealeafnation.com/2014/03/map-half-of-chinas-gdp-comes-from-major-cities/, accessed on March 31, 2014.

8. McKinsey Global Institute, *Urban World: Mapping the Economic Power of Cities* (McKinsey, 2011).

9. Milton Kotler, "A Tale of Two Cities: New Market Economy or Old?" February 24, 2013, http://mkotlerchinablog.blogspot.com/2013/02/a-tale-of-two-cities-new-market-economy.html.

10. McKinsey Global Institute, *Cities and the Rise of the Consuming Class* (McKinsey, 2012).

11. Gabriel Zucman, *The Missing Wealth of Nations* (Paris, France: Paris School of Economics, February 25, 2013).

12. McKinsey, *Urban World*, 2011.

13. Vidur Saghal, in discussion with Milton Kotler, 2013.

14. PricewaterhouseCoopers, *The BRICs and Beyond: Prospects, Challenges, and Opportunities*, http://www.pwc.com/gx/en/world-2050/the-brics-and-beyond-prospects-challenges-and-opportunities.jhtml

15. PricewaterhouseCoopers, *Cities of Opportunity 2012*, http://www.pwc.com/us/en/cities-of-opportunity/

16. McKinsey, *Urban World*, 2011.

17. Developed regions compose the United States and Canada, Western Europe, Australasia, and Japan and South Korea.

18. Local records office of Guangdong, China. Retrieved by Milton Kotler on August 4, 2011.

19. Yue-man Yeung, Joanna Lee, and Gordon Kee, *Eurasian Geography and Economics* (New York: Taylor & Francis, 2008).

20. Central Intelligence Agency, *CIA World Factbook*, 2012, https://www.cia.gov/library/publications/the-world-factbook

21. Jane Jacobs, *Cities and the Wealth of Nations* (New York: Random House, 1984).

22. McKinsey, *Urban World*, 2011; and *Cities and the Rise of the Consuming Class*, 2012, p. 3.

23. U.S. Census Bureau, "Census Bureau Projects U.S. Population of 315.1 Million on New Year's Day," December 27, 2012.

24. Richard Florida, "The Developing World's Urban Population Could Triple by 2210," *The Atlantic*, February 20, 2014, http://www.theatlanticcities.com/housing/2014/02/developing-worlds-urban-population-could-triple-2210/8431/.

25. McKinsey, *Urban World*, 2011.

26. McKinsey, *Cities*, 2012.

27. McKinsey, *Urban World*, 2011.

28. Ibid.

29. Ibid.

30. Jane Jacobs, *Cities and the Wealth of Nations*.

31. Jane Jacobs, *The Death and Life of Great American Cities* (New York: Random House, 1961).

32. McKinsey, *Urban World*, 2011.

33. http://en.wikipedia/wiki/List_of_countries_by_exports

34. Ibid.

35. McKinsey Global Institute, *The World at Work: Jobs, Pay, and Skills for 2.5 Billion People* (McKinsey, June 2012).

36. McKinsey, *World at Work*, 2012.

37. McKinsey, *Urban World*, 2011.

38. Organisation for Economic Co-operation and Development, OECD Employment Outlook 2013, http://www.oecd.org/employment/emp/oecdemploymentoutlook.htm.

39. McKinsey, *World at Work*, 2012.

40. McKinsey Global Institute, *Preparing for China's Urban Billion*, 2009.

41. McKinsey, *World at Work*, 2012.

42. Brad Plumer, "Three Reasons the U.S. Workforce Keeps Shrinking," *The Washington Post* Wonkblog, September 6, 2013, http://www.washingtonpost.com/blogs/wonkblog/wp/2013/09/06/the-incredible-shrinking-labor-force-again/.

43. The World Bank, "Employment to Population Ratio," 2014, http://data.worldbank.org/indicator/SL.EMP.TOTL.SP.ZS

44. U.S. Census Bureau, *Annual Survey of Manufactures*, 2014.

45. Dieter Ernst, "China's Innovation Policy Is a Wake-up Call for America," East-West Center, May 2011, http://www.eastwestcenter.org/sites/default/files/private/api100_0.pdf.

46. All-China Federation of Industry and Commerce, 2012.

47. Thilo Hanemann, "Chinese FDI in the United States: Q3 2013 Update," Rhodium Group, October 25, 2013, http://rhg.com/notes/chinese-fdi-in-the-united-states-q3-2013-update.

48. "Haier and Higher: The Radical Boss of Haier Wants to Transform the World's Biggest Appliance-Maker Into a Nimble Internet-Age Firm," *The Economist*, October 12, 2013, http://www.economist.com/news/business/21587792-radical-boss-haier-wants-transform-worlds-biggest-appliance-maker-nimble.

49. Stuart L. Hart, *Capitalism at the Crossroads* (Wharton School Publishing, Pearson Education, 2007).

50. Shen Jingting, "ZTE Invested $1.4 Billion in R&D This Year," China Daily, October 30, 2013, http://www.chinadaily.com.cn/china/2013-10/30/content_17069929.htm.

51. Battelle, 2014 Global R&D Funding Forecast, December 2013, www.battle.org

52. McKinsey, *Urban World*, 2011.

53. Wall Street Journal Market Watch, www.marketwatch.com, December 3, 2013.

54. Deutsche Bank Media, "Deutsche Bank Releases 2014 Renminbi Forecast," January 13, 2014, https://www.db.com/medien/en/content/3862_4234.htm.

55. SWIFT, "Will Europe Overtake Asia in RMB Trade Settlement?" October 29, 2013, http://www.swift.com/about_swift/shownews?param_dcr=news.data/en/swift_com/2013/RMB_Europe_over take_Asia_RMB_trade_settlement.xml.

56. "2012 ODI Hits Record High," *People's Daily*, China, September 2013.

57. Congressional Reference Service, *U.S. Direct Investment Abroad* (2012).

58. U.S. Department of Labor, Bureau of Labor Statistics, "Table 4.5. Gross Private Domestic Investment: 1992, 2002, 2012, and projected 2022," January 2, 2014, http://www.bls.gov/emp/ep_table_405.htm.

59. United Nations Conference on Trade and Development, Global Investment Trends Monitor, "Global FDI Rose 11%; Developing Economies Are Trapped in a Historically Low Share," January 2014.

60. "Foreign Direct Investment," *The Economist*, October 2012.

61. "Capital Inflows," Globalization 101, http://www.globalization101.org/capital-inflows

62. McKinsey, *Urban World*, 2011, and *Cities and the Rise of the Consuming Class*, 2012, p. 49.

63. McKinsey, *Urban World*, 2011.

64. Ibid.

65. Ibid.

66. Compiled from U.S. Fortune 500 company reports, 2013.

67. Ibid.

Chapter 2   How City Metropolitan Regions Compete in the Global Economy

1. Bruce Katz and Jennifer Bradley, *The Metropolitan Revolution* (Washington, DC: Brookings Institution, 2013), 41.

2. Global Cities Initiative, *The Ten Traits of Globally Fluent Metro Areas* (Washington, DC: Brookings Institution, 2013).

3. Katz and Bradley, *The Metropolitan Revolution*, 52.

4. Denver Relocation Guide, "Top 25 Employers in Denver," http://www.denverrelocationguide.net/2013/Largest-Employers-in-Denver-Colorado/

5. Contemporary writers on cities, like Benjamin Barber (*If Mayors Ruled the World*, Yale University Press, 2013), have a benign view of city interdependence. They overlook the aggressive history of annexations by powerful cities that encompass weaker adjacent cities and towns as a result of war (Europe) and politics (United States). For a review of city imperialism, see Milton Kotler, *Neighborhood Government* (Bobbs Merrill, 1969; currently Lexington Press).

6. World Urbanization Prospects, 2007 revision (online data), and Japan Statistics Bureau-Keihin'yō Major Metropolitan Area, www.stat.go.jp/data/kokusei/2000/final/zuhyou/092.xls.

7. PriceWaterhouseCoopers, "Table: Top 30 Urban Agglomerations by Projected Average Real GDP Growth, 2008–2025," *UK Economic Outlook*, November 2009, http://www.pwc.com/en_GX/gx/psrc/pdf/ukeo_largest_city_economies_in_the_world_sectioniii.pdf.

8. Brookings Institution, "Global City GDP 2011–2012," accessed December 26, 2012.

9. CNNMoney, "Global 500," http://money.cnn.com/magazines/fortune/global500/2009/cities/.

10. Mumbai Plan, Department of Relief and Rehabilitation, Government of Maharashtra, http://mdmu.maharashtra.gov.in/pages/Mumbai/mumbaiplanShow.php, accessed April 29, 2009.

11. Deborah L. Wetzel, Lincoln Institute of Land Policy, "Metropolitan Governance and Finance in São Paolo," Conference Paper, 2013, http://www.lincolninst.edu/pubs/2316_Metropolitan-Governance -and-Finance-in-S%c3%a3o-Paulo.

12. Diann Daniel, "Geek America: The Top 10 U.S. Cities for Technology Jobs," *CIO*, http://www.cio.com/special/slideshows/top_10_ cities_for_tech_jobs/slide10#slideshow_viewer.

13. Richard Pérez-Peña, "Alliance Formed Secretly to Win Deal for Campus," *New York Times*, December 25, 2011, http://www .nytimes.com/2011/12/26/education/in-cornell-deal-for-roosevelt -island-campus-an-unlikely-partnership.html?_r=0.

14. The Port Authority of New York and New Jersey, www.panyny.com

15. Municipio of Panama, http://municipio.gob.pa/, accessed June 26, 2010.

16. Darcy Crowe, "Panama's Economy to Extend Strong Growth in 2013," *Wall Street Journal*, March 16, 2013, http://online.wsj.com/news/articles/SB10001424127887324532004578364710313021 902.

17. Ryan Holeywell, "Panama Canal Expansion Has U.S. Ports Rushing," *Governing*, July 2012, http://www.governing.com/panama-canal-expansion-has-ports-rushing.html.

18. Qaswar Abbas, "Pakistan's Gwadar Port May Get Special China Status," *Mail Online India*, August 31, 2013, http://www

.dailymail.co.uk/indiahome/indianews/article-2408121/Pakistans-Gwadar-port-special-China-status.html.

19. Gwadar Private Scheme Information Center, Chinese Interest and Investment, http://gwadarprivatescheme.wordpress.com/chinese-investment/, accessed November 20, 2013.

20. Jenny E. Scheid, "Incentives Attract New Downtown Businesses," *Las Vegas Review-Journal,* September 26, 2013, http://www.reviewjournal.com/business/economic-development/incentives-attract-new-downtown-businesses.

21. Kurt Badenhausen, "The Best Places for Business and Careers," *Forbes,* August 7, 2013, http://www.forbes.com/best-places-for-business/.

22. Madhavi Acharya-Tom Yew, "Coca-Cola Canada Unveils New King Street Headquarters," *The Star,* April 4, 2013, http://www.thestar.com/business/2013/04/04/cocacola_canada_unveils_new_king_street_east_headquarters.html.

23. Louisa Peacock, "Singapore Number One Destination for Investment Bankers," *The Telegraph,* February 17, 2011, http://www.telegraph.co.uk/finance/jobs/8329383/Singapore-number-one-destination-for-investment-bankers.html.

24. Michael Porter, *Competitive Advantage* (New York: Free Press, 1985).

25. Matt Houston, "A Boom in Houston Is Led by the Energy Industry," *The New York Times,* December 4, 2012, http://www.nytimes.com/2012/12/05/realestate/commercial/houstons-boom-is-led-by-the-energy-industry.html?pagewanted=all.

26. Ibid.

27. Joseph Szczesny, "Milestone: China Now General Motors' Biggest Market," CNBC.com, July 8, 2013, http://www.cnbc.com/id/100870316.

28. "Six of the Top Ten Logistics/Distribution/Shipping Hubs Are Located in the South," MHI, August 24, 2011, http://www.mhi .org/media/news/10898.

29. John Studzinski, "Germany Is Right: There Is No Right to Profit, but the Right to Work Is Essential," *The Guardian*, February 5, 2013, http://www.theguardian.com/commentisfree/2013/feb/06/ germany-success-humanity-medium-firms.

30. Angelo Young, "$724,000 for a Ferrari? China's Rich Are Getting Shafted Buying Luxury Cars, but Who's Ripping Them Off?" *International Business Times*, July 31, 2013, http://www.ibtimes.com/ 724000-ferrari-chinas-rich-are-getting-shafted-buying-luxury-cars -whos-ripping-them-1365037.

31. Suzanne Kapner, Biman Mukherji, and Shelley Banjo, "Before Dhaka Collapse, Some Firms Fled Risk," *The Wall Street Journal*, May 8, 2013, http://online.wsj.com/news/articles/SB1000142412 78873247666045784588024238734488.

32. George L. Kelling, "How New York Became Safe: The Full Story," *City Journal*, http://www.city-journal.org/2009/nytom_ny-crime- decline.html.

33. Adam Cohen and Elizabeth Taylor, *American Pharaoh: Mayor Richard J. Daley, His Battle for Chicago and the Nation* (New York: Little, Brown, 2000).

34. Steve Wilhelm, "Phil Condit, Who Took Boeing to Chicago, Reflects on How a Different Home Changed the Company," *Puget Sound Business Journal*, June 17, 2011, http://www.bizjournals.com /seattle/print-edition/2011/06/17/phil-condit-who-took-boeing- to.html?page=all.

35. Jose Pagliery, "8 Most Business-Friendly Cities," *CNNMoney.com*, June 20, 2013, http://money.cnn.com/gallery/smallbusiness/2013/ 06/18/best-places-launch-cities/8.html.

36. Joyce Lau, "Juilliard to Bring New York-Style Teaching to China," *New York Times*, January 28, 2013, http://www.nytimes.com/2013 /01/29/world/asia/29iht-educside28.html.

Chapter 3 The Real Generators of Wealth: Global Multinational Company Investment

1. Richard F. Weingroff, "Public Roads, Federal-Aid Highway Act of 1956: Creating the Interstate System," NationalAtlas.gov, 1996, http://www.nationalatlas.gov/articles/transportation/a_highway .html.

2. Federal Highway Administration, Office of Highway Policy Information, "Table HM-20: Public Road Length (2012)," October 2013, http://www.fhwa.dot.gov/policyinformation/statistics/2012 /hm20.cfm.

3. Federal Highway Administration, Office of Highway Policy Information, "Table VM-1: Annual Vehicle Distance Traveled in Miles and Related Data," March 2013, http://www.fhwa.dot.gov/policy information/statistics/2011/vm1.cfm.

4. Richard F. Weingroff, "The Greatest Decade 1956-1966," Federal Highway Administration, Highway History, https://www.fhwa.dot .gov/infrastructure/50interstate.cfm.

5. http://en.wikipedia.org/wiki/Three_Gorges_Dam (Chinaneast.xin huanet.com)

6. Paul Calore, "What the Hoover Dam Cost to Build," WhatIt Costs.com, http://historical.whatitcosts.com/facts-hoover-dam-pg2 .htm.

7. Organisation for Economic Co-operation and Development (OECD), *Pension Funds Investment in Infrastructure: A Survey*, September 2011, http://www.oecd.org/futures/infrastructureto 2030/48634596.pdf.

8. Public Works Financing, "2011 Statistical Survey of Public-Private Partnerships Worldwide," October 18, 2011, http://pwfinance.net/document/October_2011_vNov202011.pdf.

9. OECD, *Pension Funds*.

10. Transurban, "495 Express Lanes," http://www.transurban.com/269.htm.

11. Routes Online, "China Investing in New Airport for Myanmar's Capital," July 11, 2011, http://www.routesonline.com/news/37/momberger-airport-information/117878/china-investing-in-new-airport-for-myanmars-capital/.

12. Eiffage, "Millau Viaduct," http://www.eiffage.com/cms/en/le-groupe-eiffage/millau-viaduct.html

13. Areva, "Structure of the Partnership for Hinkley Point C Project," http://www.areva.com/EN/news-9986/structure-of-the-partnership-for-hinkley-point-c-project.html

14. Gaurav Raghuvanshi, "Rolls-Royce Pushes Focus on Singapore," *Wall Street Journal*, September 15, 2013, http://online.wsj.com/news/articles/SB10001424127887323595004579070744175876558.

15. The U.S. Small Business Administration, "Summary of Size Standards by Industry Sector," http://www.sba.gov/content/summary-size-standards-industry

16. McKinsey Global Institute, *Urban World: The Shifting Global Business Landscape* (McKinsey, October 2013).

17. Phil Rosenthal and Ray Long, "ADM Announces It Is Moving Headquarters to Chicago," *Chicago Tribune*, December 18, 2013, http://articles.chicagotribune.com/2013-12-18/business/chi-adm-headquarters-chicago-20131217_1_incentives-state-tax-credit-headquarters.

18. David Barboza, "Chicago, Offering Big Incentives, Will Be Boeing's New Home," *New York Times*, May 11, 2001, http://www.nytimes.com/2001/05/11/business/chicago-offering-big-incentives-will-be-boeing-s-new-home.html.

19. Colum Murphy, "GM to Move International Headquarters to Singapore From Shanghai," *Wall Street Journal*, November 13, 2013, http://online.wsj.com/news/articles/SB10001424052702303289904579195351521001492.

20. Dan Ritter, "The Auto Industry's 5 Largest Market Share Shifts in 2013," Wall St. Cheat Sheet, January 25, 2014, http://wallstcheatsheet.com/stocks/the-auto-industrys-5-largest-u-s-market-share-shifts-in-2013.html/?a=viewall.

21. David Gelles, "New Corporate Tax Shelter: A Merger Abroad," *New York Times,* October 8, 2013, http://dealbook.nytimes.com/2013/10/08/to-cut-corporate-taxes-a-merger-abroad-and-a-new-home/.

22. Makiko Kitamura, "Perrigo to Buy Elan for $8.6 Billion, Get Irish Domicile," Bloomberg, July 29, 2013, http://www.bloomberg.com/news/2013-07-29/perrigo-to-buy-elan-for-8-6-billion-get-irish-domicile.html.

23. Charles Riley, "Pfizer Eyes AstraZeneca for $100 Billion Acquisition," CNNMoney.com, April 28, 2014, http://money.cnn.com/2014/04/28/news/pfizer-astrazeneca/.

24. Nathalie Tadena, Jason Dean, and Leslie Scism, "Aon Shifts Headquarters to London," *Wall Street Journal*, January 24, 2012, http://online.wsj.com/news/articles/SB10001424052970204542404577158633936346056.

25. Ann Davis, "Ensco Opts to Move to U.K.," *Wall Street Journal*, November 9, 2009, http://online.wsj.com/news/articles/SB10001424052748703808904574525981001767654.

26. Brett Clanton, "Another Houston Oil Firm Moves Its Headquarters Overseas," *Houston Chronicle,* December 12, 2008, http://www.chron.com/business/article/Another-Houston-oil-firm-moves-its-headquarters-1769131.php.

27. David Wethe, "Noble Corp.'s London Move May Cut Its Tax Bill in Half," Bloomberg, July 1, 2013, http://www.bloomberg.com/news/2013-07-01/noble-corp-s-london-move-may-cut-its-tax-bill-in-half.html.

28. McKinsey, *Urban World*, 2013.

29. Ibid.

30. Ibid.

31. McKinsey Global Institute, *Urban World: Mapping the Economic Power of Cities* (McKinsey, March 2011).

32. Ibid.

33. James Politi, "Barack Obama Mounts Big Push to Bolster FDI in US," *Financial Times*, October 27, 2013, http://www.ft.com/cms/s/0/c5119344-3f0a-11e3-b665-00144feabdc0.html.

34. OXFAM, "The World's Top 100 Economies: 53 Countries, 34 Cities, and 13 Corporations," October 19, 2011, http://oxfamblogs.org/fp2p/the-worlds-top-100-economies-53-countries-34-cities-and-13-corporations/.

35. Vincent Trivett, "25 US Mega Corporations: Where They Rank if They Were Countries," *Business Insider*, June 27, 2011, http://www.businessinsider.com/25-corporations-bigger-tan-countries-2011-6?op=1.

36. Global 500, *CNNMoney*, July 26, 2010, http://money.cnn.com/magazines/fortune/global500/2010/performers/companies/biggest/.

37. McKinsey, *Urban World*, 2011.

38. "Hyundai Motor Eyes Major Expansion With New Plant in China," Reuters, March 26, 2014, http://www.reuters.com/article/2014/03/26/hyundai-plant-idUSL4N0MM4XM20140326.

Chapter 4   How Multinational Companies Target Global City Markets for Expansion

1. Jack Ewing and David Jolly, "Europe Remains G.M.'s Weak Spot," *New York Times*, February 15, 2012, http://www.nytimes.com/2012/02/16/business/global/europe-remains-gms-weak-spot.html?pagewanted=all.

2. Paul A. Eisenstein, "China to Limit Car Sales in Fight Against Air Pollution," NBC News, July 2013, http://www.nbcnews.com/business/autos/china-limit-car-sales-fight-against-air-pollution-f6C10599665.

3. Amit Bhasin, "The Fall of the Rupee: Is Policy Paralysis the Culprit?" Public Policy, http://stdwww.iimahd.ernet.in/pubpol/july_2012_fall_of_indian_rupee.html.

4. Malavika Vyawahare, "India Ink: Falling Rupee Puts Brakes on India's Auto Industry," *New York Times*, September 5, 2013, http://india.blogs.nytimes.com/2013/09/05/falling-rupee-puts-brakes-on-indias-auto-industry/?_r=0.

5. Mercer, "2014 Quality of Living Worldwide City Rankings–Mercer Survey," February 19, 2014, http://www.mercer.us/press-releases/quality-of-living-report-2014.

6. Nirmalya Kumar and Jan-Benedict E.M. Steenkamp, *Brand Breakout: How Emerging Market Brands Will Go Global* (Palgrave Macmillan, June 18, 2013).

7. Much of this chapter is based on updating a previous book by one of the authors: Philip Kotler, David Gertner, Irving Rein, and Donald Haider, *Marketing Places, Latin America* (Makron and Paidos, 2006).

8. International Monetary Fund, "Latin American Growth to Edge Higher in 2013—IMF Survey," May 6, 2013, http://www.imf .org/external/pubs/ft/survey/so/2013/car050613a.htm.

9. McKinsey Global Institute, *Building Globally Competitive Cities: The Key to Latin American Growth* (McKinsey, August 2011).

10. Jeremy Palaia, "Latin American Consumer Market Projected to Reach 661 Million People at Combined GDP of $15.14 Trillion in 2025; Highest Number of High Net Worth Individuals in Brazil," PR Newswire, January 9, 2013, http://www.prnewswire.com/ news-releases/latin-american-consumer-market-projected-to-reach -661-million-people-at-combined-gdp-of-1514-trillion-in-2025- highest-number-of-high-net-worth-individuals-in-brazil-1862559 32.html.

11. McKinsey, *Building Globally Competitive Cities*, 2011.

12. Global Intelligence Alliance, "Latest Insights: Latin America," http://www.globalintelligence.com/geographies/latin-america/.

13. Andres Oppenheimer, "Latin America's Fastest-Growing Economies of 2013," *The Miami Herald*, April 24, 2013, http://www .miamiherald.com/2013/04/24/3362939/andres-oppenheimer- latin-americas.html.

14. Government of Canada, Consulate General of Canada in Miami, "South Florida as a Gateway to Latin America and the Caribbean," January 8, 2014, http://www.can-am.gc.ca/miami/highlights-faits/ 2014/Gateway-Porte.aspx?lang=eng.

15. Shelly K. Schwartz, "What's the Next Global Manufacturing Superpower?" CNBC.com, September 18, 2012, http://www.cnbc .com/id/49007307.

16. Michigan State University, Global Edge, "Mercosur: History, 2013," http://globaledge.msu.edu/trade-blocs/mercosur/history.

17. McKinsey, *Building Globally Competitive Cities*, August 2011.

18. PricewaterhouseCoopers, "Global City GDP Rankings 2008–2025," American Chamber of Commerce of Mexico, Monterrey.

19. Tom Orlik, "No Way for Huawei in U.S.," *Wall Street Journal,* October 11, 2012, http://online.wsj.com/news/articles/SB10000 872396390444799904578049520739337306.

20. Bloomberg, "U.S. National-Security Clearance of Softbank: Sprint Deal Hits Huawei," *South China Morning Post,* May 31, 2013, http://www.scmp.com/business/companies/article/1249878/us-national-security-clearance-softbank-sprint-deal-hits-huawei.

21. CNNMoney, "Fortune 500 companies—Illinois," May 21, 2012, http://money.cnn.com/magazines/fortune/fortune500/2013/full_list/.

22. United States Census Bureau, Population Division, "Chicago SMSA 2012 Population Estimates," March 2013, http://www.census.gov/compendia/statab/cats/population/estimates_and_pro jections--states_metropolitan_areas_cities.html.

23. Chengcheng Jiang, "The Juilliard School Bets on China, Builds Outside Beijing," *TIME,* July 30, 2012, http://world.time.com/2012/07/30/the-juilliard-school-bets-on-china-builds-outside-beij ing/.

24. Greg Hinz, "ADM to Move Headquarters to Chicago," *Crain's Chicago Business,* December 17, 2013, http://www.chicagobusiness.com/article/20131217/BLOGS02/131219778/adm-to-move-headquarters-to-chicago.

25. "Chile and Mexico Lead Latin Charge to Market as Cross-Over Investors Return," *EuroWeek,* London, 785, January 10, 2003, 1, 18.

26. http://www.chileinvestmentforum.cl/

27. Ibid.

28. The World Bank, Doing Business, "Ease of Doing Business in Singapore," 2014, http://www.doingbusiness.org/data/exploreeco nomies/singapore/.

29. Alice Baghdijian, "Singapore to Emerge as Top Finance Hub by 2015: Study," Reuters, July 4, 2013, http://in.reuters.com/article/2013/07/04/singapore-swiss-funds-idINDEE9630AX20130704.

30. "Mozambique: Many Businesses Dissatisfied With Public Administration," All Africa, March 3, 2013, http://allafrica.com/stories/201303030211.html.

31. KPMG, "Global Cities Investment Monitor 2013: New Rankings, Trends and Criteria," http://www.kpmg.com/FR/fr/IssuesAndIn sights/ArticlesPublications/Documents/Observatoire-des-Investiss ements-Internationaux-principales-metropoles-mondiales-2013 .pdf

32. http://www.asiaweek.com/asiaweek/features/asiacities/ac1999/data/introduction.html

Chapter 5   How Cities Compete to Attract Midsize and Large Multinational Companies

1. Erik Heinrich, "Would Getting the Olympics Be Good or Bad for Chicago?" *TIME*, September 30, 2009, http://content.time.com/time/business/article/0,8599,1926505,00.html.

2. Jon Hilkevitch, "Dan Ryan Cost Drives Toward $1 Billion," *Chicago Tribune*, September 17, 2006, http://articles.chicagotribune .com/2006-09-17/news/0609170356_1_contracts-road-project-ryan-project.

3. BJ Lutz, "Chicago Lost: Five Reasons Why," NBC Chicago, October 2, 2009, http://www.nbcchicago.com/news/local/Why-Chicago-Lost-2016-Olympic-Bid-63050927.html.

4. Michael Richardson, "Singapore Industrial Park Flounders: A Deal Sours in China," *New York Times*, October 1, 1999, http://www .nytimes.com/1999/10/01/business/worldbusiness/01iht-suzhou .2.t.html; also, "Suzhou Industrial Park Is a Success," *The Straits Times*, October 2006.

5. Suzhou China, "Dushu Lake Higher Education Town," November 11, 2011, http://www.suzhou.gov.cn.

6. Patrick McGeehan, "City's Virtues to Be Sold in New Global Ad Campaign," *New York Times*, October 11, 2007, http://www.nytimes.com/2007/10/11/nyregion/11promo.html?_r=0&gwh=599E515BA816A03CCB8C54F31151FB9A&gwt=pay.

7. Jim Yardley and Gardiner Harris, "2nd Day of Power Failures Cripples Wide Swath of India," *New York Times*, July 31, 2012, http://www.nytimes.com/2012/08/01/world/asia/power-outages-hit-600-million-in-india.html?pagewanted=all&gwh=CBE8DC580C44ED18BB2FAFA3D1D362FB&gwt=pay.

8. Jason Belcher, "Eastern Kentucky's Economic Woes Are Not Unique," *Floyd County Times*, 2012, http://floydcountytimes.com/news/letters/2421324/Eastern-Kentuckys-economic-woes-not-unique.

9. Colum Murphy and Rose Yu, "Can Wuhan Become the Detroit of China?" *Wall Street Journal China*, October 17, 2013, http://blogs.wsj.com/chinarealtime/2013/10/17/can-wuhan-become-the-detroit-of-china/.

10. Rohit Arora, "Top U.S. Cities for Small Business Growth in 2013," FOX Business, May 7, 2013, http://smallbusiness.foxbusiness.com/finance-accounting/2013/05/07/top-us-cities-for-small-business-growth/.

11. "Mayors and Mammon," *The Economist*, July 13, 2013, http://www.economist.com/news/business/21581695-city-leaders-are-increasingly-adopting-business-methods-and-promoting-business-mayors-and-mammon.

12. Ibid.

13. Ibid.

14. Nancy Scola, "Bringing Chinese Investment to American Cities," National League of Cities, 2013, http://www.nlc.org/find-city-solutions/city-solutions-and-applied-research/economic-development/global-economic-linkages/bringing-chinese-investment-to-american-cities.

15. Ben Rooney, "How Tel Aviv Became a Tech Hub," *Wall Street Journal Tech Europe,* January 27, 2012, http://blogs.wsj.com/tech-europe/2012/01/27/how-tel-aviv-became-a-tech-hub/.

16. Qiu Bo and Li Yu, "Chengdu Seeks UK Investment," *China Daily USA*, March 27, 2014, http://usa.chinadaily.com.cn/epaper/2014-03/27/content_17383479.htm.

17. Olivia Goldhill, "Google Wins Final Approval for Huge British HQ," *The Telegraph*, May 1, 2014, http://www.telegraph.co.uk/finance/newsbysector/constructionandproperty/10290136/Google-wins-final-approval-for-huge-British-HQ.html.

18. Sara Corbett, "How Zappos' CEO Turned Las Vegas Into a Startup Fantasyland," *Wired*, January 21, 2014, http://www.wired.com/2014/01/zappos-tony-hsieh-las-vegas/.

19. "Mayors and Mammon," *The Economist*, July 13, 2013.

20. *Buenos Aires Herald*, May 2, 2014

21. Philip Kotler, Donald H. Haider, and Irving Rein, *Marketing Places: Attracting Investment, Industry, and Tourism to Cities, States, and Nations* (New York: The Free Press, 1993).

22. Accessed December 16, 2002, http://www.brol.com/trv_cty02weather.asp?ID=17

23. "1957: Dreaming Up Brasília," *The Economist*, London, 353, no. 8151, December 31, 1999, 57.

24. San Francisco Center for Economic Development, ChinaSF, http://sfced.org/china-sf/

25. Aaron Maasho, "Ethiopia Signs $800 Million Mobile Network Deal With China's ZTE," Reuters, August 18, 2013, http://www.reuters.com/article/2013/08/18/us-ethiopia-china-telecom-idUSBRE97H0AZ20130818.

26. Sam Shead, "Chinese Refuse to Open the Mysterious Tomb of Their First Emperor and the Remaining 6,000 Terracotta Soldiers," *London Daily Mail*, August 17, 2012, http://www

.dailymail.co.uk/sciencetech/article-2189908/Some-things-best-left-untouched-Why-Chinese-ignoring-best-secret-tomb.html.

27. "Sanya Tourism Industry Shows Strong Growth in 2013," *Sanya News*, January 18, 2014, http://www.whatsonsanya.com/news-29847-sanya-tourism-industry-shows-strong-growth-in-2013 .html.

28. "Sanya Tourism Revenue Hits RMB10.989 Billion in Q1 of 2014," *Hainan News*, April 22, 2014, http://en.visithainan.gov.cn/en/ newsview_3349.htm.

29. NG Careers blog, "The 15 Best Companies to Work for in Nigeria," December 13, 2012, http://blog.ngcareers.com/295/the-15-best-companies-to-work-for-in-nigeria/.

30. Global Finance, www.globalfinance.gr

31. NG Careers blog, December 13, 2012.

32. "Fifth Avenue The World's Most Expensive Shopping Street," *Huffington Post*, May 25, 2011, http://www.huffingtonpost.com/2010/ 09/21/the-worlds-most-expensive_1_n_733301.html#s142754title =Cartier.

33. Benita Hussain, "World's Best Cities for Architecture Lovers," *Condé Nast Traveler*, July 7, 2013, http://www.cntraveler.com/daily-traveler/2012/06/cities-architecture-design-lovers-photos.

34. Christina Larson, "China Gives Teeth, Finally, to Beijing's New 'War on Pollution'," *Bloomberg Business Week*, April 28, 2014, http://www.businessweek.com/articles/2014-04-28/china-gives-teeth-finally-to-beijing-s-new-war-on-pollution.

35. Taís Fuoco, "GM Prepares Brazil Investment Plan Surpassing $3.2 Billion," Bloomberg News, July 27, 2011, http://www .bloomberg.com/news/2011-07-27/gm-prepares-brazil-investment-plan-surpassing-3-2-billion.html.

36. "The Biggest Startup Community in the World," http://www.start
    upchile.org/

37. Frank Teng, "Santiago, Chile: Ingredients for a Smart City," Meet-
    ing of the Minds, February 5, 2014, http://cityminded.org/santiago-
    chile-ingredients-smart-city-10307.

38. Boyd Cohen, "Filling South America With Smart Cities,"
    Co.EXIST, August 24, 2012, http://www.fastcoexist.com/1680388/
    filling-south-america-with-smart-cities.

39. Ibid.

40. *The Street*, June 2010.

41. "Energy Futures and Urban Air Pollution," The National
    Academies Press, 2007, http://www.nap.edu/openbook.php?record
    _id=12001&page=229:Ch. 8

42. Dan Bobkoff, "From Steel to Tech, Pittsburgh Transforms Itself,"
    NPR, December 16, 2010, http://www.npr.org/2010/12/16/13190
    7405/from-steel-to-tech-pittsburgh-transforms-itself.

43. Matthew Gower, "Mexico's 50 Most Prestigious Foreign Compa-
    nies," *Business Mexico*, 12, no. 8, July 2002, 32–43.

44. World Scientific, www.worldscientific.com

45. "The 10 Major IT Hubs in India – Ranking," *Outsourcing Journal*,
    February 3, 2012, http://outsourcing-journal.org/india-2/674-the-
    10-major-it-hubs-in-india-ranking.

46. Brian Blackstone and Vanessa Fuhrmans, "The Engines of
    Growth," *Wall Street Journal*, June 27, 2011, http://online.wsj.com/
    news/articles/SB1000142405274870350910457632964315391
    5516.

47. McKinsey Global Institute, *Urban World: Mapping the Economic
    Power of Cities* (McKinsey, March 2011).

48. Greg Brown, "A City Transformed by a Fish . . . Worries That the
    Boom Won't Last," *Business Week*, 36–65, January 24, 2000, 4.

49. McKinsey, *Urban World*, 2011.

50. Bureau of Transport Statistics, 2012.

51. Ying Yiyuan, "Private Sector Contributes Over 60% to GDP," CCTV.com English, February 26, 2013, http://english.cntv.cn/program/bizasia/20130206/105751.shtml.

52. Yvette Ousley, "Thank$, Uncle Walter Annenberg Pledges $50m It's for Reform of City Schools," Philly.com, January 27, 1995, http://articles.philly.com/1995-01-27/news/25713545_1_walter-h-annenberg-new-schools-peddie-school.

53. Rahim Kanani, "What Ever Happened to Mark Zuckerberg's $100M Gift to Newark?" *Forbes*, September 12, 2013, http://www.forbes.com/sites/rahimkanani/2013/09/12/what-ever-happened-to-mark-zuckerbergs-100m-gift-to-newark/.

54. Justin Harper, "Australia Launches 'Golden Ticket' Visa for Millionaires: Wealthy Foreigners Willing to Invest Millions in Australia Can Be Fast-Tracked for a Visa," *The Telegraph*, November 28, 2012, http://www.telegraph.co.uk/finance/personalfinance/expat-money/9705707/Australia-launches-golden-ticket-visa-for-millionaires.html.

55. Steve Wilhelm, "Phil Condit, Who Took Boeing to Chicago, Reflects on How a Different Home Changed the Company," *Puget Sound Business Journal*, June 17, 2011, http://www.bizjournals.com/seattle/print-edition/2011/06/17/phil-condit-who-took-boeing-to.html?page=all.

56. Ibid.

57. "Interview With Phil Condit," *Puget Sound Business Journal*, June 2011.

58. "World Cities Culture Report Explores 12 of the World's 'Most Important Cities'," *Huffington Post*, August 22, 2012, http://www

.huffingtonpost.com/2012/08/22/world-cities-culture-report_n_1821200.html.

59. Amcrican Chamber Mexico, "Monterrey," http://www.amcham.org.mx/about-us/Monterrey.aspx#sthash.rjwRrYdm.dpbs

60. Charles Piggott, "Mexico: Monterrey's Moment," *LatinFinance*, 125, March 2001, 80.

61. Tecnológico De Monterrey, http://www.itesm.mx/wps/portal/english/!ut/p/c5/04_

62. Julian Dowling, "Northern Star," *Business Mexico*, 11, no. 7, July 2001, 48–52.

63. INCAE Business School, http://www.incae.edu/en/; also FT Business School rankings, Global MBA Ranking 2013. INCAE ranked 90th worldwide in 2013: http://rankings.ft.com/businessschoolrankings/incae

64. Andrew Bounds, "Central America's Great Survivor: Business Education: INCAE Has Endured Revolutions and Funding Crises but Has Managed to Maintain the Highest Standards," *Financial Times*, April 1, 2002, 8.

65. Coordination for the Improvement of Higher Education Personnel, http://www.capes.gov.br/

66. National Council for Scientific and Technological Development, http://www.cnpq.br/

67. "Open Doors 2003: International Students in the U.S.," Institute of International Education, http://opendoors.iienetwork.org/?p=36523

68. Jonah Newman, "Almost One-Third of All Foreign Students in U.S. Are From China," *The Chronicle of Higher Education*, February 7, 2014, http://chronicle.com/blogs/data/2014/02/07/almost-one-third-of-all-foreign-students-are-from-china/.

69. "Special Reports: Economic Impact of International Students," Institute of International Education, 2014, http://opendoors .iienetwork.org

70. Wang Hongyi, "More Chinese Students Return to Find Work After Studying Abroad," *China Daily*, October 17, 2013, http://www .chinadaily.com.cn/china/2013-10/17/content_17038151.htm.

71. Demetrious G. Papdemetriouc and Madeline Siumption, "The Role of Immigration in Fostering Competitiveness in the United States," Migration Policy Institute, 2011.

72. Carol Morello and Dan Keating, "D.C. Region's Asian Population Is up 60 Percent Since 2000, Census Data Show," *Washington Post*, May 26, 2011, http://www.washingtonpost.com/local/dc-regions-asian-population-is-up-60-percent-since-2000-census-data-show/ 2011/05/25/AGvgndBH_story.html.

73. "The Americas: Making the Most of an Exodus: Emigration from Latin America," *The Economist*, 362, no. 8261, February 23, 2002, 66.

74. Norman Crampton, *The Best Small Towns in America* (Englewood Cliffs, NJ: Prentice-Hall, 1993), 394.

75. Morello and Keating, "D.C. Region's Asian Population," 2011.

76. James Marshall Crotty, "Should Cash-Strapped Public Schools Sell Seats to Foreign Students?" *Forbes*, March 15, 2012, http:// www.forbes.com/fdc/welcome_mjx.shtml.

77. Graham Webster, "Why Are the Chinese Investing in Toledo?" *CNN Money*, June 20, 2012, http://finance.fortune.cnn.com/2012/ 06/20/toledo-china-real-estate/.

78. Timothy Williams, "In Blue-Collar Toledo, Ohio, a Windfall of Chinese Investments," *New York Times*, December 26, 2013, http://www.nytimes.com/2013/12/27/us/in-blue-collar-ohio-a-win

dfall-of-chinese-investments.html?_r=0&gwh=02D3E372CDE9
CFB1FD35AC5DF65D8966&gwt=pay.

79. Webster, "Why Are the Chinese Investing in Toledo?" 2012.

Chapter 6   How a Nation Can Help Its City Economies

1. BlackNews.com, "Not Just Detroit; 7 Other U.S. Cities Have Also Filed for Bankruptcy Since 2010," *New Pittsburgh Courier*, December 29, 2013, http://newpittsburghcourieronline.com/2013/12/29/not-just-detroit-7-other-u-s-cities-have-also-filed-for-bankruptcy-since-2010/.

2. Stephen Moore, "20 Cities That May Face Bankruptcy After Detroit," NEWSMAX, August 8, 2013, http://www.newsmax.com/US/cities-bankruptcy-after-detroit/2013/08/06/id/519081/.

3. Military.com, Naval Base San Diego, http://www.military.com/base-guide/naval-base-san-diego

4. Stephanie Bloyd, "The List: Wichita's Largest Employers," *Wichita Business Journal*, July 26, 2013, http://www.bizjournals.com/wichita/subscriber-only/2013/07/26/the-list---wichitas-largest-employers.html.

5. Lockheed Martin, http://www.lockheedmartinjobs.com/locations-southwest.asp

6. U.S. Census Bureau, "2003–2006 Economic Trends Report," http://www.census.gov/econ/census/data/

7. Brian M. Rosenthal, "States Salivating for Boeing 777X Feast," *Seattle Times*, November 20, 2013, http://seattletimes.com/html/localnews/2022293812_boeingotherstatesxml.html.

8. "Ruling Against China on Trade Is Another Victory for the US," *The Vindicator* (Vindy.com), March 29, 2014, http://www.vindy.com/news/2014/mar/29/ruling-against-china-on-trade-is-another/.

9. Shelly Banjo, "Wal-Mart Pulls Back in India: U.S. Company Ends Venture With Bharti, Will Focus on Wholesale, Not Retail," *Wall Street Journal*, October 9, 2013, http://online.wsj.com/news/articles/SB10001424052702303382004579124703326968442.

10. Milton Kotler, *Neighborhood Government* (Bobs-Merrill, 1969).

11. Dana Bash, Ed Henry, Suzanne Malveaux, and Deirdre Walsh, "UAE Firm to Transfer Port Operations to 'U.S. Entity'," CNN .com, March 10, 2006, http://www.cnn.com/2006/POLITICS/03/09/port.security/index.html?section=cnn_us.

12. Donald Cohen, "Cities Need to Weigh Costs of Private Partnerships," NYT Dealbook, July 23, 2013, http://dealbook.nytimes .com/2013/07/23/cities-need-to-weigh-costs-of-private-partner ships/?_php=true&_type=blogs&_r=0.

13. "Top 10 Military Cities," http://www.allmilitary.com

14. Military.com, "Top 10 Cities for Defense Jobs," http://www .military.com/veteran-jobs/search/aerospace-defense-jobs/top-defense-job-cities.html

15. Center on Budget and Policy Priorities, "Policy Basics: Where Do Our Federal Tax Dollars Go?" March 31, 2014, http://www .cbpp.org/cms/?fa=view&id=1258.

16. Thomas Harding, "Chinese Nuclear Submarine Base," *The Telegraph*, May 1, 2008, http://www.telegraph.co.uk/news/worldnews/asia/china/1917167/Chinese-nuclear-submarine-base.html.

17. GlobalSecurity.org, "King Khalid Military City (KKMC) Al Batin, Saudi Arabia," http://www.globalsecurity.org/military/facility/kkmc .htm.

18. Friedman Foundation for Educational Choice, *The Role of Government in Education* (1962), http://www.edchoice.org/The-Friedmans /The-Friedmans-on-School-Choice/The-Role-of-Government-in-Education.aspx.

19. "National Rankings: Best High Schools," *U.S. News & World Report*, 2014, http://www.usnews.com/education/best-high-schools/national-rankings

20. University of California, 2011–2012.

21. Robert Hill, "In a Cost-Reduction Move, the University of Pittsburgh Combines Key Administrative Functions of Its Bradford and Titusville Regional Campuses Under the Leadership of Pitt-Bradford President Livingston Alexander," University of Pittsburgh, News Services, May 7, 2012, http://www.news.pitt.edu/BradTitusComb.

22. Johns Hopkins University, About Johns Hopkins University, http://webapps.jhu.edu/jhuniverse/information_about_hopkins/

23. Crain's Chicago Business, http://www.chicagobusiness.com/.

24. Aaron M. Renn, "The Second-Rate City?" *City Journal*, Spring 2012, http://www.city-journal.org/2012/22_2_chicago.html.

25. *The Guardian*, February 2010.

26. Libby A. Nelson, "Half of $1 Trillion in Federal Student Loan Debt Not Repaid," Politico, August 8, 2013, http://www.politico.com/story/2013/08/student-loan-debt-95213.html.

27. Chris Gautz, "State Adopts German Apprenticeship Model," Crain's Detroit Business, May 30, 2013, http://www.crainsdetroit.com/article/20130530/NEWS/306029990/#.

28. Joel Kotkin, "The Surprising Cities Creating the Most Tech Jobs," *Forbes*, November 20, 2013, http://www.forbes.com/sites/joelkotkin/2013/11/20/the-surprising-cities-creating-the-most-tech-jobs/.

29. Allie Bidwell, "College Enrollment Falls for Second Year in a Row," *U.S. News & World Report*, December 12, 2013, http://www.usnews.com/news/articles/2013/12/12/college-enrollment-falls-for-second-year-in-a-row.

30. Ronald Roach, "U.S. International Education Enrollment Reaches All-time High," *Diverse*, November 11, 2013, http://diverseeducation.com/article/57394/.

31. Greg Toppo, "Public Schools Recruiting International High Schoolers," *USA Today*, February 24, 2014, http://www.usatoday.com/story/news/nation/2014/02/23/public-schools-selling-seats/5553119/.

32. QS:Top Universities, "Worldwide Universities Rankings: Study in China," http://www.topuniversities.com/where-to-study/asia/china/guide

33. Institute of International Education, Center for Academic Mobility Research, "U.S. Students in China: Meeting the Goals of the 100,000 Strong Initiative: A Pilot Study on U.S. Student Participation in Education Abroad Activities in China," http://www.iie.org/Research-and-Publications/Publications-and-Reports/IIE-Bookstore/US-Students-in-China

34. Laura McMullen, "Which Cities Have the Best Hospitals?" *U.S. News & World Report*, July 16, 2012, http://health.usnews.com/health-news/best-hospitals/articles/2012/07/16/which-cities-have-the-best-hospitals.

35. Singapore Medical Tourism, "My Med Holiday," http://www.mymedholiday.com/country/singapore

36. John Cimble, "Bangkok Capitol of Thailand and Facelift Surgery," Articles Factory, November 2011, http://www.articlesfactory.com/articles/health/bangkok-capitol-of-thailand-and-facelift-surgery.html.

37. John Benson, "Medical Tourism: Latin America Is a Prime Destination," Inside Costa Rica, May 6, 2014, http://insidecostarica.com/2013/07/10/medical-tourism-latin-america-is-a-prime-destination/.

38. Editorial Board, "The Affordable Care Act Comes in with Better-Than-Expected Numbers," *Washington Post*, April 17, 2014, http://www.washingtonpost.com/opinions/the-affordable-care-act-comes-in-with-better-than-expected-numbers/2014/04/17/0db87 4aa-c4df-11e3-b195-dd0c1174052c_story.html.

39. "Obamacare and Employment: Grim Prognosis," *The Economist*, February 5, 2014, http://www.economist.com/blogs/democracyina merica/2014/02/obamacare-and-employment.

40. Michael Niebauer, "D.C. Far Outpaces Nation in Personal Earnings," *Washington Business Journal*, December 17, 2013, http://www.bizjournals.com/washington/blog/2013/12/dc-far-outpaces-nation-in-personal.html.

41. Edward Wong, "One-Fifth of China's Farmland Is Polluted, State Study Finds," *New York Times*, April 17, 2014, http://www.nytimes.com/2014/04/18/world/asia/one-fifth-of-chinas-farmland-is-polluted-state-report-finds.html.

42. Heather Timmons and Malavika Vyawahare, "India's Air the World's Unhealthiest, Study Says," *New York Times*, February 1, 2012, http://india.blogs.nytimes.com/2012/02/01/indias-air-the-worlds-unhealthiest-study-says/.

43. Tristan Edis, "The 7 Who'll Pay Half the Carbon Tax Bill," *Climate Spectator*, November 19, 2013, http://www.businessspectator.com.au/article/2013/11/19/7-wholl-pay-half-carbon-tax-bill.

44. Neil Winton, "Tesla Success Forces Long-Term Skeptics to Relent, a Bit," *Forbes*, March 17, 2014, http://www.forbes.com/sites/neil winton/2014/03/17/tesla-success-forces-long-term-sceptics-to-relent-a-bit/.

45. Sam Frizell, "General Motors Bailout Cost Taxpayers $11.2 Billion," *TIME*, April 30, 2014, http://time.com/82953/general-motors-bailout-cost-taxpayers-11-2-billion/.

46. Pamela Engel and Rob Wile, "11 American Cities That Are Shells of Their Former Selves," *Business Insider*, June 26, 2013, http://www.businessinsider.com/american-cities-in-decline-2013-6.

47. Tom Phillips and Lanzhou Xinqu, "From Sand to Skyscrapers: Inside China's Newest City as 400 Million Move to Towns," *The Telegraph*, June 17, 2013, http://www.telegraph.co.uk/news/world news/asia/china/10123620/From-sand-to-skyscrapers-Inside-Chinas-newest-city-as-400-million-move-to-towns.html.

Chapter 7   The Responsibilities of Companies and Cities

1. Gianluca Mezzofiore, "Bangladesh Dhaka Garment Factory Fire: Gap, Next and Primark Among Brands Caught in Deadly Blaze," *International Business Times*, October 9, 2013, http://www.ibtimes .co.uk/walmart-george-bangladesh-garment-factory-fire-dhaka-51 2562.

2. Anna Mukai, "Toyota China Sales Decline Slows as Anti-Japan Boycotts Fade," Bloomberg, December 3, 2012, http://www .bloomberg.com/news/2012-12-03/toyota-china-sales-decline-slows-as-anti-japan-boycotts-fade-1-.html.

3. Amelia Gentleman, "Indians Protest Wal-Mart's Wholesale Entry," *New York Times*, August 10, 2007, http://www.nytimes.com/2007/08/10/business/worldbusiness/10walmart.html?_r=0.

4. Sumitomo Electric, "Our Volunteer Staff Making a Social Contribution: Renovating an Elementary School in Thailand," January 4, 2014, http://global-sei.com/smile/2014/01/10_1014.html.

5. "POSCO: Selected as 'Excellent Company in Corporate Social Responsibility Management'," 4-Traders.com, November 15, 2013, http://www.4-traders.com/POSCO-6494927/news/POSCO --Selected-as-Excellent-Company-in-Corporate-Social-Responsibility-Management-17466082/.

6. Meera Mohanty, "Odisha Officials Say Posco Not Helping Its Own Cause," *The Economic Times* (India), January 18, 2014, http://economictimes.indiatimes.com/industry/indl-goods/svs/

metals-mining/odisha-officials-say-posco-not-helping-its-own-cause/articleshow/28979449.cms.

7. Richard M. Locke, "The Promise and Perils of Globalization: The Case of Nike," Industrial Performance Center, Massachusetts Institute of Technology Working Paper Series, July 2002, http://ipc.mit.edu/sites/default/files/documents/02-007.pdf.

8. Nilanjana Bhowmick, "Bangladesh's Garment Factories Still Unsafe for Workers, Says Report," *TIME*, March 12, 2014, http://time.com/21038/bangladeshs-garment-factories-still-unsafe-for-workers-says-report/.

9. Meet Puerto Rico, http://www.meetpuertorico.com/nav/facilities

10. Alen J. Shienman, M&CEvents, June 2012

11. Megha Bahree, "Wal-Mart's Path to Power in India Hits Its Limits: The Lawyers," *Wall Street Journal*, April 1, 2013, http://online.wsj.com/news/articles/SB10001424127887324373204578373830411211410.

12. David Barstow and Alejandra Xanic van Bertrab, "The Bribery Aisle: How Wal-Mart Got Its Way in Mexico," *New York Times*, December 17, 2012, http://www.nytimes.com/2012/12/18/business/walmart-bribes-teotihuacan.html.

13. Matthew Pennington, "India Defends Rules for Foreign Retailers," APNews, October 10, 2013, http://bigstory.ap.org/article/india-defends-rules-foreign-retailers.

14. Megha Bahree, "Wal-Mart's Path to Power."

Chapter 8 How Marketers Manage the City-Centered Global Economy

1. Morgan Brennan, "The 20 Cities With the Most New Construction," *Forbes*, March 3, 2012, http://www.forbes.com/pictures/mhj45eegjl/introduction-51/.

2. Metro Atlanta Chamber, "2013 Mid-Year Metro Atlanta Rankings," http://www.metroatlantachamber.com/docs/resources/metro-atlanta-rankings-(2013).pdf?sfvrsn=0

3. http://en.wikipedia.org/wiki/List_of_metropolitan_areas_of_the_United_States

4. http://en.wikipedia.org/wiki/List_of_U.S._metropolitan_areas_by_GDP

5. City Mayors, "The 150 Richest Cities in the World by GDP in 2005," http://www.citymayors.com/statistics/richest-cities-2005.html

6. http://en.wikipedia.org/wiki/List_of_U.S._cities_with_significant_Chinese-American_populations#California_-_Greater_Los_Angeles

ADDITIONAL REFERENCES

Banfield, Edward. (1974). *The Unheavenly City Revisited*. Prospect Heights, IL: Waveland Press.

Banfield was a rationalist in his approach to urban planning. He saw city evolution as a function of changes in demography, technology, and economics—not in government planning and programs. His first edition in 1970 was written at a terrible time for U.S. cities. Middle-class families and companies were fleeing the violence and turmoil of American cities and moving to the suburbs.

The recent resurgence of some cities, but by no means all, is a result of changes once again in demography, technology, and economics. The decline of two-parent households, a new wired generation, and the expansion of multinational companies for new production centers and markets are far greater causes of urban revitalization than government planning and programs.

The poor moved to older suburbs where the middle class once lived or to many towns and cities that could not revitalize, but could sustain them on welfare. Banfield did not live to see the astonishing rise of the multinational companies and their market empowerment of cities, as well as their massive reduction of poverty in the developing world. Multinational companies have also stimulated a cultural work ethic in countries for which there was no earlier impulse, for want of economic opportunity. The developed world is slowly deleveraging its welfare supports for fiscal reasons. This may initiate enough economic growth to keep ahead of the developing economies.

Barber, Benjamin. (2013). *If Mayors Ruled the World: Dysfunctional Nations, Rising Cities*. New Haven, CT: Yale University Press.

It is important to read Barber's book to get a sense of how cities across the world are associating to share knowledge and action to meet urban social, environmental, crime and security, infrastructure, information, human rights, and cultural diversity problems. He has excellent case examples of selected cities, whose mayoral leadership has bypassed the bureaucratic restraints of state and central governments to solve some of these problems. The book is a fine compendium of city interdependence—what cities can accomplish by talking to each other and acting together while nations fail to solve city problems.

Barber cites the same data of urbanization and metropolitan organization as the authors of this book do, but he does not address the economic imperatives of city economic growth. All cities are competing for multinational investment to generate jobs, income, and tax revenues. Barber does not address the city market and multinational drivers of the world urban economy. His neglect of the economic issue of competition among cities for private and public investment is a black hole in his analysis. The thrust for economic development and competition for investment is where the massive energy of city life really exists, while inter-city association can be very helpful on peripheral but nonetheless important issues.

Barber proposes an ideal global city governance infrastructure, albeit short of sovereignty, that he feels can help cities solve their problems and also be reconciled with the power reality of sovereign nations. This is an important ideal, based on the numerous inter-city associations that currently exist and the magnitude of global city markets. Our book propounds a different premise of city dynamics. We live in a global market economy of multinational companies and global city markets that compete for investment and profit. City competition in a free market is as fierce as the competition of nations for power. Their fundamental interests are competitive, not cooperative. Mayors are political animals who are as hungry for power as multinational companies are hungry for profits. They are only problem solvers to the extent of furthering their power ambitions.

The greatest value of expanded inter-city association and voluntary rule-making is to create a forum of power balance with multinational companies that are playing off one city against another for investment incentives to further their global expansion. Barber dwells in a sustainability sphere, whereas the authors deal with the rough-and-tumble of political power and business. Both premises need a hearing.

Duany, Andres, Elizabeth Plater-Zyberk, and Jeff Speck (2000). *Suburban Nation: The Rise of Sprawl and the Decline of the American Dream.* New York, NY: North Point Press.

The authors value their friendship with Andres Duany and his DPZ team in Miami. As global cities concentrate private wealth, company headquarters and top management, and creative people in the city center, they face the problem of providing enriched middle-class housing for companies' workforces in outlying districts of the city center.

The professional talent that must populate multinational operations requires more than the boring suburban sprawl of past decades. They desire affordable new district towns that are culturally rich and physically refreshing. This is what Duany designs. Cities and metros that aim to attract multinational companies must support new town development that has aesthetic and intellectual appeal. Companies compete for top management with money. They must compete for their technical and middle managers with exciting and affordable living communities for their families.

Duany is not focusing on Richard Florida's small segment of the single, high-rise creative class that can afford small spaces in the city center, but on the larger number of family staff members who power multinational company operations, whether at headquarters or at divisions and branches throughout the world. The competition for this talent will rest on land development that surrounds the central city. An exciting downtown that these families cannot afford will not attract these people. Metro area councils must control developers and hold them to a code standard that makes their metro region competitive for multinational investment.

Duany has worked and written consistently on the theme of walkable towns that are difficult for families to leave for attractive offers elsewhere. Multinational location decisions concern the quality of life of the main body of their professional workforce, not just its elite creative class that can afford to live downtown.

Florida, Richard. (2002). *The Rise of the Creative Class: And How It's Transforming Work, Leisure, Community, and Everyday Life*. New York, NY: Basic Books.

It is important to read Florida's major book and subsequent writings, because of his view of the salutary effects of the creative class on urban revitalization. By *creative class*, Florida refers to a new generation of educated, well-paid young professionals in entertainment, software, and social media industries who have moved to city centers and spurred real estate investment in high-end housing and high-end entertainment and retail venues. This creative segment of the population has grown from the information technology industry and has a new set of social norms that diverge from the vastly larger landscape of conventional families living in the outlying neighborhoods of central cities and their suburbs.

Florida does an excellent job of portraying this new generation segment, but his hypothesis that this segment can revitalize city and metro economies is a bit farfetched. The segment is small in the urban population of city regions, and its economic output is too small to drive economic growth for the large city and metro populations. Its impact on city life and economy cannot meet the economic needs of a vast, financially strained metropolitan population. In fact, the creative class that Florida celebrates is just another generational stage of earlier central city gentrification in the 1970s and 1980s that drove the black poor out of the city. This stage is driving the white middle class communities out of the city.

The creative class—and its ultimate industry of entertainment and tourism—may be a temporary godsend to municipal finance and real estate developers, but it is no foundation for the renewed economy of large city populations. The only basis for economic renewal that touches the lives of most city people are large-scale industrial investments that only multinational companies can provide. Mayors should not divert their primary mission of attracting multinational industry to their cities for large-scale employment for the sake of a good-looking, well-spoken, and highly mobile small segment of creatives. What happened to the creativity of community small businesses, scientists, and entrepreneurs?

Glaeser, Edward. (2011). *Triumph of the City: How Our Greatest Invention Makes Us Richer, Smarter, Greener, Healthier, and Happier*. New York, NY: Penguin.

Glaser is a good antidote to the nostalgia of Lewis Mumford. Instead of longing for what no longer exists, Glaeser analyzes the reality of modern urbanization and celebrates its essential economic, intellectual, and social value. Glaeser argues that dense cities attract human capital and foster innovation. Human capital, more than infrastructure, builds economic prosperity. He rejects Jane Jacobs' praise of neighborhood for community life and sees instead that the personal proximity of creative minds and their digital connectivity is a new basis of community.

Glaeser's work reflects a real change in human consciousness brought about by mass education and information technology. We are no longer a romantic generation of Mumford's time. We are a digital generation where mind subordinates nature. Innovation, not the Lake Country of Wordsworth, is the thrill of modern existence for current and forthcoming generations. Smart minds are the flora of the modern age. The more that educated, creative people live closer together, the better.

The paramount problem of cities is their spatial limit. The rich move to the brilliant culture of great central cities, which forces creative minds into suburban wastelands. This intellectual disaster can only be solved by building more urban skyscrapers. Build up, not out.

Jacobs, Jane. (1984). The Economy of Cities *and* Cities and the Wealth of Nations:
Principles of Economic Life. New York, NY: Vintage Random House.

Any book on the economy of cities has to recognize the pioneering work of Jane Jacobs. Her book *The Economy of Cities* was conjoined with Milton Kotler's book *Neighborhood Government* in a double book selection of the Urban Affairs Book Club back in 1969. Jane's great strength was her probative mind, which got to the root of what cities were really about—namely the primary drivers of economic development through import substitution, consumption, trade, and investment—what we now call GDP. Her later books amplified this thesis, and our book carries the evolution of the economy of cities to its present global scale.

Katz, Bruce, and Jennifer Bradley. (2013). *The Metropolitan Revolution: How Cities
and Metros Are Fixing Our Broken Politics and Fragile Economy*. Washington, DC:
Brookings Institution Press.

The Brookings Institution is to be congratulated for supporting the Metropolitan Policy Program and the groundbreaking research and insightful analysis of Bruce Katz and Jenifer Bradley. Their book adds the formal context of metropolitan organization to core municipal cities that accounts for the economic growth of cities. The Metro areas, commonly referred to as Standard Metropolitan Statistical Areas (SMSAs), give historic cities the added market scale that drives their urban economies.

The city in today's economic sense is not just a municipality; it is a coordinated economic and political region of the historic core city and surrounding jurisdictions, often adjacent to other city regions. The historic municipal city throughout the world has emerged as a regional financial, entertainment, cultural, university, and high-end residential and retail center, whereas surrounding suburbs attract manufacturers, vast estates of middle-class and affordable housing, and the commercial businesses that support these sprawling communities.

The book is a well-researched argument for greater economic, political, and social initiative at the metro level to solve the host of problems of America's highly urbanized society that neither state nor federal governments can effectively manage.

Machiavelli, Niccolò. (2014/1520). History of Florence. Create Space Independent Publishing Platform.

Urban planning and business management have been notoriously weak in their treatment of the force of personal political power that drives city form and function. Their training in this matter is constitutional or formalistic, which is a far cry from the real brutality of political power in city life. Careers are ruined and businesses fail because they are unprepared about learning to deal with power. Whatever knowledge they eventually gain, whether they succeed or fail, is a result of experience, not education.

One has to turn to political literature to grasp the powerful dimension of political power in the life of cities. There is no better primer on what they will face than Machiavelli's *History of Florence*, published in 1520. The methods and objectives of power may have changed, but not its ruthless nature and force.

For those with a weaker stomach, I advise reading *Plunkitt of Tammany Hall: A Series of Very Plain Talks on Very Practical Politics*, by William Riordan, published by Signet Classics.

McKinsey Global Institute, McKinsey & Company, New York, NY

Our book draws heavily on the comprehensive and richly varied research of the McKinsey Global Institute, to which our endnotes attest. We particularly recommend three of their reports that document the concentrated economic power of 600 global cities and the 8,000 multinational companies that power these cities: *Urban World: Mapping the Economic Power of Cities*; *Urban World: Cities and the Rise of the Consuming Class*; and *Urban World: The Shifting Global Business Landscape*.

Some of these reports are based on 2007 data, before the financial crisis of 2008. Therefore, their projections to 2025 may be skewed on the upside. Nonetheless, their invaluable data on the economic growth of cities in the developing world are likely to hold, because growth rates in the developing world held up more strongly than in the developed world in the aftermath of the financial crisis. It is more likely they overestimate the long-term economic power of European and North American cities.

Micklethwait, John, and Adrian Wooldridge (2003). *The Company: A Short History of a Revolutionary Idea*. New York, NY: Random House.

An understanding of the vast power of today's multinational companies and the issues they face requires a broader context of their evolution from the earliest forms of joint-stock corporations. From their ancient origins, the company has evolved into many forms, the multinational being the most powerful descendant. Micklethwait and Wooldridge present the evolution of company organization and its permanent tension between sovereign warrant and private right—between shareholder interest and wider stakeholder interest. Much has happened in the last decade since this book was written to further increase the scale, scope, and origin of multinational companies, but history is a good foundation for evaluating its benefits and pondering its future transformation.

Mumford, Lewis. (1961). *The City in History*. New York, NY: Harcourt.

Lewis Mumford is the grandfather of city history. His classic work is a panoramic vista of the different forms and functions of the city over time, at least to the time of its publication. Much has changed in cities over the past 50 years. Mumford favors the organic city of limited size that balances nature and technology. Today we call this ideal balance livability and sustainability. The book is important to read as an historical and idealistic counterpoint to the contemporary reality of massive cities and their interlocked metropolitan areas.

The tragic irony is that the small cities that Mumford advocates cannot support the competition of global multinational companies that drive the economies of cities to an ever-increasing urban scale of industry, service, energy, talent, consumer markets, and financial investment. His ideal small cities are now economically decaying under the forces of economic globalization. The social and environmental relations that Mumford sought in city design 50 years ago are nostalgic reminders of a bygone age. Human relations in today's vast urban technopolis will have to find their personal touch in neighborhood decentralization and in the social media of a digital world. We cannot move cities backward in time.

Roach, Stephen. (2009). *The Next Asia: Opportunities and Challenges for a New Globalization*. Hoboken, NJ: Wiley.

As authors, we spend a great deal of time in Asia. We are grateful to the small set of economists who truly understand the rising economic power of Asia and how the West has to peacefully accommodate. Chief among our mentors is Stephen Roach, formerly at Morgan Stanley and now at Yale University. Roach has the most astute understanding of the changing world landscape of economic power and its opportunities and threats. He understands the dynamic economic power of the East, and he knows that Asia's economic growth comes from the demographic and market forces of Asian cities and the long-suppressed merchant spirit of the people—long suppressed and now aided and abetted by central government policies.

Sassen, Saskia. (2012). *Cities in a World Economy* (4th ed.). Los Angeles, CA: Sage.

Saskia Sassen has been very helpful in understanding how dispersed global companies have concentrated their service functions in top global cities. City growth is no longer a function of production growth. For many multinational companies, their service sector employment and cost exceeds their production sector. As companies move out of direct production and assembly, their service sector of research, design, finance, procurement, logistics, communications, and marketing increases in size and concentrates its operations scale in top global cities.

Our only concern is that Sassen should update her charts in new editions to capture the emerging economic power of global cities in the developing economies. We also take issue with her nomenclature.

Today, every city is global. One has only to see the devastation of certain cities that have lost their industry to other shores to realize that no city can escape the global drivers of its business. There is no longer such a thing as an indigenous business.

Subramanian, Arvind. (2011). *Eclipse: Living in the Shadow of China's Economic Dominance*. Washington, DC: Peterson Institute for International Economics.

Arvind Subramanian's 2011 book *Eclipse: Living in the Shadow* of *China's Economic Dominance* was the first macroeconomic document to muster the evidence of China's imminent dominance in trade, wealth, and finance. He understands the importance of China's steady policy of fueling the enormous dynamo of China's productive cities. As a scholar, he has the practical wisdom of knowing what every businessman in China knows—that the Yuan will soon be convertible and challenge the reserve status of the dollar.

Vernon, Raymond. (1998). *In the Hurricane's Eye*. Cambridge, MA: Harvard University Press.

Raymond Vernon of Harvard was the keenest analyst of multinational companies. His two books, *Sovereignty at Bay* and *In the Hurricane's Eye*, are scholarly watersheds in the globalization of large companies. He masterfully tracks the growth of MNCs since the end of World War II and the tension of industry's advance from home countries to host countries. National governments have been trying to preserve their control of economic development against the onslaught of MNC investment and its global reach. Their regulatory balance against the power and political influence of MNCs has had its ups and downs, with shifting periods of nationalization, regulatory constraints, and open-door investment. However, the trends in the 1990s give greater weight to the MNC power.

Professor Vernon died in 1999, and we have missed his analysis of global trade and investment policy over the past 15 years. But as nations have declined in their fiscal capacity to stimulate domestic growth since the fiscal crisis of 2008, the power of MNC investment in host countries has only become more dominant. Vernon was also prescient in noting the growing role of local-level government in bypassing nations for MNC investment attraction. We document the advance of this trend. We hope another scholar will pick up the ball of MNC analysis now that the brilliant Raymond Vernon has passed.

Wasik, John F. (2006). *The Merchant of Power: Sam Insull, Thomas Edison, and the Creation of the Modern Metropolis*. New York, NY: Palgrave Macmillan.

This well-researched and well-written book presents the reader with a case study of three central elements of city economic development: innovation infrastructure, business organization, and politics. Sam Insull was Edison's secretary and accountant, who implemented his master's electrical inventions into the massive electrical infrastructure of Chicago and its far-reaching surrounding towns and beyond.

Insull's private companies powered the growth of Chicago as America's second largest city, and they vividly illustrate the gap between innovation and implementation—and the central role of infrastructure in the growth of city economies. Insull created vast publicly listed holding companies, encompassing his many companies that collapsed under the weight of the Great Depression. His enemies, the advocates of public infrastructure ownership, hounded him through the courts, but he exited with acquittal. Chicago would not be what it is today without the financial ingenuity and persistence of Sam Insull. In the current developed world intellectual climate of regrettably low esteem for entrepreneurship, Insull is an insult, but he was a hero of economic growth.

INDEX

Note to the reader: All Multinational Companies (MNCs) are in **bold**; all cities are in *italics*.